# Life
## at the
# MARMONT

# Life
# at the
# MARMONT

**by**
**Raymond R. Sarlot**
**and**
**Fred E. Basten**

ROUNDTABLE PUBLISHING, INC.
Santa Monica    California

ROUNDTABLE PUBLISHING, INC.
933 Pico Boulevard
Santa Monica, CA 90405

*First Printing, 1987*

Library of Congress Catalog Card Number—87-061784

*All photos are from the Chateau Marmont Collection, unless credited.*

PRINTED IN THE UNITED STATES OF AMERICA

# Acknowledgements

When we first contacted Ginger Rogers for her remembrances about Chateau Marmont, she commented, "If only the walls could talk!"

The walls didn't talk, but hundreds of people did: former and current guests, staff members, and others who have been close to the Hollywood community over the years. Without their generous contributions, this book never would have been possible.

For opening doors, offering suggestions, and providing leads that proved invaluable to the researching of the Marmont story, we thank Rutanya Alda, Lu Artz, Sandy Arcieri, DeWitt Bodeen, Ward Byron, Richard Bright, Nancy K. Campbell, Dona Carn, Margaret Cormier, Thomas DeLong, Suzanne Jierjian, Mary A. Fischer, George Fisher, Bill Hickman, Edgar Kahn, Terry Kingsley-Smith, Dorothy A. Kuhn, Elmo Legg, Jona Liebrecht, Banks Montgomery, Tom Owen, Audrey Plant, Barbara Platoff, Mary Carol Rassett, Liz Roberson, Katie Roper, Leah Rozen, and Rosa Lee Sonney.

For sharing a part of their lives, and memories, we are especially indebted to the Arngrim family (Alison, Norma, Stefan, and Thor), Lauren Bacall, Hermione Baddeley, Billy Barnes, Greg Bautzer, Anne Baxter, Regina Bernstein, Bill Boling, Larry Bordeaux, Yul Brynner, Donald Carroll, Morgan Cavett, Richard Chamberlain, Quentin Crisp, John Crosby, Dolores Dorn-Heft, Glenn Ford, Jim Frank, Nicolas Gessner, Alex Gildzen, Guilford Glazer, James Haake, Sherry Hackett, Richard Haydn, James Hill, Doug Horowitz, Dr. Robert Horowitz, John Howell, Pam Hughes, Alexander Ives, Burl Ives, Jill Jackson, Henry Jaffe, Gavin Lambert, Burton Lane, Esther Long, Mary Loos, Louis Malle, Walter Matthau, Loren Michaels, Inez Monter, George Montgomery, Ken Murray, Connie Nelson, Barry

# ACKNOWLEDGEMENTS

Norcross, Robert Osborne, Bernard Owett, Elsie Ferguson Pendleton, Joan Penfield, Tom Rafter, Tony Renis, Lynn Redgrave, Lee Remick, Ginger Rogers, Dawn Sandor, Natalie Schafer, Gwen Seager, Wallace Seawell, Martha Scott, Tom Sefton, Steffi Sidney, Inger Simonsen, James Gordon Smith, Donald Spackman, Michael Stewart, Alan Sues, Donald Sutherland, Noelly Tomayo, Casey Tibbs, Marc Wanamaker, Ilenna Welch, Tom Wheat, Boyd Willet, Marie Windsor, Joanne Woodward, and Eleanor Zee.

For their candid observations, anecdotes, and continued moral support, we are grateful to a special group of friends who asked to remain anonymous.

For their cooperation in helping track down and verify statistical data relating to the Marmont's early days, as well as its celebrity clientele, our sincere appreciation to the keepers of the reference files at the *Los Angeles Times,* the Academy of Motion Picture Arts & Sciences, and the Los Angeles and Santa Monica Public Libraries.

For the files of Corinne Patten, which she generously left to the hotel. Corinne had hoped to one day write a book about her experiences at the Marmont. Extensive use of her detailed memoirs was invaluable.

For the opportunity of speaking often with a truly amazing lady, Ann Little, before she passed away. Though her remembrances were of times long past, she related them with such vividness that one almost believed that they had happened yesterday.

Above all, for her faith in this book, and her enormous contributions throughout its preparation, our deepest appreciation to Carmel Volti. Carmel's friendship, enthusiasm, and colorful revelations about the Marmont filled each day with discovery and joy.

Finally, we must acknowledge Chateau Marmont itself, for graciously enduring Hollywood's many changes to link the past with the present.

—Raymond Sarlot & Fred E. Basten

# Contents

CONTENTS

# Foreword

When my partner, Raymond Sarlot, and I bought Chateau Marmont in 1975, we had heard most of the legends about the hotel and its famous guests. The so-called tales of the Marmont had been circulating for so long that they had come to be accepted as fact.

The story of Chateau Marmont is practically a capsule history of Hollywood itself, from the decline of silent pictures and the start of "talkies" through the glamorous golden era, and beyond. As the movie capital prospered, so did the Marmont. When Hollywood hit hard times, the hotel struggled as well. Somehow, they have both survived the seasons of change to become legends in their own time.

Like Hollywood, Chateau Marmont has attracted the most celebrated and talented names in show business and the arts: writers, producers, directors, and stars. They came to Hollywood to work and to be seen. They came to the Marmont to live in seclusion.

For most of its nearly sixty years, the Marmont has been one of Hollywood's best-kept secrets, a Gothic-inspired hideaway within the land of glitter and hype. The celebrities who made the Marmont their home away from home were attracted by its privacy and Old World charm. Others were fascinated by its fabled past. Even today, it is not unusual for visitors to request suites that were once occupied by such stars as Jean Harlow, Greta Garbo, and Marilyn Monroe.

One of the legendary tales of the Marmont had it that Rudolph Valentino was an early visitor to the hotel. Old-timers swear they saw the dashing screen idol at several of the Marmont's grand-opening parties. A great bit of Hollywood history, Ray and I thought on first hearing. We didn't know until later that Valentino had been dead nearly two-and-a-half years when the hotel opened in 1929.

According to legend, Clark Gable proposed to Carole Lombard in the

Marmont penthouse. (Gable never lived at the Chateau Marmont, although he was no stranger around the hotel, particularly during Jean Harlow's heralded honeymoon stay.)

There were other tales with romantic connections making the rounds. Humphrey Bogart and Lauren Bacall, it was said, trysted at the Marmont, away from the jealous eyes of Mayo Methot. ("Not true," insists Bacall.) It was at the Marmont that Paul Newman proposed to Joanne Woodward. (Woodward calls that "pure Hollywood legend," but confirms that she met her husband at the hotel.) And, of course, it was from the balcony of their suite that an angry Lucille Ball threw a valise jammed with money at Desi Arnaz, showering dollar bills over Sunset Boulevard. (No one was witness to that momentous event.)

It has been said that Chateau Marmont was named for British actor Percy Marmont. (The name was actually taken from the street that fronts the hotel—Marmont Lane.)

Steve McQueen started his own legend at the Marmont. Whenever he was having differences with his wife, Neile, he would alert the Hollywood trade papers that he had moved into the hotel. (The switchboard would light up for days with calls asking for McQueen, but the elusive actor had never signed in. He simply used the hotel as a decoy while hiding out elsewhere.)

There were stories about Lyda Roberti, the platinum-blonde singing star of 1930s musicals (contrary to rumor, she died suddenly at her Hollywood hills home, not at the Marmont), and tennis star Bill Tilden, said to be the pro at the hotel during his Hollywood days (the Marmont has never had a tennis court).

The stories are contagious. One, in particular, could be heard everywhere, it seemed. "Greta Garbo owns the Marmont!" Everyone believed it—and why not? The statement, fact or fiction, somehow gave the hotel a cachet.

Rumors were certainly flying when Ray Sarlot and I took over in 1975. There were fears that the hotel would be leveled to make way for a new development. Chateau Marmont had become a losing proposition. It was in sorry shape, inside and out, from years of neglect. But tearing down the Marmont was not in our plans. The building may have become a fading flower, but it was still architecturally magnificent. And its clientele, despite the grim surroundings, had remained fiercely loyal.

Ray and I regarded our new acquisition as an investment, nothing more. It wasn't until Ray moved in and the renovation began that our thinking began to change. The Marmont, we discovered, was a most friendly castle. The atmosphere was warm, and genuinely real. We fell in love with the place.

As the months passed, we met many of the Marmont's guests. There were regulars, wonderful people like Tony Randall, Maximillian Schell, Colleen Dewhurst, Carol Lynley, Richard Gere, Donald Sutherland, Diane Keaton, Lauren Hutton, Lee Grant, Loren Michaels, and Robert DeNiro. There were newcomers, and future friends, as well: moviemakers Henry Jaglom, Louis Malle, Claudia Weill, Bernardo Bertolucci, Peter Weir, Brian DePalma, Danny Selznick, James Jarmusch, and Terry Gilliam; artists Claes Oldenburg, Jasper Johns, Ellsworth Kelly, Roy Lichtenstein, David Hockney, Robert Rauschenberg, and Edward Ruscha; sculptors Edward Kienholz, and Eduardo Paolozzi; composers, singers, and musicians Peter Allen, Eddie Money, John Kander, Charles Aznavour, Sting and Sade.

Through our new associations we discovered more and more about the people who came to visit. The more we heard, the more intrigued we became. Still, we knew so little about the hotel's history. How did the Marmont come to be? we wondered. Who built it? What was it like during the early days? Who were the guests then? Were the legends true—or not?

We set out to uncover the real mystery behind the Marmont. Four years later, we had amassed a wealth of material. The result is this book.

Welcome to life at the Marmont!

—Karl Kantarjian

# Life
## at the
# MARMONT

Prominent Los Angeles attorney Fred Horowitz returned from France in 1926 with a dream. (*Courtesy of Dr. Robert Horowitz*)

Title box from original blueprints, dated December 27, 1927.

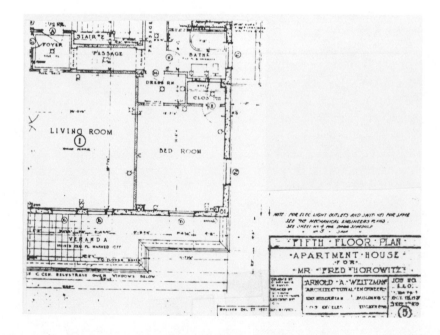

# Prologue

## The Continental Touch

On an overcast morning in November, 1926, a chauffeur-driven towncar motored westward along Sunset Boulevard through Hollywood. At the intersection of Sunset and Laurel Canyon, the paved roadway ended. The vehicle paused briefly before crossing onto a narrow two-lane strip of dust-covered oil and macadam, then continued onward another several hundred yards. There it pulled to a stop near the weed-covered hillside.

Inside the towncar were Fred Horowitz of Los Angeles, Inez Fredericks of New York City, and Florence E. Dean of San Francisco. At thirty-one, Fred Horowitz was a prominent local attorney, already gaining a reputation for his "tough as nails" approach. He had recently returned from a tour of the Continent, a trip that was less a vacation than a mission. He had long dreamed of creating and owning the most unique and fashionable apartment house in Hollywood and had turned to the foreign capitols of Europe for inspiration. The idea was hardly original. He was following the lead of the booming motion picture industry, which was discovering many of its greatest stars in exotic overseas locales.

Traveling through the French countryside along the Loire, Horowitz had seen a magnificent chateau with towers and terraces, arched Gothic windows and walkways. He was so impressed with the ornate structure, that he photographed it from various angles. When he returned to the U.S., he showed the photographs to his longtime friend, Miss Fredericks. Not only was the wealthy socialite interested in helping finance Horowitz's venture, but she had a friend in the fur business, Miss Dean, who owned a vacant parcel of land in the Hollywood hills. In exchange for a partnership,

Florence Dean was all too willing to donate her site. Horowitz would not commit himself until he had seen the property.

Now the stockily built, five-foot-ten Horowitz moved with determination along the rutted dirt edge of Sunset Boulevard. He walked with a slight limp, due to a childhood accident, but nothing could hold him back. He focused his deep-set eyes on a narrow, winding fork in the road. It turned upward, curving sharply until it connected with another narrow byway. A small signpost identified the deserted streets as Marmont Lane and Monteel Road. Horowitz stopped. He was standing at the northwest corner of Florence Dean's land.

Except for a handful of houses scattered in the hills, the immediate area was undeveloped, covered with tinder-dry sagebrush and tumbleweed. Below, on the flatlands, stood a general store and a construction site. The former estate of film star Alla Nazimova, on the far side of Sunset, was undergoing changes. Around its enormous swimming pool, a complex of villas (to be named the Garden of Allah) was taking shape. The view of the sprawling city, from the faraway mountains to the sea, was breathtaking.

Horowitz pulled the snapshot from his coat pocket and held it up, as if to visualize the illustration of his beloved French chateau against the setting. A moment later he waved to the towncar parked at the bottom of the hill and hollered, *"Yes!"*

The only opposition to Horowitz's planned venture came from his law partner in the firm of Willebrandt, Horowitz, and McCloskey—the distinguished Mable Walker Willebrandt. As former United States Attorney General in charge of prohibition enforcement, and at the time the Supervisor of the Bureau of Federal Prisons, Mrs. Willebrandt had established herself as one of the nation's most respected women; her opinions were not to be dismissed lightly. "You have no experience in property management," she told her associate without hesitation. She also feared that a multiple-story apartment building, as envisioned by Horowitz, would not be popular among Southern Californians, who favored less formal garden-court living.

Horowitz pointed to the motion picture industry, enjoying its most successful year ever, which was attracting top creative talent from the east. "These people—directors, writers, actors—are arriving in droves every day," he argued, "and they'll be looking for a touch of home."

From their Los Angeles offices in the downtown Union Bank building, Horowitz could see clusters of giant outdoor movie sets, replicas of frontier towns, jungle villages, and ancient cities. He spoke of the expanding studios of Warner Brothers, Paramount, Metro-Goldwyn-Mayer, and of the new complex Fox was building on the west side of town. He spoke too of the need for luxury furnished apartments. "In good times like these," he said, "people want the best." He would not be discouraged.

Shortly after the first of the year, Horowitz commissioned his brother-in-law, European-trained architect Arnold A. Weitzman, to design a seven-story, L-shaped building that would capture the flavor, in every detail, of the original chateau in France. Weitzman was instructed to work directly from Horowitz's photographs, and within a budget of $350,000. With its main entrance opening onto Marmont Lane, the new structure would be called Chateau Marmont. (The names Chateau Sunset and Chateau Hollywood had been rejected.)

Weitzman spent more than a year developing plans for the new Chateau Marmont, which called for forty-three spacious view apartments of one to six rooms each, with living rooms ranging in size from fifteen by twenty to seventeen by thirty-two feet. There were specifications for individual balconies and terraces; separate service entrances; a revolutionary ventilating system, powered by fans in the roof, to change the air in each of the kitchens at twenty-second intervals; an expansive main-floor drawing room and lobby, with high-beamed ceilings; a basement garage, with parking for forty-six cars; elevators; courtyard gardens; and a vaulted arcade, flanked by columns, leading from the street to the main entry. Decorative filigree masonry and bas-relief, copied faithfully from Horowitz's photos, were penciled in to adorn the facing of the structure.

Unlike the original chateau, the plans called for steel and concrete construction throughout, with banded steel casements to render it, in the architect's words, "absolutely Los Angeles' first earthquake-proofbuilding." Said Horowitz proudly, "Chateau Marmont will be constructed without regard to expense, but with the desire to achieve an ideal—that of completing the most dignified apartment house in the state."

In February, 1928, Fred Horowitz gave his final approval to Weitzman's blueprints, and on March 6, the city issued a building permit. W. Douglas Lee, whose firm was responsible for the design, engineering, and construction of many of Los Angeles' finest commercial and industrial structures, was hired as contractor to personally supervise construction. Ground-breaking ceremony, took place on April 3, 1928.

By December, work was progressing so smoothly that Horowitz was able to bring in artisans to handpaint intricately designed murals on the ceilings of the main-floor drawing room, lobby, and exterior arcade, already

Grand Opening ad, February 2, 1929.

Decorous initial "h" on building's upper facade is a lasting reminder
of the Marmont's creator, Fred Horowitz.

being lauded as the finest of its kind in the country. There were other extravagances—rich, rare woods, ornate wrought iron, imported tiles, and stained glass. On a front-facing exterior tower wall, Horowitz personally guided the installation of an ornamental shield, surrounded by a flourish of concrete ribbon, containing a large baroque style letter "H."

Horowitz was particularly proud of the sharply pitched, angular roof, which had been installed by a company he had brought to California from Pennsylvania, along with its workers. Jay Horowitz, Fred's brother, was a quality-control expert and had been hired to oversee the project in that capacity. One day, Jay climbed to the roof with a ten-pound sledgehammer to test the finished job. He reportedly hammered away, but was unable to dislodge any of the slate shingles.

So much attention was spent on embellishments that Horowitz and his partners were suddenly faced with a budget so slim that little was left for the purchase of furnishings. A call to the factories of Grand Rapids, Michigan, resulted in the buy-out of serviceable but undistinguished stock pieces at cut-rate prices. The oriental rugs that graced the floors of many apartments were not a special purchase, however. By necessity, they came from the private collections of Fred Horowitz and Inez Fredericks.

Chateau Marmont officially opened for inspection on February 1, 1929. Visitors were warmly greeted in the lobby by Horowitz and his partners, who stood before an impressive line-up of smiling, crisply-dressed maids and the newly hired resident manager, Mrs. Blanche Bryson. Over three-hundred people passed through the Marmont that day, including a large number of reporters from the local press. While the general reaction was positive and, at times, even glowing, there were few sign-ups for apartments. Comments of "exorbitant" or "outrageous" were not uncommon in response to the rents, which peaked at $750 per month.

The first few days may have been a disappointment to the owners, but Horowitz remained undaunted. Many of the early visitors, he realized, were not in a financial position to afford Chateau Marmont living; they had come simply to satisfy their curiosity.

Following the opening, *Saturday Night*, a popular weekly tabloid of the day, touted Chateau Marmont as "Los Angeles' newest, finest, and most exclusive apartment house." The article went on at length to describe the Marmont's notable and distinctive features, including its unique location. "The property is superbly situated," the paper reported, "close enough to active business to be accessible and far enough away to insure quiet and privacy."

The accolades in *Saturday Night* and other publications generated such interest in the Marmont that initial resistance began to crumble. Over the next few months, so many affluent newcomers signed long-term leases that only a handful of vacancies remained. In October, however, disaster struck. The sudden collapse of the stock market sent residents fleeing in panic, their fortunes having evaporated overnight.

Mabel Walker Willebrandt wasted no time in advising her law partner to shut down the Marmont. She had learned that the Beverly Hills Hotel, in the center of America's richest village, had already closed its doors and that the Garden of Allah, which had been open since early 1927, was on the verge of bankruptcy. Fred Horowitz refused to listen. "Then get some help," she prodded, "someone with experience in property management."

Ben Weingart was known as a shrewd real-estate developer and investor. Born dirt-poor, he had accumulated vast holdings during his forty-one years (in time, he would own more rental units than Conrad Hilton) and, in the process, had learned the entrepreneurial rules of survival, including how to hustle for a living. Since the Crash, Weingart had expanded his considerable interests by taking on the management of "troubled" properties.

Weingart demanded complete authority, which Fred Horowitz gladly surrendered to save his investment. (Weingart's name became so associated with the Marmont it was assumed he had bought control.) No guarantees were made, but Weingart's track record and reputation provided more than a measure of hope.

Three afternoons a week Ben Weingart arrived unannounced at Chateau Marmont with a long checklist of items demanding his attention. He moved from floor to floor casting his critical eyes in every direction. Nothing escaped him, least of all idle maids, who had little to do with vacant apartments on every level. The number of staff members was quickly cut in half. Manager Blanche Bryson became another casualty, but for a far different reason.

Weingart's reputation as a ladies' man was surpassed only by his business acumen. He loved women, and they adored him. Even in an age of chivalry, he was a rare commodity—a gracious gentleman of the old school. Few females could resist his charm, or the sight of his dated but still elegant turn-of-the-century appearance, set off by winged collars, high button shoes, and, on occasion, a beret worn at a rakish tilt.

When Ben Weingart came to Chateau Marmont, he had been married more than a dozen years. In the fall of 1928, he began a serious relationship with a divorcee named Hazel Walsh. There were other romantic involvements as well, mistresses he had installed as managers within his various enterprises around Hollywood and Los Angeles. His comment, "Here's to our wives and sweethearts, may they never meet," was said with a twinkle—and an undertone of apprehension.

To replace Blanche Bryson, Weingart brought in Emma Lovell. Her heavily mascaraed eyes, salon-dyed black hair, and black satin dress projected a menacing appearance that seemed appropriate for the dreary times. Residents who dared approach Lovell found her to be courteous and sympathetic to their needs, but only Ben Weingart knew her truly warm side. Three afternoons a week, following his rounds, he would disappear into her first-floor apartment. They would not be seen again until the dinner hour, when he would rush off to be with his wife.

The slim savings realized from staff firings and other cuts in expenses did little to console Fred Horowitz, who was growing increasingly unhappy with the unprofitable Marmont. He spoke with Inez Fredericks in New York. "We'll give it one more year," she told him, "and no longer."

Neither would admit that they had gambled on a dream, and lost.

In October, 1931, the beleaguered owners of Chateau Marmont sold their holdings to Albert E. Smith for $750,000 cash. Included in the package was the site, purchased from Miss Florence Dean. Reporting the sale of the Marmont, and the staggering amount paid for it, considering the times, a Los Angeles newspaper facetiously posed the question: "Did anyone say Depression?"

Whatever disappointment Fred Horowitz and his partners may have felt in their failure to make a go of the Marmont was undoubtedly mollified by the profit they made on their relatively short-term investment—a very healthy three-hundred thousand or so, after deductions for expenses.

The local papers identified the new owner, fifty-six-year-old Albert E. Smith, as a former motion picture producer and investor. He was much more. As co-founder of Vitagraph, one of the most prolific and successful pioneer motion picture production companies, Smith and his partner, fellow Englishman J. Stuart Blackman, had been powerful forces in the fledgling film industry, rivaling Cecil B. DeMille and D. W. Griffith. Smith's Vitagraph releases were the most popular among cinema audiences of the early silent era and his discoveries the most famous. It was Smith who gave starts to Florence Turner (the "Vitagraph Girl"), Rudolph Valentino, Clara Kimball Young, Adolphe Menjou, Norma Talmadge, John Bunny, and Maurice Costello. His career as a filmmaker spanned nearly thirty years, culminating in 1925 with the sale of Vitagraph to Warner Bros. (In 1947, Smith was honored with a special Academy Award as one of a small group of pioneers "whose belief in the new medium and whose contributions to the development blazed the trail along which the motion picture has progressed in their lifetime, from obscurity to worldwide acclaim.")

With the sale of Vitagraph to Warner Bros., Smith began dabbling in real estate, first in land, with the sprawling La Cumbra Rancho near the old Douglas Fairbanks property outside Rancho Santa Fe, then in rental properties. He acquired the neglected forty-eight apartment Bryn-Carlton in Hollywood and gave it new life with his artistic touches, turning a white elephant into a swank moneymaking operation. Proud as Smith was of his accomplishment, he later admitted that the Bryn-Carlton was "not in the same class as Chateau Marmont."

The transformation of the Bryn-Carlton had come during a period of high and fast spending, when times were good and getting better. Now Hollywood, like America, was in the doldrums. Motion picture box-office receipts were the worst on record and dropping. Theaters were closing every day; those that managed to stay open did so by sharply cutting admission prices or staging "giveaways" to lure customers. Even the few people who had money were reluctant spenders. As a way of life, "easy come, easy go" had become a thing of the past.

Chateau Marmont represented a special challenge for Albert Smith, one he accepted willingly. He loved a good fight, any excuse to keep him active and stir his creative juices. But the fact remained that his seven-story castle on the hill, Hollywood's most distinctive new building, was nearly empty.

Despite a worsening economy, Smith could see only positive times ahead. The 1932 Olympic Games were coming to Los Angeles, an event that would attract hundreds of thousands of visitors. Smith optimistically told one reporter, "I've already had telephone calls and letters from people all over the United States, even from abroad, asking about rentals in Los Angeles for the Olympics. I'm satisfied that many of these people will remain in Southern California after their summer visit—and that means Los Angeles' rental properties will soon command premium prices."

Olympics crowds would not spell a cure-all for troubled Los Angeles property owners, Smith felt certain. But the visitors would surely give the local economy a much-needed shot in the arm. If Chateau Marmont was to attract its share of Olympics riches, changes had to be made.

Smith spent long hours pondering Marmont policy. Until now, leases were required on all apartments. But leases meant long-term commitments, and in these times of tight money even the mention of the word brought

The Vitagraph man—Albert E. Smith, creator of "the Marmont look." (*Courtesy of James Gordon Smith*)

The spacious main-floor drawing room, newly refurbished with precious antiques, early 1930s.

Stylized Chateau Marmont dominated
1931 ad.

Catered meals were prepared for guests in the Marmont's new
kitchen during the 1930s.

fear to the eyes of prospective renters. Wouldn't it be far more appealing to eliminate all strings and offer accommodations on a monthly, weekly, even daily rental basis? Smith was willing to bet that it would. In effect, the change in policy would turn the Marmont from an apartment house into a hotel.

Of concern too was Chateau Marmont's management team of Ben Weingart and Emma Lovell, which had been retained after the changeover in owners. Weingart ran a tight ship, watched expenses with a hawk's eye, and, with his own vast real-estate holdings, undoubtedly possessed more expertise in property management than anyone in California. Lovell was efficient and dependable, despite a sinister appearance; her rapport among both guests and staff could not be faulted. Yet their preoccupation with routine responsibilities, and often with each other, left little time or energy for the all-important pursuit of new business. Albert Smith found Weingart, who insisted on doing things his own way, unapproachable to suggestions.

Although Smith had no intention of moving into the Marmont—he had a home in Hollywood where he lived with his wife and children—being an absentee owner, as his predecessors had been, was out of the question. Weingart, therefore, was expendable. As for Lovell, her loyalty extended to only one person—the man who had hired her, the man who shared her bed three afternoons a week. Smith's only option was to relieve them both of their duties.

With unemployment at a record high, the finest in managerial talent was available and begging. But Smith's first choice to fill his vacant management post could claim no prior experience. She was an actress, a one-time leading lady in silent serials and westerns. She had starred opposite William S. Hart and Wallace Reid and, as the Indian maiden, Naturitch, in DeMille's classic, *The Squaw Man.*

Albert Smith had known Ann Little for nearly twenty years, since her start in films. He admired not only her considerable talents but her professionalism. She was a tireless worker, bright and dedicated. Friends and co-workers spoke of her in glowing terms. Her fans were legion.

Since her retirement from films in 1925, Ann Little had been appearing in local stage productions, most recently with the Henry Duffy Players at Hollywood's El Capitan Theater. Smith found her there and made her an offer on the spot. To sweeten his proposal, he threw in free room and board at the Chateau.

Ann Little was intrigued. At forty, she was ready for a career change. Show business had lost its excitement for her, and the thought of a steady salary was hard to resist. Too, the accommodations Smith so generously offered could be shared with her ailing mother. A strict Christian Scientist, Little insisted on caring for the elderly woman herself.

But Ann Little didn't jump at Smith's offer. She had visited friends at the Marmont and had seen not only the main-floor drawing room but several suites. "I was less than impressed," she remembered years later. "The building itself was grand, unlike anything I'd ever seen before. And while it was all clean and new, it needed fixing up. The furniture was bad. I told Mr. Smith that I couldn't work for him unless he redid the place. How I had the nerve I'll never know!"

Little's honesty only strengthened Smith's belief that she was right for the job. The furnishings *were* atrocious, he agreed, and inappropriate for the Marmont's unique architectural styling. The furnishings in all the suites were bland, lacking drama and imagination. Even the penthouse needed attention. He would begin work immediately, he promised Little, if only she would say yes to his offer. She accepted.

Albert Smith didn't look upon the job of refurbishing the Marmont's spacious suites as a formidable task. A lover of art and fine furnishings, he had honed his considerable decorating skills during the transformation of the Bryn-Carlton. He had been assisted then by his wife, Lucille, a former Vitagraph actress known professionally as Jean Page. Together the Smiths had acquired many valuable pieces by attending estate auctions.

Albert and Lucille Smith went into the furniture business in a big way, and riches were to be had for a song. The Depression had closed many mansions in the most exclusive areas of Los Angeles. They attended auctions along Adams and Los Feliz Boulevards and traveled to nearby Glendale and Pasadena, where they purchased rare and imported antiques by the carload—artifacts by the finest French, English, Italian, and Oriental craftsmen. There were pieces of every size, from end tables and curio cabinets to massive armoires, even babygrand pianos.

To house their precious treasures, Albert Smith leased a large warehouse on Western Avenue, moving pieces into the Marmont as needed. A skilled photographer (his development of a special motion picture camera had propelled him into the film business), he would shoot and catalog each piece so that guests could make substitutions from his photo file if they were dissatisfied with particular furnishings in their suites. Chateau Marmont's lavishly decorated and individually different rooms quickly became another of its distinct features. Without realizing it, Albert Smith had created "the Marmont look."

In his attempt to make the Marmont the finest apartment-hotel in Hollywood, Smith continued his spending spree. He fully equipped the kitchen, off the newly refurbished main-floor drawing room, and instructed Ann Little to hire a cook experienced in international cuisine. Her choice was Golan Banks, a man of East Indian and South African heritage, who had worked for years on the Continent.

Although the Marmont had no formal dining room, Ann Little inaugurated a policy of serving catered meals to guests in their suites. Full course dinners, offering a range of entrees, were priced for one dollar and twenty cents (similar meals, without the frills, were offered after serving hours to staff members for thirty-five cents). "Guests would call me in the morning," Little recalled, "to say they were having friends in for dinner that evening. Most of them hadn't even bothered to prepare a menu. They knew Golan would come up with something extraordinary—and that it would be served in an elegant fashion."

At midday on Sundays, a formally-set dining table would appear in the main-floor drawing room, next to one of the towering swag-draped Gothic windows overlooking the garden. The table was reserved exclusively for Albert and Lucille Smith and children Ronald, James Gordon, Kathleen, and Albert. There, fresh from church, they would enjoy a full-course family dinner in the British tradition. Their fare of minted roast lamb, mashed potatoes, green peas, and ice cream never varied from week to week.

Following the meal, the Smiths would relax on the drawing room's stylistic new French settees, where "Father," impeccably dressed as always, from starched collar to spats, enjoyed his cigar. Somehow the conversation always turned to the magnificent framed prints of English country scenes and historic landmarks adorning the walls. They had come from all over the world, sent by members of Smith's large family—eight brothers and a sister—still living in Europe.

In addition to Golan Banks, other newcomers joined the Marmont staff. A security man, Charles, was hired to patrol the stairways and corridors at regular intervals. Many suites were still unoccupied, but a number of guests took time to comment how much safer they felt with Charles making his rounds.

Eddie worked the elevator. A polite young man with an easygoing personality and a smile that never dimmed, he soon became one of the Marmont's most popular employees.

Additional maids were brought in to augment a too-thin crew. New faces included Heddy, Anna Maria, and Elsa.

Ned joined the night staff as desk clerk. After several months on the job, however, he was caught stealing from the cash drawer. Ann Little fired him on the spot, but Albert Smith refused to prosecute. The loss of Ned dropped the staff count to twenty-five.

To help promote the Marmont, Smith hired an advertising writer with the improbable name of Ben Allah Newman. Soon ads began appearing in local publications, touting Hollywood's newest wonder, the elegant Chateau Marmont. Newman's *piece de resistance* was a lavishly illustrated brochure headlined *Designed for Living*, which described "stunning suites of rare refinement and charm" and "comfort highlighted by the choicest pieces of yesteryear's furniture craftsmen." Of the breathtaking vistas from the Marmont's windows, Newman wrote poetically, "A pleasant panorama of people and cars and places of interest for the daylight hours. By night, Hollywood's most breathtaking view. For vast miles stretches a veritable carpet of flickering lights and colors." Gracing the cover was a finely detailed pen and ink drawing of the Marmont under a halo of billowy white clouds. A simplified version of his romanticized design was later adapted as the official logo; only the cars parked outside the main entry are updated from time to time.

Ann Little's name appeared prominently as resident manager on all advertising and promotional pieces. It was Newman's idea. He believed that her still-solid reputation among fans and studio personnel would attract attention and interest. Little appreciated the gesture, but then again she found few things wrong with Newman's work. With the engaging writer also living gratis at the Marmont, they were frequently seen in each other's company. Newman resisted any involvement, preferring only her friendship and nothing more.

With the exception of Albert Smith, Ben Allah Newman probably knew Ann Little better than anyone at the hotel. A very private person, she rarely talked about her personal life. Although she had never married, rumor had it that at one time she was Mrs. Allan Forrest, wife of the silent screen actor. Such talk was dismissed with a simple but firm, "Not true." Even casual conversation concerning her movie days was avoided. "I try not to live in the past," she modestly told a friend. "I've even destroyed all my old scrapbooks and clippings."

One day a visiting reporter from the Los Angeles *Times* spotted Ann Little behind the Marmont's front desk. Surprised to find her there and retired from acting, he requested an interview. She declined at first, then agreed only if she could offer advice to her former colleagues. "There are too many stars who fall from the big time into extra work," she said for the record. "I want to tell them to get busy, especially in these hard times, and make a life for themselves. That's what I'm doing."

Chateau Marmont was one subject Ann Little enjoyed discussing. She thrived in her position as manager and eagerly embarked on chatty guided tours with prospective guests, starting with the penthouse. Albert Smith had primed her to push the lofty six-room suite. "That's our bread and butter," he told her. "As long as the penthouse is rented, we'll do just fine." She wasn't always successful in 'selling' such large-scale accommodations, but she kept enough other suites occupied to more than make up for the loss in income.

Few people could resist Little's charm and forthright approach. "We offer the best service in town," she promised newcomers, "and all the privacy in the world. Give us a week, and you won't want to leave." And they didn't. Guests at the Marmont were so pampered that many delayed their departures. Those unable to stay seldom failed to return. Said Little proudly, "We killed them with kindness."

As summer approached, visitors began flooding Los Angeles for the Olympic Games. Throughout the competition, and for many months afterward, the Marmont was filled to capacity.

It was as Albert Smith had predicted months earlier.

Sunset Boulevard winds through eastern half of "No Man's Land,"
circa 1931. Chateau Marmont rises above roadway at far right.
(*Courtesy of Bison Archives*)

# PART I

# WELCOME TO THE MARMONT

Equestrian group parades along Sunset Boulevard's landscaped
bridle path in Beverly Hills, late 1920s.

Switchboard operator Carmel Volti (*right*) and co-worker Gerdye
LaCoste take a break on the Marmont lawn, early 1930s. (*Courtesy
of Carmel Volti*)

As down-and-out America moved into the 1930s, Hollywood had become a land of dreams, a symbol of luxury, glamor, and hope.

The image that Hollywood projected, and indeed promoted, was misleading. Hollywood was simply a work town, one in transition, and none too secure, having just begun to recover from its first industry panic, the coming of sound. The studios were grinding out talking pictures as fast as they could be shot. Most of them were pretty bad, although the public, still fascinated by the fact that pictures talked at all, was not yet that critical. Still, the nation's woeful economy was reflected at the box office, where brief flurries of business were followed by seemingly endless slumps. For the most part, the great stars of yesterday had faded into a silent world of oblivion. The search was on for new stars. New faces with voices.

On the outskirts of town, and somewhat above it all, Chateau Marmont seemed far removed from the dizzying Hollywood scene. The fact that the hotel was practically "in the country" was of great concern to many incoming visitors who longed to be closer to the action, either because of a burning curiosity or out of necessity.

Of all the questions asked by newcomers to the Marmont, and Hollywood, the most common began with the words, "How far...?" How far, they wanted to know, was it from the hotel to Paramount, or MGM, or Columbia? How far to the plush movie palaces, such as Grauman's Chinese Theater, where the spectacular premieres were held? How far to Hollywood and Vine? To those inquiries, and others, Ann Little had a stock reply. "We're fifteen minutes from everywhere," she would say. She wasn't exaggerating by much.

The line did not originate at the Marmont. It came from the Sunset Boulevard boosters, a small group of merchants dedicated to dispelling the notion that the two-mile stretch of roadway fronting their businesses (Chateau Marmont included) led through an area commonly referred to as "No Man's Land."

In a way, the phrase was quite accurate. Sandwiched between the city limits of Los Angeles to the east and Beverly Hills to the west, this portion of Sunset Boulevard and its environs constituted a tract of unincorporated county territory, unattached to either city and entirely independent of their codes and ordinances.

Being under the county's administration had its disadvantages. The boosters watched in frustration as road crews from the surrounding cities made constant improvements to the boulevard—but the work never progressed beyond the county lines. On the Los Angeles side, trolley tracks had been installed so that passengers could ride in comfort aboard Pacific Electric Red Cars to the Gardner Street depot, a point several miles east of the Marmont. From there, a "dinky" carried more adventurous travelers to the city limits—or "the end of civilization" — just past Laurel Canyon.

On the Beverly Hills side, a bridle path, enhanced with rustic arches and flowering shrubs, divided the road. "Ye Bridle Path," as it was called, not only fostered local interest in horseback riding but camouflaged the old P.E. tracks. Since the discontinuance of trolley service in that area, influential residents had been up in arms, calling the neglected median strip an eyesore.

The unincorporated portion of Sunset Boulevard had its own eyesores. On rainy days, cascading waters from the hillsides turned the street into a sluggish river of mud. Clean-up crews, under-manned and under-equipped, appeared only to shovel the ooze onto the already treacherous soft shoulders, creating small mountains of muck that made parking impossible and foot traffic disappear.

Old-timers in the area were accustomed to such inconveniences. They could remember a time, shortly before the turn of the century, when there was no roadway at all. They could remember, even more vividly, teams of workmen arriving several years later to slash a byway through the hilly countryside, carving out portions of mountain as they zigzagged westward to the ocean. At the right hour of day, said the old-timers, "you would swear the road disappeared into the sunset."

It didn't take long for the newly named Sunset Boulevard to attract developers. But they came to Los Angeles and Beverly Hills, not to No Man's Land. The stretch of roadway that ran between the two cities was considered little more than a connecting link—a convenience that also offered an eye-filling "rim of the world" view of the vast flatlands below.

The first real sign of commercial activity—and elegance—came to the area in 1924, two years before Fred Horowitz discovered his site for Chateau Marmont. Francis S. Montgomery began construction on four "Champs Elysee-style" store buildings, each containing six shops. He called his project Sunset Plaza. It was situated on both sides of the street in the very heart of "the link."

Hollywood agents were the next to arrive, chased out of their Los Angeles offices in the early 1930s, when the city clamped a $100 business tax on artists' representatives.

The Hollywood agents ascended on Sunset Boulevard in impressive numbers. High-powered names like Jessie Wadsworth, Vic Orsatti, Leon

Lance, Maggie Ettinger, Bessie Loo, and Harry Eddington, came west to open up shop where restrictions were far fewer. The advantages offered by the county were beginning to outweigh the disadvantages. As Jessie Wadsworth later remarked, "County license fees and taxes were far lower than they were in Los Angeles or Beverly Hills, and rents were so much cheaper. The whole atmosphere was more liberal. Besides, most of my clients lived in the vicinity and drove along Sunset going to and from the movie studios. It was a central location in a far-flung business. As the saying went, we were fifteen minutes from everywhere."

Each of the agents brought along an impressive clientele, the top names in motion pictures. That fact was not lost on Billy Wilkerson, whose recently launched industry trade paper, *The Hollywood Reporter*, was flourishing.

Wilkerson drew even more celebrities to the area when he created Cafe Trocadero on vacant land just east of Sunset Plaza. From its dazzling opening night party in 1934, hosted by producer Myron Selznick, the "Troc" became a mecca for the film colony.

Gambling was a natural for the free-wheeling, free-spending atmosphere of No Man's Land. Night after night, famous formally clad patrons roamed freely through the elegant salons of the country's newest, most lavish gambling casino, the Clover Club. The illicit hillside operation had quickly become a favorite haunt of the big spenders, while being virtually ignored by the authorities. That it was run by a burly former Los Angeles vice-squad officer made little or no difference.

The hillsides along No Man's Land—the future Sunset Strip—had yet to be developed when Carmel Volti made her way to Chateau Marmont in 1930. At that time, that portion of Sunset Boulevard was still a neglected section of roadway, and Ben Weingart, between trysts with his mistress-manager, Emma Lovell, was striving to save the hotel for owner Fred Horowitz. Carmel had only recently come to Hollywood from Diamondville, Wyoming, after detouring briefly in Utah. Like other young women who come to Hollywood from towns throughout the country, Carmel had a dream—although hers was quite different from most.

In the small mining town of Diamondville, Carmel's father spent his days delivering bread, freshly baked by his brother, to the miners' wives; her mother worked in the general store, selling everything from groceries to work clothes. Carmel wanted none of that. Her ambition was to become a switchboard operator for the telephone company. "We didn't have many luxuries or necessities, but for some reason we were one of the few families to have a phone." The wall-mounted contraption fascinated her.

# WELCOME TO THE MARMONT

There was no place in or around Diamondville for Carmel to pursue her dream; she had to wait until she was seventeen, when her parents pulled up stakes and moved to Salt Lake City. But the big town brought disappointment rather than the start of a career. The personnel director of the phone company took one look at Carmel's smallish size and sighed, "Heavens no—your arms are much too short to reach the switchboard."

It wasn't until Carmel came to California and the Marmont that she was given a chance—and she made the most of it. Except for time out to marry and have a child, she worked at the Marmont for forty-three years, far more than any other employee. During that time, she firmly established herself, not only as the hotel's Number One telephone operator, but as "The Voice of the Marmont."

Carmel Volti was the first of the legendary "Marmont ladies" to work at the hotel, and throughout the 1930s she would witness both the glamor and the hard times this period would bring. She would also welcome some very special guests to her place of employment.

Nellita Choate Thomsen, *nee* Pauline Payne. (*Courtesy of Larry Bordeaux*)

# Chapter 1

## Fifteen Minutes From Everywhere

## Mrs. Thomsen

Everybody thought they knew Nellita Choate Thomsen. They had discovered, for example, that she was the daughter of an aristocratic Southern family, the William L. Choates of Chesterfield County, Virginia, and a direct descendant of the emminent lawyer-orator-statesman, Rufus Choate, legendary patriarch of the illustrious Choates of Boston. They had learned, not necessarily indirectly, that she was born "within the shadows of Jefferson's glorious Monticello," that she was a superior hostess (her lavish society parties, catered by the Marmont, were the talk of Hollywood), and a devoted patron of the arts. The Marmont's charter guest was not only blue blood but blue book.

Everyone who came in contact with Nellita Choate Thomsen, even the most casual acquaintance, had to admit that she was not the typical society matron of the day. The most obvious difference was her age. When Nellita and her husband, wealthy manufacturing jeweler-turned-architect, Carl H. Thomsen, moved to Chateau Marmont shortly after its opening in February, 1929, she had been out of college less than seven years; her numerous impressive accomplishments at Stanford were still fresh, beacons for other young women to follow. And, unlike her colleagues, she zealously avoided recognition for her philanthropic endeavors. Photographers found her more slippery than the F.B.I.'s most wanted criminals when they aimed cameras in her direction. Even her closest friends were at a loss to explain why she refused to allow her lovely likeness to appear in print.

# WELCOME TO THE MARMONT

At Stanford, according to her yearbook, "Nellita was one of the most popular and brilliant girls on the campus. In addition to winning the Phi Beta Kappa key for scholarship in her junior year, she participated in college dramatics, assisted in editing one of the college journals, was a member of the Women's Conference and Kappa Kappa Gamma sorority."

More than anything Nellita loved to write, and she used her considerable talents to voice her opinions on raging campus issues in the pages of the *Stanford Illustrated Review.* No person or subject intimidated her. When an editorial authored by a prominent professor infuriated her, she countered: "The literary tone of the *Illustrated Review* should not be lowered by illiterate contributors." When the Women's Conference attempted to control the actions of her classmates, she wrote: "The Conference is involving itself in endless complexities when it attempts to arbitrarily establish laws of good taste. Provincialism, restraint, puerile rules, and the stupid compliance to such regulations are not worthy of the Real Stanford Woman who, regardless of a few foolish exceptions, is capable of thinking for herself, deciding for herself, and acting for herself." When the university fixed the number of women students at five hundred, commonly referred to as the Stanford Five Hundred, she lashed out: "The education of both sexes must be equally full and complete. The rights of one sex, political or otherwise, are the same as those of the other sex and this equality of rights must be fully recognized!"

At the Marmont, Nellita was considerably less outspoken, at times quiet as a sponge. In fact, it was her willingness to act the role of a sympathetic listener, coupled with her ability to respond with only the most appropriate comments or questions, that earned her so many friends.

Her genuine fondness for people made it seem perfectly natural when she appointed herself to the unofficial position as the Marmont's "official greeter." She made it her business to meet all incoming guests, and no one, least of all the celebrated who held a special attraction for her, escaped her most gracious welcome. It wasn't long before she charmed her way into their confidences, in the process discovering fascinating stories and tidbits of information beyond her wildest imagination.

What the guests failed to discover about Nellita was that she led a double life. As Pauline Payne she was a crackerjack reporter for the Hearst newspapers, often competing with Adela Rogers St. Johns covering scandalous trials and sensational happenings within the motion picture industry. Her daily syndicated column, "The Merry-Go Round," reached millions of devoted followers across the nation, who doted on her outspoken revelations, scoops unwittingly provided, in large part, by her unsuspecting neighbors at the Marmont. After all, she had a wealth of intriguing and ever-changing subjects only scant seconds from the doorway of her suite.

Jean Acker had been a leading lady in silent films long before she registered at Chateau Marmont. But her greatest claim to fame came as a result of her marriage to a bit player named Rudolph Valentino in 1919 and their divorce, following his incredible success with *The Sheik*, in 1921. Jean Acker never relinquished her married name, using it not only in private life but as a screen credit. Mrs. Rudolph Valentino, as she insisted on being addressed, confided to Nellita Choate Thomsen that she locked her sensuously handsome husband out of their secret honeymoon hideaway on their wedding night. "That was the end of him," Mrs. Valentino boasted. "He thought more of making love to the camera than to me!"

George Hill, the distinguished director, became the first occupant of the penthouse in mid-1929. At the time, he was moving from one Frances Marion-scripted film, *The Big House*, to another, *Min and Bill* (both would be among MGM's biggest hits in the coming year), and entertaining friends Lila Lee, Marie Dressler, and Louella Parsons. But it was with Miss Marion, the recent widow of cowboy star Fred Thomson, that he became romantically involved. Their courtship began on the set of *The Secret Six*, their fifth teaming, and soon adjourned to the Marmont. As plans for their wedding were being arranged, Hill was involved in a horrifying accident that resulted in the death of a family of Japanese immigrants. Although Hill was held blameless, he could not wipe the tragedy from his mind; it remained with him constantly even after his eventual marriage to Frances Marion. One morning in 1934, while lying in bed with his wife at their Malibu beach house, George Hill stuck a pistol in his mouth and shot himself.

Blonde, dimpled character actress Minna Gombel was happily single when she moved to the Marmont in 1930. But her days as one of Hollywood's most eligible bachelor girls were numbered when she met successful San Diego banker, Joseph W. Sefton. Their courtship was far from typical, as Hollywood courtships go; it dragged on for nearly two years, hampered in part by Sefton's out-of-town business responsibilities. When at last Minna said "I do," she gained not only a husband but a young son, Tom, from Sefton's earlier marriage.

For a time, the newlywed Seftons seemed idyllically happy, although they were rarely together. Minna's film commitments kept her in Hollywood, forcing her husband to travel back and forth on weekends to be with her.

With each extended parting, Minna's smile became less radiant, her laugh less jovial. Ultimately, the marriage could not survive the on-again, off-again relationship, leaving the once-dimpled darling of the screen a sad and broken woman. "It was no wonder," Nellita Thomsen remarked rather pointedly, "that she played brassy, hardbitten faded blondes so well in her later films."

Another of Nellita's early neighbors at the Marmont was Clara Clemens, the daughter of Mark Twain, who signed in only days after the death of her husband, famed pianist-conductor, Ossip Gabrilowitsch. Prior to her arrival, during the dark months of Ossip's illness, when doctors gave him little hope, they had sought spiritual methods of healing through Christian Science. At the Marmont, Clara found being alone impossible and turned to Ann Little for consolation, begging to know if she could talk with her husband. "Is he near?" she asked repeatedly. "Will he return to see me?" But it was with Nellita Thomsen that Clara spent many lonely hours, particularly during early evenings. With only a single dim light burning, Clara would tearfully reminisce about happier days, as a Victrola mournfully cranked out the strains of Ossip's classical recordings. When it was impossible for Nellita to be near, Clara would try to seek solace at her baby-grand piano. An accomplished pianist herself, she often played through the night, sobbing quietly as she delicately fingered the compositions that were her dear husband's favorites.

For nearly a decade, starting in mid-1929, the enormously wealthy Theodore Whites and their entourage occupied two-thirds of the second floor. (In adjoining smaller suites lived a maid, cook, nurse, and chauffeur.) Mr. White was a brilliant civil engineer, whose most challenging accomplishment, the designing of the Los Angeles freeway system, was still years away; Mrs. White was an exquisitely beautiful heiress from Sweden. It was not the Whites who intrigued Nellita Thomsen, but the "children," to whom the stunning Swede played surrogate mother.

In one of their nearby suites, stripped of all Marmont furnishings and completely redecorated for the comfort of its occupants, lived a menagerie of fanciful, exotic pets, birds of every size and color, and a long-haired monkey with huge glistening eyes, which Mrs. White cradled in her arms as if she had given birth to it.

Stan Laurel, the wispy, featherbrained member of the screen's most successful comedy team, continually frustrated Nellita Thomsen in her attempts to "welcome" him. "He opens his door at the Marmont only to admit the liquor man," she wrote of the forever drunk comedian.

Nellita didn't see much of Katharine Hepburn either, not that she would have recognized her if she did. Hepburn's striking face, with its wide eyes, high cheekbones, full mouth, and angular jawline may have attracted attention on the east coast, where she had appeared in theatrical productions, but she was unknown at the Marmont when she strode through the lobby one July afternoon in 1932. Still, she didn't go completely unnoticed. Tall, leggy, spattered with freckles, and dressed in an expensive-looking but unflattering gray silk suit (her traveling outfit), she wore her long, frizzy hair pulled severely back and stuffed under a large saucer hat. Even more distinctive was the eye-patch she wore.

Hepburn, at twenty-four, had been summoned to Hollywood by RKO for her first motion picture, *A Bill of Divorcement*. During the long train trip west, she had injured her eye. The accident had happened as she and her constant companion, American Express heiress Laura Harding (who registered with Hepburn at the Marmont), stood on the windy platform of the train's observation car. A "speck of something" had flown into her eye. In trying to remove it, she had scratched the retina.

The bothersome eye-patch was soon discarded; at least, she was not wearing it the morning after her arrival at the Marmont. Hepburn's eye was quite swollen, but apparently that was of little concern to her, judging by the rest of her appearance. The odd-looking gray suit had been replaced by pants and an old, oversize man's sweater, gathered and held in the back by a large safety pin.

Hepburn did travel in style, however. The car that took her and Laura Harding to the studio that morning was an elegant, enormous Hispano-Suiza limousine, driven by a liveried chauffeur. The classic automobile was undoubtedly more famous, at that point, than Hepburn. It had been used by Greta Garbo in *Grand Hotel* earlier in the year.

Katharine Hepburn and Laura Harding remained at the Marmont less than a week before moving to a small cottage in one of the nearby canyons. Mrs. Hearst stayed considerably longer.

The very elegant and lovely Mrs. Hearst, estranged wife of one of William Randolph Hearst's sons, was at the Marmont while awaiting her divorce and a huge settlement. "She looks like a Ziegfeld girl as she descends the staircase to the lobby, her hair adorned with delicate ostrich plumes," Nellita Thomsen revealed in her column. She didn't report that, until Mrs. Hearst received her settlement, which was being fiercely contested, she was virtually without funds. Nor did Nellita mention Mrs. Hearst's desperate attempts to obtain ready cash while awaiting the court's decision.

One day, after collecting her mail from the front desk, the exquisitely gowned Mrs. Hearst encountered the security man, Charles, in the corridor leading to her suite. "I must discuss a delicate and private matter with you," she said, inviting him inside. She poured herself a cordial and offered Charles a cigarette from the coffee table humidor. Before he could strike a match, she was grasping his arm and ranting, "I'm absolutely desperate. You must help me!"

Thinking Mrs. Hearst feared for her safety, Charles urged her to explain. But it was no threat, imagined or real, that had her so distraught. "I'm destitute," she cried, "absolutely penniless. Mr. Hearst has left me without a cent, and I don't know where to turn. If you could loan me a small amount until I receive my fortune . . . "

Charles politely excused himself. He didn't even attempt to explain his own financial plight, the sacrifices he and his family were having to endure while living on the meager earnings provided by his part-time job; he felt fortunate indeed to be working at all in these uncertain times. Charles tried to forget the incident, but he could not, and the longer it stayed with him the angrier he became. After days of deliberation, he decided he had to tell someone. And so, in strictest confidence, he reported to the Marmont's private ear, Nellita Choate Thomsen.

Exotic Mexican actress, Raquel Torres, refused to admit that her career was on the wane. She had achieved overnight stardom with her first film, *White Shadows of the South Seas*, but subsequent roles were impressive mainly because of her beauty. At the Marmont, she was her own best publicity agent. "I am very busy with many new roles," she would say. To further enhance the illusion, she repeatedly left word at the front desk to stuff her mail box with messages so she would appear "in demand." That was especially important on days when her phone seldom rang, which was often.

Mary Astor, a favorite of moviegoers since the early 1920's, arrived at the Marmont in an ambulance during the winter of 1935. Stricken with pneumonia while filming a trouble-plagued feature on location at Lake Tahoe (the company was snowed in and everyone came down with the flu, including one crew member who died), she was rushed back to Los Angeles to recuperate. The Marmont was not her first choice. She had wanted to return to her comfortable home in Toluca Lake to be near her young daughter, Marylyn, but that was impossible. Her estranged husband, obstetrician Dr. Franklyn Thorpe, happened to be in residence at the home at the time. "She looked so frail—that lovely woman—that we were afraid we might lose her," remembered Ann Little, "but that phone call seemed to renew her spirits." The call came from Dr. Thorpe to advise Astor that he was abandoning their home for a place in town, one closer to his office. Mary Astor departed Chateau Marmont within the week, still frail but "more determined than ever that her marriage was over." In the months to follow, she would need all her strength. Ahead were a bitter court battle over the custody of Marylyn and the publication of alleged extracts from her diary detailing indiscretions with many notables—particularly her illicit love affair with writer George S. Kaufman. It would become the most publicized scandal of the 1930's.

"Garbo's wonderful agent, Harry Eddington, has taken a suite at Chateau Marmont," Nellita Thomsen told her readers. She also labeled him a "top-flight flirt," when she learned he was screening prospective clients ("beautiful young things") within the confines of his luxurious new quarters. Only days earlier, she had received a tip that his estranged wife was shopping for marked-down items in the May Company basement.

There were other notable early guests:

Singer Lanny Ross, during the filming of *Melody In Spring* and *College Rhythm;* author James Hilton, while preparing the screenplay of *Camille* (with Frances Marion and Zoe Akins); actress-comedienne Ina Claire and her maid, Lena Hopnon; Broadway choreographer Robert Altman, for his first Hollywood film assignment, *Strike Me Pink;* actors Lee Tracy, Conrad Nagel, and Louis Sobol; actresses Estelle Taylor and Enid Markey.

Alan Napier, Norma Vareen, and Larry Adler(the harmonica virtuoso) first came to the Marmont during the Depression, years before it was fashionable for the British crowd. "They were such nice people," Ann Little remembered, "so refined and elegant. And those beautiful voices. Everyone was a little envious of the way they spoke."

When Ned Sparks, the stone-faced character actor, moved into Chateau Marmont in the early 1930's, he brought with him a droopy-eyed companion, a beagle, who bore an uncanny resemblance to his master. Little did Sparks realize that he was starting a trend with pets, one that would nearly get out of hand in the coming years. As any number of guests have commented: "Everybody had *something*."

One early guest had a bushy Spitz, who was trained to stand at the elevator every morning at eight o'clock. "It was the most amazing little animal," Ann Little recalled. "A houseboy would meet the dog at the elevator, take it downstairs, and walk it all around the block. When they returned, he would put the dog in the elevator and send it back upstairs. That went on like clockwork for months. Then we had the Theodore Whites, with their

their parrot and monkey. They always kept their pets inside, thank Heavens!"

The Ritz Brothers—Al, Jimmy, and Harry—were a top attraction in vaudeville, night clubs, and on the musical stage, when they signed with Twentieth Century-Fox in 1935, to spark up some of the studio's song-and-dance productions with their zany antics. Over the next four years, throughout their stay at Fox, the comic trio not only called the Marmont home, but romped through the corridors and lobby at will—singing, dancing, clowning—while rehearsing new routines for the screen.

If it sounds like the brothers played havoc with the hotel's cherished tranquility, oldtimers swear "not so." Anyone who had the good fortune of witnessing the Ritzes' hijinks contends that there was nothing raucous or ill-mannered about them. "They were nice, polite men, with a high-class act," observers recall. "They left the slapstick and physical insanity to the Marx Brothers."

As the Marmont's charter guest, Nellita Choate Thomsen considered herself blessed. She had witnessed the creation of "the Marmont look"—which she unhesitatingly accredited to Albert E. Smith—and she felt at least partially responsible for helping establish the hotel's show business connection. These early days at the hotel, as she would discover later, were the highlight of her life.

# Mr. Murray

It was a typical chilly day in early March, but the temperature was the last thing on the mind of comedian Ken Murray. He was living in luxury high above Sunset Boulevard on the tenth floor of the appropriately named Sunset Tower, an Art Deco column of concrete located less than a curving mile west of Chateau Marmont. The lavish apartment wasn't Murray's. It belonged to Richard Dix, the ruggedly handsome hero of silent films, who let Murray "camp out" whenever he came to town, which, lately, was often.

Ken Murray was spreading his show business wings, turning from vaudeville, where he had been the youngest entertainer on the Keith circuit, to motion pictures. Now, after four films in less than three years, and more planned, he was starring on his own network radio show as well.

Juggling his many activities left twenty-nine-year-old Murray with few idle moments. But he was never too busy for his favorite pastimes—photographing Hollywood's elite in unguarded moments, usually at play, and entertaining the most attractive of movieland's leading ladies.

On the afternoon of March 10, 1933, Ken Murray had reached one of his avocational plateaus. Secluded in his borrowed high rise apartment, he was playing host to the quintessential flapper of more than a dozen films, the vivacious Sue Carol. Before she could say "showtime," Murray had her nestled snugly in his lap, as a projector cranked out the latest of his amusing self-shot productions.

But the day had more in store for Murray than hot times and home movies. At 5:15 P.M., Sunset Tower lurched with a jolt, nearly catapulting a startled Miss Carol from Murray's arms. Pictures danced off the walls, and furniture tumbled, as the lofty structure began to sway like a wagging finger in the sky.

A massive earthquake, its epicenter located less than fifty miles to the south, in the Long Beach area, was rocking Hollywood. The first shock lasted a suspense-filled, and seemingly endless, eleven seconds.

When the movement at last subsided, Murray and his terrified guest darted for the door. "We ran for our lives," he reported, "without even thinking to grab a coat or sweater. And was it cold outside!"

The elevator wasn't running, so they were forced to descend ten flights of stairs to ground level. Midway there, however, Murray stopped. "As frightened as I was," he remembers. "I kept hearing a voice telling me, 'You shouldn't have left that way!' It was crazy but, at that moment, I wasn't thinking about aftershocks or crumbling buildings. I only knew that I had to go back upstairs."

In those days, Murray admits, he had a phobia about leaving a room cluttered and unkempt. So strong were his feelings that he was compelled to send Sue Carol on her way, while he returned to the tenth-floor apartment. There, within its cracked plaster walls, he straightened pictures, uprighted overturned chairs, tables, and lamps, even emptied ashtrays. "I just couldn't leave the place in a mess," he explained.

Outside, traffic clogged dusty Sunset Boulevard. Residents, who only moments earlier had run screaming and crying from their hillside homes, now huddled in small groups along the roadside hoping to find solace among friends and neighbors. There were famous faces in the crowd. On the walkway near the Garden of Allah stood actors Charlie Butterworth, Louis Calhern, and Willard Keefe, author Ward Morehouse, screenwriters Robert Benchley and Edwin Justers Mayer, and Lela Rogers, whose dancing daughter, Ginger, had yet to return from the studio where she was working.

Ken Murray wandered along the boulevard until he reached Chateau

# WELCOME TO THE MARMONT

Marmont. He had heard that the Marmont was "built like a rock," and he found the words comforting now that he was no longer enchanted with sky-high living.

The lobby of the Marmont seemed strangely calm. There were no signs of the quake nor any indication of panic by the small gathering of guests who sat, chatting idly, in the drawing room. Everyone appeared oblivious to the commotion in the streets.

As manager Ann Little remembered the catastrophic event: "I had just come downstairs after fixing a big bouquet of red roses for an incoming guest, when I felt the building starting to sway. My first thought, oddly enough, was of the flowers. I told myself, 'Oh, no, the roses have toppled.' But when I went upstairs to check, they were exactly as I'd left them. Nothing was broken, nothing had even moved. The swaying had been so gentle. The most frightening thing was seeing the trees outside. They were shaking so wildly their leaves were falling like confetti. But inside we were just fine."

Ken Murray registered instantly.

Over the next few years, Murray frequently made the Marmont his Hollywood headquarters, usually for a week or two at a time. It was on one of his visits that he was in for the shock of his life, a far different kind of jolt than he received that fateful March day in 1933.

"I was engaged to a beautiful girl then, a very big movie star, and I had just returned after being on the road. She didn't like my traveling so much, but it was part of my job, something we had to live with."

To celebrate his homecoming, Murray planned a festive night on the town with his illustrious fiancee. During the evening, however, he sensed something was wrong. "She acted happy to see me and insisted she loved me more than ever, but I couldn't get really close to her. She seemed restless and preoccupied." At that point Murray suggested driving her home. It was earlier than planned, but she didn't argue. "When we reached the Los Feliz district, were she lived, she made me promise to phone her the minute I got back to the Marmont. I guess she could tell how disappointed I was over the way the evening had gone. She seemed so concerned about me I couldn't refuse. Besides, I was still stuck on her."

Eager to hear his betrothed's voice again, Murray raced through the streets of Hollywood. Reaching the Marmont, he rushed to his upstairs suite and placed his call with the switchboard operator. "I heard a click," he recalls, "then another click. All of a sudden I was cut into a conversation already in progress. I could hear my fiancee talking with another man, and she was saying, 'He'll probably be gone in a day or two, then we can be together. Tonight? It was awful. I couldn't wait to get away.' "

Murray put the receiver down, unable to listen any more. He was crushed.

"I kept asking myself why I had to hear her say those things? Why, at that moment, did the lines get crossed? It was a one in a million fluke."

Not much later, Murray's phone rang. It was his fiancee, wondering why he hadn't called her.

"I tried," he said, "but your line was busy."

"My line busy?" she replied lightly. "Really?"

"That's right, and you know how my imagination runs wild. I kept thinking you'd found somebody new, and you were telling him, 'Ken will be gone in a day or two, then we can be together. Tonight? It was awful. I couldn't wait to get away.' " He repeated verbatim the bit of conversation he had overheard. Then he waited for an explanation.

She responded without a second's pause. "You *do* have an active imagination, darling. *You're* my one and only. I just wasn't myself tonight, but tomorrow will be different. I will see you tomorrow, won't I?"

"Of course," Murray answered, as sincerely as possible.

He had no intention of seeing her, ever again. "Early the next morning, I checked out of the Marmont, drove to Union Station, and boarded a train for Houston. I had to change the scenery."

Changing the scenery was the easy part. Forgetting the hurtful incident was more difficult. Murray's beautiful love-of-his-life was constantly in the headlines. The papers played up her latest films, her trend-setting fashions, and her romantic escapades with her newfound love. "She married the guy on the phone," Murray admits. Then he adds philosophically, "but I was the lucky one after all. Once she landed him, she turned right around and sued for divorce."

# Mr. and Mrs. Rosson

On the afternoon of September 20, 1933, a black Pierce Arrow touring car, its wire wheels reflecting the hot California sun, made its way up Marmont Lane and parked directly in front of the colonnaded entry to Chateau Marmont. From the driver's side stepped a nattily attired middle-aged man of medium height, with slicked-back hair and a small, dark mustache. He paused briefly to straighten his coat and tie, then smiled in the direction of the passenger door before moving on alone. It was impossible to determine the object of his attention inside the car. Despite the temperature, the side windows were sealed and covered with roll-up shades.

Anyone who had seen a newspaper over the past few days would have recognized the man immediately as Harold Rosson, one of Hollywood's ace cameramen. His photo had been featured prominently on front pages across the country, along with his new bride, the curvaceous and controversial platinum blonde film sensation, Jean Harlow. Their surprise elopement on Monday, just two days earlier, had made headlines.

The newlyweds had come to the Marmont, bypassing the revitalized Garden of Allah and nearby Sunset Tower, in search of a honeymoon suite. It was Hal's choice. He had had a soft spot in his heart for the Marmont ever since he learned of Albert E. Smith's take-over. It was Smith who had given Rosson his first break in show business, hiring him as a teenage bit player with Vitagraph in 1908, then grooming him for a career behind the camera, one that in time surpassed even his mentor's expectations.

Rosson's ties with the past were strengthened considerably when he discovered another familiar face from his Vitagraph days waiting to greet him in the lobby. Ann Little, whom he had known for over twenty years, had been anxiously watching his arrival from the main-floor drawing room windows. Surprised to see her, he asked incredulously, "What are *you* doing here?'

Never one for explanations, she answered simply, "Oh, I'm just here."

"Well, isn't this like old home week!" he beamed, warmly, taking her hand. "Jean and I are going to love this place." The question of available accommodations wasn't even raised. In 1933, vacancy signs were still as common as bread-lines and five-cent apples.

It was fifteen minutes later when Harold Rosson, accompanied by Ann Little, returned to his bride. Jean Harlow was still seated in the touring car, only now she was in clear view next to an open window. Few people would have guessed her identity. A floral silk scarf covered all but a wisp of her glowing blonde locks, and dark glasses shielded her bedroom eyes. She smiled graciously, as Rosson introduced her to the manager, then asked, "What'd you find—anything?"

With one hand, Rosson teasingly jangled the keys to Suite 3BC. He followed with a sweep of his arm, pointing to the third floor windows that stretched nearly the entire length of the Marmont's north-south wing. "Swell," Jean said, nodding in the direction of the building, "I want to hear all about it."

Ann Little invited Jean inside, but she declined. "I'll take a rain check," Jean signed, sounding wilted. "I'd better get home before I keel over." She pulled a small square of chiffon from her handbag and dabbed at her forehead.

Home for Harlow was her newly completed neo-Georgian mansion less than ten miles away. Perched on a rise overlooking the imposing Bel Air gate at Beverly Glen Drive and Sunset Boulevard, the huge two-story home, painted the color of whipped cream, stood as a monument to America's reigning sex symbol. With its shimmering swimming pool, bridged lily pond, and more than an acre of lush landscaping, Jean Harlow had surrounded herself with more luxury than she had ever dreamed possible. Only one thing was missing—privacy.

Building and furnishing a house from scratch was the idea of Jean's agent and discoverer, Arthur Landau, who firmly believed that such an undertaking would provide her some much-needed stability following the tragic suicide of her former husband, Paul Bern.

Jean had initially resisted Landau's suggestion, fearing a large place would attract her possessive mother, "Mama Jean," and opportunistic stepfather, Marino Bello. Landau pushed his case and won—and Jean never forgave him. Immediately upon completion of the Beverly Glen estate, in late December, 1932, Mama Jean and Marino moved in, lock, stock, and barrel. Then they took control, bankrolling their spending sprees with Jean's money. Despite their hovering, often smothering presence, Jean actually began to form an attachment to what she laughingly called "my house."

Living with the Bellos was difficult enough, without a husband. With one, it was impossible. Jean publicly stated that "any man capable of putting up with Mama and Marino is not a man I would want in marriage." Harold Rosson showed his mettle early on. After only two days of strained connubial bliss at Beverly Glen, he issued an ultimatum: "*They* go or *we* go!" Jean opted for the easy way out. Pulling up roots would be far less complicated than a confrontation with her imperious mother and stepfather.

It would be a full week before the Rossons took occupancy of 3BC at the Marmont, but Jean didn't wait that long to acquaint herself with her new surroundings. Less than twenty-four hours after Hal had signed the guest registry, a revitalized Jean appeared at the front desk. She was accompanied not by her husband, whom she claimed was working, but by a stately blonde woman and a suavely handsome man who identified themselves as Mr. and Mrs. Bello. "We're here to look around," Jean told Ann Little. "Is my rain check still good?"

The Harold Rossons (*front*) and Marino Bellos in a rare snapshot taken the day Hal and his bride, Jean Harlow, checked into Chateau Marmont. (*Courtesy of Sandy Arcieri*)

The bedroom in the Rossons' honeymoon suite contained twin beds until Mama Jean stepped in.

Clark Gable's nights with Harlow at the Marmont sparked talk that they were more than "just friends."

"Good as gold," Little answered, beckoning them upstairs.

Jean smiled. The Bellos registered no emotion.

As manager Little remembered: "Mrs. Rosson acted more than pleased with her accommodations. She went from room to room, commenting, 'This is perfect—just perfect.' The remark seemed quite natural at the time." The Bellos, she said, exchanged disapproving glances, but for the most part, kept silent. "They appeared to be biting their tongues."

The only negative comment came from Jean's mother. Stepping into the master bedroom, she gasped, "Twin beds! Wait until some nosey reporter gets ahold of *that!*" A call to the switchboard brought a strapping young man on the run, who removed the small dividing bedstand and secured the two bed frames snugly together. The result was one bed of mammoth proportions, a playground worthy of a sex siren.

Suite 3BC at the Marmont was actually two adjoining suites, connected by a long central hall. It contained a foyer, a large high-ceilinged living room (with a hidden Murphy bed and a flickering antique *faux* fireplace, fronted by a petit point screen), a separate dining room and terrace (reached through French doors), kitchen, master bedroom, and two full "his and her" baths, each with its own dressing room. French windows throughout opened to sweeping views: the city to the south, the ocean to the west. The suite was elegantly furnished with period pieces of the Chippendale style, upholstered in muted tones of blue and beige. Contrary to legend, nothing was "Harlow white," not even the walls, which were painted a soft sand to match the draperies and carpeting.

The layout was especially appealing to honeymooners, as the master bedroom, located at the far end of the central hallway, was completely isolated from the rest of the suite. It even had its own private entrance leading to the outside corridor.

On Friday, September 22, Jean brought in suitcases packed with clothes and personal effects, and boxes of books. The cookbooks went in the kitchen, the others lined shelves in the living room. Glamorous publicity photos framed in silver were placed on tables in every room. Sprigs of trailing ivy graced the fireplace mantel, along with an ornate rococo clock. Soon deliveries arrived from the most fashionable shops along Wilshire Boulevard, gifts of liquor, china, monogrammed towels and pillowcases purchased by the Bellos. The bills arrived within the month, addressed to Jean Harlow Rosson, in care of Chateau Marmont.

Next came cases of canned tomato juice, cartons of raspberries, bags of celery, carrots, watercress, and endive, and bottles of skimmed milk—

all part of Jean's "complexion diet," a beauty secret she generously shared with her inquiring maid, Anna Maria.

From the start, the Rossons were rarely alone. Visitors arrived all hours, laden with housewarming presents: flowers, liquor, and candy. Those able to time their arrivals to the dinner hour were often invited to join Jean and Hal in a meal, especially prepared and served from the Marmont kitchen, most often baked fish and steamed fresh vegetables. Jean personally consulted with cook Golan Banks on several occasions to make certain he understood the restrictions of a healthful diet. Said Banks, following one of their meetings, "It's a wonder how such a gracious lady can portray the sinister, sinning vixens she does on the screen. She must be a wonderful actress."

Each morning Harold Rosson would leave at dawn for MGM, where he was starting *This Side of Heaven*. Jean was currently "between pictures," having completed her latest film, *Bombshell*, on which Hal was the cameraman, just prior to their elopement. But she kept busy in other ways, usually in her suite at the Marmont. There were sessions with interviewers, photographers, her hairdresser, and masseuse, and meetings with advertisers, representatives from Max Factor's "Society Make-up" and Lux Soap, products Jean was endorsing. It was impossible to keep track of the comings and goings, as many visitors never passed through the lobby, making their way upstairs directly from the garage. At times, late arrivals were seen entering the door marked 3B, which led directly into the Rossons' master bedroom.

Hal faithfully returned to the Marmont each evening. That was not always the case with Jean, whose affable husband was often left to make excuses with the switchboard. She's running late tonight, he would say, or she's visiting her mother at Beverly Glen.

In the eyes of the general public, the Rossons were hopelessly in love. Newspapers and magazines ran photos of the honeymoon couple sharing adoring glances, holding hands, and playfully embracing at filmland functions. "Hal's the one great emotion in my life," Jean told a reporter. Insiders at the Marmont knew better. Passing through the lobby, the couple rarely spoke to one another. They kept their hands to themselves, and their glances were straightforward.

The morning after the Rossons' arrival, one of the third-floor maids came across a startling discovery. In the master bedroom, she found only one slept-in bed; in the living room, she found another. The Murphy bed, she reported later, was used every night, even on those occasions when Jean failed to return to the hotel. The news spread like wildfire among the help.

There was another discovery: a chain latch had been installed on the doorway leading from the master bedroom to the rest of the suite.

As the days passed, Jean grew progressively edgy, and there was talk that she was feuding with her MGM bosses, particularly Louis B. Mayer, over her demands for a new contract and a hefty salary increase. Although she never spoke of her disenchantment with the studio, or a possible suspension should she fail to soften her stand, she did mention the possibility of someday making films on her own. "I have such wonderful plans for the future," she said one afternoon, stopping to pick up her mail. A message from Mayer's secretary brought a sudden droop to her famous arched brows, and her voice hardened as she added, "That day may not be far away. Then the lion will *really* have something to roar about."

By the end of the month, Jean's struggles with the studio appeared to be resolved. On the morning of September 29, massive floral arrangements began arriving from the powers at MGM. From Louis B. Mayer came dozens of long-stemmed white roses. From Irving Thalberg a breathtaking creation of orchids, birds of paradise, and anthuriums. From director Victor Fleming came lilies of the valley. Clark Gable sent a rainbow of gladiolas. The Rosson suite at the Marmont looked like a hothouse in full bloom.

The occasion for the outpouring was twofold. Although no proclamation had been given, it was clearly Jean Harlow weekend in Hollywood. On Friday afternoon, she received the star treatment at Grauman's Chinese Theater, where her hand and footprints were immortalized in cement for her screaming fans. The following evening, wrapped in luxurious white fur and shimmering satin, Jean returned to Grauman's movie palace for the premiere of *Bombshell*. She was mobbed by reporters and photographers as she made her way along the red carpet into the theater. All but lost in the crowd were Harold Rosson and Mama Jean. Marino Bello failed to appear.

Two weeks later, three days shy of their one-month anniversary, the Rossons departed the Marmont for an announced evening of celebration, only to return earlier than expected. Jean did not look well. Hal commented, as he helped his wife from the garage to the elevator, that she probably had too much excitement for one day. That afternoon, they had joined friends to attend a college football game at the Los Angeles Coliseum.

By midnight, Jean's condition had worsened. Hal kept the Marmont switchboard lighted with calls for extra blankets, hot water bottles, and "anything from the kitchen to ease her queasiness." When Jean began complaining of extreme stomach pains, he reached for the phone again, this time to summon a doctor.

In those days, and for the next forty-two years, all outgoing phone calls had to be placed through the switchboard, which was manually operated, using a series of plugs and switches. An enterprising operator could easily listen in on calls, and was often compelled to if the situation had the ring of an emergency.

Hal sounded frantic, but he was stopped short of making his contact by Jean's mother; her incoming call tied up the line. He begged her to hang up so he could call for medical assistance. "A doctor?" she screamed. "Never!"

"You're only making things worse," Hal told her. "Please, for Jean's sake, she needs help." He was silent for a moment, then cried, "My God, she's barely conscious!"

Mama Jean would not give in. Her parting words were a threat to call Arthur Landau. " *He knows ,*" she ranted. "Arthur will tell you. You're going against all my beliefs!"

Hal barely had time to catch his breath before the phone rang. It was Louis B. Mayer. He had just heard from Arthur Landau. "I never know whether to believe that Bello woman or not," he snorted. After having it confirmed that Jean was indeed seriously ill, he told Rosson to sit tight. "*I'll* get her a doctor," he said. "The finest—at once!"

Mama Jean hadn't fired all her guns. She had an ally, Ann Little, at the hotel. Since their first meeting, a bond had formed between the two women, sparked by a deep mutual involvement in Christian Science. She wasted no time in reaching the manager. "If a doctor comes in asking for Jean," she told Little by phone, "stall him until I get there. I don't want any doctor touching my baby."

Ann Little had been awakened from a sound sleep by Mrs. Bello's call. By the time she dressed and reached the lobby, a man carrying a black bag was stepping into the elevator. She called out, but it was too late. One of the desk clerks on duty remembered: "Miss Little always had the sweetest disposition. She never lost her composure or said a cross word. But she came close to it that night."

The doctor was hovering over Jean's pale, bent form on the living-room sofa before Mama Jean could stop him. She pleaded first with him, then with Harold Rosson, to let her call in a Reader. "She's my daughter," she cried. "I know what's best for her!"

The doctor continued his examination without interruption. "My orders come from a higher source," he said firmly.

In the doctor's rush to reach Jean, the door to 3BC was left wide open. Hearing the commotion, a small crowd of fascinated onlookers gathered outside in the corridor. They had to be separated to carry Jean's limp body out on a stretcher.

Jean was taken by ambulance to Good Samaritan Hospital, where she was operated on that evening for acute apendicitis. At the end of her two-week stay, Harold Rosson reported that his wife was in excellent spirits and able to walk short distances without assistance. "She's still a little wobbly," he told Ann Little, "but she hasn't lost her spunk."

The news from Jean's mother wasn't as glowing. "The baby is weak and confused. She could stay in that hospital forever and never receive the attention she needs." Mama Jean refused to believe that her daughter's condition had been life-threatening, or that an operation had been necessary.

Certainly Jean was now strong enough to return to the Marmont. There she had everything she could possibly need, including a husband. But Jean did not have the strength to refuse her mother, who insisted, against Hal's wishes, that Jean be driven directly from Good Samaritan to the house on Beverly Glen. "I will care for Jean myself, around the clock if need be," Mama Jean promised. "Jean will be her gorgeous self again in no time." Rather than accompany his wife and mother-in-law, Hal went straight from the hospital to MGM.

Jean's convalescence probably would have been smoother had she been on better terms with her studio. But her problems continued. Until her demands for a new contract had been met, she would not read another script. In turn, Mayer promptly took her off the payroll.

With Jean on Beverly Glen and Hal at the Marmont, columnists began to speculate that the Rossons had parted. Jean laughingly told reporters, "C'mon fellas, when would Hal have time to play nursemaid to me? He's a busy guy. Listen, he's working on a film now and has two more all set to go. I sure miss being with him, but we talk every night. I couldn't go to sleep without hearing Hal's voice." If Hal did talk to his wife, it wasn't from the Rosson suite at the hotel. Except for an occasional business call, his line was never busy.

It was shortly after midnight on New Year's Eve when Jean returned to Chateau Marmont for the first time in two months. Hal had picked her up at the place on Beverly Glen, after attending a small celebration hosted by the Bellos. Eddie, the elevator man, later recalled Harlow's homecoming: "They were in the garage, waiting for a hand with her grips, when

I saw them. I welcomed Mrs. Rosson back and wished them both a Happy New Year. Usually she was real friendly, but not this time. She smiled a little and thanked me, but she didn't say another word. It was that way all the way up to the third floor— quiet. The two of them just stood apart in the elevator. There was something bad going on between them. You could feel the cold." Two days later, Harold Rosson, carrying a small suitcase, stopped at the front desk to leave word that he could be reached at the studio if necessary.

The afternoon of Rosson's departure, Jean called the switchboard with two requests. She wanted guard chains attached to her doorways leading into the outside corridor and brighter light bulbs for her ceiling fixtures, especially those in the long dim hall that stretched from one end of her suite to the other. Earlier, more than one person had commented on seeing lights burning throughout the night in the Rosson suite whenever Jean was in residence. It was given no thought because of her many visitors, but Jean claimed that she was deathly afraid of the dark.

Later that same afternoon, a drunken Marino Bello staggered into the lobby, where he was intercepted by the secuirty man, Charles, and assisted to the front desk. A quick call to 3BC brought an immediate response from Jean. "I do not want to see him," she said emphatically. "He is not to come upstairs—*ever!*" The dictum, even though tactfully rephrased for Bello's benefit, set off sparks. He all but exploded.

A man of impressive stature, Marino Bello could easily have forced his way past the smaller Charles, but his assault was verbal, not physical. And he unleashed his anger on his celebrity stepdaughter, whom he frequently referred to as "that tramp."

According to Bello, Jean never loved Harold Rosson. The marriage had been arranged by Louis B. Mayer to save the studio, and its Platinum Bombshell, from another raging sex scandal, one that could have been fatal for all concerned on the heels of Paul Bern's shocking suicide only a year earlier.

When Harlow should have been in widow's weeds, Bello raged in a voice filled with contempt, she was picking up men in bars, on street corners, even around darkened studio sound stages. (Jean occasionally left word at the front desk that she had "gone fishing." At the time, no one realized that "fishing" was Jean's euphemistic term for manhunting.)

It wasn't until Mayer learned of an involvement with one of his leading actors, the husband of a wealthy socialite, that Mayer stepped in, fearing an alienation of affection suit. Bello said Mayer had wanted to make an "event" out of his star's wedding to the highly respected Rosson, and to cash in on the positive publicity, but Jean double-crossed him and eloped. "The little tramp made a fool of Mayer—but he is getting even with her now. He is getting his revenge." Bello laughed hysterically as he collapsed in a chair. After several cups of coffee, he was put in a cab and sent to Beverly Glen.

It was growing dark when Clark Gable arrived, carrying a small bunch of flowers. Whether Jean had invited him to keep her company during an evening alone or whether he invited himself is uncertain, but Gable was admitted without hesitation. He remained, not only for a steak dinner, but for breakfast, both meals coming from the hotel kitchen. When he appeared again the next night, and the next, night after night, Ann Little speculated as to the depth of their friendship.

Between 1931 and 1933, Clark Gable and Jean Harlow had appeared together in three films. Their smoldering love scenes had been so convincing that rumors of an affair had run rampant throughout Hollywood. Harlow then denied any involvement, limiting her comments to, "Clark is extremely protective and likes to playfully kid around." Now she wasn't talking. But she didn't hesitate grabbing his arm, locking it in hers, while walking through the Marmont lobby, or aggressively stealing a kiss in the elevator.

For the first time since coming to the Marmont, Jean openly displayed her sexuality. With Harold Rosson on the scene, she had kept her sizzling screen image under wraps. Now, dressed in filmy low-cut blouses or baring halters, she not only looked but acted the part. The celluloid Bombshell had sprung to life.

Even Gable made no attempt to downplay his physical appeal. He often wore his shirts unbuttoned, and his trousers were always tightly belted to accentuate his trim waist and broad shoulders.

The nights Harlow and Gable spent together at Chateau Marmont led insiders to believe the two stars were much more than just playmates. Said one: "It was the real thing all right. No telling what might have happened between them if she had had control of her life. But, of course, she never did."

In late January, Jean left for Washington, D.C., to join a galaxy of stars attending a birthday ball honoring President Roosevelt. Fours days after her return, Mama Jean informed manager Little that her daughter was moving back to the Beverly Glen house, "where we can keep an eye on her." Harold Rosson, she said, had taken a room at the Hollywood Athletic Club. With the news came a request for empty cartons and "a couple of strong backs."

Jean's return to her mother's protective arms was followed by an announcement in the nation's press. "It was wrong for Hal and me to live together," Jean said, "when we are so obviously incongenial. We simply were not meant for each other." She filed for divorce on March 11, 1934.

Jean Harlow's stormy off-and-on stay at Chateau Marmont had ended abruptly. But her presence within its secluded rooms and corridors would linger forever.

Above a Gothic arch, a ribbon of concrete framed the letters
M-A-R-M-O-N-T.

Colonnaded entry to Chateau Marmont.

# Chapter 2

## Buon Giorno, Guten Tag, Good Morning

### Mr. Wilder

The person Ann Little hired to work the switchboard had to speak at least one foreign language. "French, German, Italian . . , *anything*," recalled Carmel Volti. "I spoke fluent Italian and a little Spanish, and was able to pick up key words and phrases in other languages day by day."

Good thing, too, because the hotel guest register was taking on a foreign flavor, recording the names of visitors fleeing the beginnings of turmoil overseas. Dita Parlo, Gustav Froehlich, and Oskar Karl Weiss made their way to the Marmont from Germany. From Austria came Fritz Rotter, Walter Reisch, Carl Esmond, Lili Darvas, and Dolly Haas.

It was in late August of 1934 that twenty-eight-year-old Billy Wilder arrived at Chateau Marmont. The tall, trim young man with the unruly carrot-colored hair and heavily accented, often unintelligible speech, appeared in a joyless mood. Without a job or prospects, and running precariously low on funds, his only possessions were one well-traveled valise and a battered 1928 DeSoto coupe, on which he was behind with his payments. The Marmont's smallest, least expensive bachelor quarters on the building's backside was the best he could afford. A room with no view (the single window opened onto a dried mass of weeds covering the hillside across Monteel Road), a hotplate for a kitchen, and a Murphy bed that occupied nearly two-thirds of the available space when lowered, it seemed an appropriate setting for his despair.

The Austrian-born Wilder had been accustomed to much better. He had not only tasted the good life, he had feasted on it.

His early success came in Berlin, after turning from newspaper reporting to writing screenplays. Between 1928 and 1933, he turned out over two-hundred scenarios for silent films—alone, as a ghostwriter, or in collaboration— including the highly praised *Menschen am Sonntag (People on Sunday)* which led to his full-time association with UFA, Germany's giant film production combine.

As Wilder's fortunes soared, so did his lifestyle. He moved into an ultra-swank apartment building on one of Berlin's most fashionable thoroughfares and furnished his flat with bold experimental designs by Mies van der Rohe. He drove a sleek new Graham-Paige convertible. He wore only the finest silk shirts and custom-made suits in the very latest styles. He dined at the best restaurants, made the rounds of all the night spots, romanced the most ravishing *frauleins*. He more than dabbled in the arts. His collection of prints and paintings included valuable works by Cezanne and Matisse.

The good life was too good to last. As Adolf Hitler and his Nazi party gained increasing control, Wilder's adopted homeland became the scene of political turmoil and rioting. Brown-shirted Storm Troopers, banded with the party's feared swastika emblem, flooded the streets at the slightest provocation.

Shortly after New Year's Day 1933, while Wilder was on a skiing holiday with Hella Hartwig, a wealthy enamored heiress from Frankfurt, the news broke that Hitler had been appointed to the powerful position of Chancellor. Wilder decided then to leave Germany while there was still time.

Wilder and his heiress fled to Paris, pausing only long enough en route for him to arrange the sale of his treasured possessions. Under less hurried circumstances he would have easily recouped his investment, and then some, but he settled for bottom dollar, happy to get that.

In Paris, amid rumors that refugees were being hunted and returned to Nazi Germany, Billy and Hella found shelter in a dingy Bohemian hangout where even *der Fuhrer* probably wouldn't have aroused the suspicion of yawning clerks. Eventually they settled at the Hotel Ansonia, a dreary underground hideaway for refugees. The roster was studded with creative aliens, including a young actor named Peter Lorre, who less than two years earlier had become an international sensation for his work in Fritz Lang's chilling masterpiece, *M*. The diminutive Lorre, and the towering Wilder, soon became fast friends. (Nearly fifty years later, during an interview with Dick Cavett, Wilder talked of having roomed with Lorre at Chateau Marmont on his arrival in 1934. At that time, however, Lorre was still in Paris; he did not come to Hollywood until the following year.)

Wilder and Hella were miserable in Paris. She detested the tawdry existence. She yearned for bright lights and fancy restaurants, shopping sprees, and high times. She wanted to get married. He found writing difficult, especially using his own name; he had no work permit. He secretly dreamed of moving on, this time to Hollywood. He had no intention of tying himself down with Hella. "I did not contemplate matrimony, then or ever," he admitted later. "I did not like the idea of marriage. It was enslavement and the end of liberty."

Wilder buried himself in work. He wrote story after story, even experimented with film direction for the first time, as a favor for a friend. (The star of the picture, *Mauvaise Graine,* was sixteen-year-old Danielle Darrieux). The friend thought so much of one of his stories, a musical *billet-doux* called *Pam-Pam*, that he forwarded a copy to another expatriate, director Joe May. May and his wife, Mia, who had starred in many of her husband's German-made spectacles, were living in Hollywood where Joe was under contract to Columbia Pictures.

Just prior to Christmas 1933, Wilder heard from Joe May. Not only were the powers at Columbia intrigued with *Pam-Pam,* May cabled, they were willing to finance Wilder's passage to Hollywood and pay him to develop a screenplay. Was Wilder interested in a short-term contract, May wanted to know. *Was he!*

Goodbye Paris. So long Hella.

The Mays welcomed Billy Wilder into their rambling Mediterranean-style Hollywood hills villa, providing him with room and board for seventy-five dollars a week, half his take-home pay from the studio. His days were filled with work, his nights devoted to play. There were girls, girls, girls; a fresh supply as near as his telephone. He loved the excitement of the film capital, and the promise his new assignment provided. He knew he belonged in Hollywood. He had to stay.

Along with expectation came deep disappointment. His finished screenplay met with little enthusiasm, and the project was dropped. His contract with Columbia came to an abrupt end. His salary stopped; he could no longer afford to live with the Mays. Only days remained before his visitor's visa would run out.

It was possible to obtain an immigration visa across the California border in Mexico. Wilder headed south and returned with the necessary papers. Now he needed an inexpensive room with privacy, where he could continue his writing. He still had his dreams and a head full of ideas. It was only a matter of time, he felt certain, until one of the studios would look favorably upon his work.

In his search for new quarters, Billy Wilder drove west along Sunset Boulevard. Passing LaBrea and the Chaplin studios, he saw a castlelike structure looming on a distant hillside. By the time he reached Laurel Canyon, it dominated his view. He was reminded of the stately baronial manors in his native Europe.

He turned his battered DeSoto up a winding sidestreet and paused before the building's main entrance. Above a Gothic archway, embedded in a curlicue of concrete, were the letters M-A-R-M-O-N-T. During his brief stay at Columbia, he had heard occasional references to a relatively new hotel bearing that name, where the management welcomed writers and entertainers. Wilder felt suddenly intimidated. Surely he could not afford to live in such a place.

Ann Little quickly calmed his fears. For less than half of what he was paying Joe and Mia May, he could take immediate possession of "our loveliest small suite." Manager Little, in her eagerness to fill the Marmont's least attractive availability, was overly generous with her description. The accommodation was hardly a suite, and far from lovely. It was simply a furnished cubicle; small, cramped, and dark. But to Billy Wilder it was the answer to his prayers, a private sliver of Heaven where he could literally hole up close to the studios and write to his heart's content.

"We didn't see much of Mr. Wilder for the longest time," Ann Little recalled. "He stayed in his room and worked till all hours of the night. I can't remember a time when I didn't see a light coming from beneath his door as I would make my evening rounds. That young man was much too hard on himself."

A former desk clerk remembers another side of Billy Wilder. "Every once in awhile, he would come out for air to pick up a newspaper or magazine and ask if we had any books he could borrow. He read a lot and listened to his radio, not so much for the news but to practice his English. He was so determined to learn. Of course, in his business, that *was* important. But what I remember most about him was that he had a very busy social life. I doubt if he dated the same girl twice. He was quite the ladies man."

Actually, during his first months at the Marmont, Billy Wilder was a solitary man. He worked feverishly without the pleasures of companionship, and often without meals. It was only after his work met with constant rejection, and he began to consider himself a failure, that he started to stray. To keep from going stir crazy, he motored to the nearby coast, taking the dusty roads to the resort areas of Santa Monica, Ocean Park, and Venice. He would waste days lying on the sandy beaches, at times lingering long past sundown to dance at the pavilions on the pleasure piers, where fun-loving girls were always plentiful. On Sunday afternoons he would journey to Santa Monica Canyon to commiserate with Greta Garbo's friend and future screenwriter, Polish-born Salka Viertel. The weekly get-togethers at Viertel's home, which had become a gathering spot for exiles, gained him new industry friends but little more.

It took just over a year and the ambitious plans of the newly formed Pioneer Pictures for Wilder's luck to change. Backed by the big money of John Hay (Jock) Whitney and his cousin Cornelius (Sonny) Vanderbilt Whitney, Pioneer was planning to move into film production with a splash. The Whitneys and their producer-director partner, Merian C. Cooper, had already made news by signing a contract with the Technicolor company, calling for the use of its revolutionary full-color process (promoted as "100% new Technicolor") in the production of eight films, "super-feature in character and especially featuring color." Until now, no studio would touch Technicolor, not after the failure of its two-color process in the late 1920s. The stars too had shied away, unwilling to risk careers that were flourishing in black and white. Only cartoonist Walt Disney had been brave enough to experiment with the new "living color."

Pioneer's heavy commitment to Technicolor and filmmaking led Billy Wilder to believe that the company might be in the market for scripts. Still striking out on his own, he had been collaborating with Oliver H.P. Garrett, a screenwriter of some note, since their chance meeting at Salka Viertel's house. The pairing had resulted in two original screenplays. Pioneer bought both of them, earning Wilder five-thousand dollars and a long-term con-tract. (In breaking the news to Ann Little at the Marmont, Wilder talked only of one figure, ten thousand dollars. He made no mention of having to split the money with Garrett. Perhaps he wanted her to feel that he had truly struck it rich, and was indeed good for all the back rent he owed.)

Flushed with sudden success, Billy Wilder made plans for a brief return to France and Austria. He wanted to see Hella; he had to see his mother and childhood friends. Now he could face them with shining eyes and bright talk of the future. "Save a place for me," he told the front desk as he departed. "I'm coming back."

He made good his promise six weeks later. It was only days before

Christmas, and the Marmont was filled to capacity for the holidays. "We don't have a thing, not a room," Ann Little advised sadly. "But don't worry, in a few weeks..."

*"Weeks?"* Wilder repeated, cutting her off. "I left word I would be coming back!" He couldn't believe what he was hearing.

"But you didn't say *when.* If only you had let us know, we would have . . . "

"I'm coming back!" he insisted. "I AM COMING BACK!"

"But . . . "

"You're telling me you don't have something? Anything?" Little shook her head.

"A closet, a corner? Who cares where?"

"I'm so sorry."

Wilder slumped like a mistreated puppy. "I've got to come back," he said pathetically. Then, in a painful way, he begged, *"Please."*

Ann Little was actually quite fond of Billy Wilder, but her interest in him was far different from that of his other female admirers. She considered him "a wonderfully inventive writer . . . , Hollywood's finest." She also regarded him as one of her regulars and a part of the Marmont family. Seeing him in such desperate straits nearly broke her heart. She could not bear to turn him away, especially over the holidays. "Well," she sighed, "let me think."

"I would rather sleep in a bathroom than in another hotel," he said quickly, trying to be helpful.

The remark, seemingly inane, sparked an idea. Adjoining the women's restroom, off the lobby, was a small vestibule. If he was willing to stay there until the first availability . . .

He moved in that very day. It wasn't much, especially after the addition of a cot, floor lamp, and chair, but at least he had a place to stretch out and store his belongings. Of course he had to sacrifice some privacy. Even years later his most vivid remembrances of Christmas 1935 were not of merrymaking and mistletoe but of interruptions and sleepless nights. He would say, "Women were coming in and peeing and looking at me funny."

Shortly after the holidays, he took possession of his very own room. He still couldn't afford a suite, but he had every confidence that day was coming soon. After all, he was busy writing at Poineer, he had the security of a contract, and all seemed right, if not with the world, with Hollywood. He had even met a girl he wanted to date more than once. He found himself growing serious about Judith Iribe.

His mother in faraway Austria was now his major concern. He had hoped to bring her back to America with him but she had refused. News reports from overseas had grown progressively worse. Her letters were optimistic, however. She implied that Hitler and his gathering army were no threat.

In early 1936, Pioneer Pictures' second feature film, *The Dancing Pirate,* opened to frosty reviews and even colder public response. Within weeks Pioneer dissolved; Jock Whitney joined David O. Selznick in the formation of Selznick International Films, and Billy Wilder hied to his sanctum at the Marmont to ponder the future. This time he didn't fret for long. Another of his collaborations, *Champagne Waltz,* was picked up by Paramount. A contract followed, earning him a spot on the studio's roster, along with over one-hundred other writers. Hardly exclusive, but at least he had a foot in the door.

As Billy Wilder's fortunes improved, so did his accommodations at the Marmont. His rooms became larger, his view more impressive. The busy thoroughfare below held a special fascination for him.

With his marriage to Judith Iribe in mid-1936, he moved into a suite and, for the first time in his life, Billy Wilder settled down. He had a new partner professionally as well- -fellow Paramount contractee, Charles Brackett. Their pairing was the start of a long and successful collaboration, one that was to end fittingly with the very stylish drama of contemporary Hollywood, *Sunset Boulevard.*

# Miss Kiesler

The man from MGM's publicity department carefully worked his way along the crowded platform to await the incoming train from New York. In his arms he carried an immense bouquet of long-stemmed red roses. Attached was a sealed envelope, hand-addressed only hours earlier by the studio chief, Louis B. Mayer, to his newest European discovery, Miss Hedwig Kiesler. The flowers and accompanying note, dated October 4, 1937, were to be presented to Miss Kiesler immediately upon her arrival in Los Angeles.

The publicity man had never seen the young Viennese actress. He knew only that he was to find, in Mr. Mayer's words, "the most beautiful creature on earth." After that his job was simple: rush her back to the executive suite at MGM, where Mayer was waiting to welcome her formally.

The glare from the strong autumn sun made it difficult to identify the

Viennese beauty Hedy Lamarr had a hectic first day in Hollywood.

incoming passengers as they departed the train. To make matters worse, most of the ladies wore face shading slouch hats in the latest broad-brimmed style. The man from MGM grew increasingly uneasy as he strained to see.

Actually he had little trouble spotting her. The jet black shoulder-length hair, the exquisitely refined features, the flawless complexion. She was even more magnificent than he had been led to believe. Classically beautiful, a Botticelli painting come to life.

He hurried to her side, introduced himself, and presented his offerings. Then, without wasting a moment, they crisscrossed through the milling crowd to the parking lot, where a studio limousine was waiting for the journey across town.

The last months had been stressful for Hedwig Kiesler. She had been living only briefly in London—after fleeing Vienna for Paris to divorce her munitions manufacturer husband—when she was introduced to Louis B. Mayer. In England to launch MGM's first British-made production, *A Yank at Oxford*, Mayer was also interviewing new talent, in the hope of augmenting his already impressive roster. Only days earlier, he had signed a young stage actress named Greer Garson.

The meeting with Mayer had been arranged by an American talent agent, Bob Ritchie, who had been captivated by Kiesler's appearance in the film, *Symphonie der Liebe* (later released as *Ecstasy*). "She's not only gorgeous, but she can act," Ritchie told Mayer. "You can make her a big star at MGM."

It was not Kiesler's acting, however, that had Ritchie (and, indeed, all of Europe) buzzing, but three torrid scenes that had her swimming nude in a lake, cavorting *dishabille* through a forest, and registering the delights of orgasm while a camera concentrated on her fabulous face.

Personally Mayer rather enjoyed witnessing such shocking displays. But he turned puritanical when it came to his own films, and he made that point clear to Kiesler from the start. Pumping himself up to his full height, which was a good head shorter than his visitor, he said in a straightlaced way, "You're lovely, my dear, but I have the family point of view. At MGM we make clean pictures. We want our stars to lead clean lives. I don't like what people would think about a girl who flits bare-assed around the screen."

By this time, as the story goes, Mayer was standing face to decolletage with Kiesler. He was staring at her cleavage when he added, "You have a bigger chest than I thought. You'd be surprised how tits figure in a girl's career."

Kiesler listened as the stocky little man offered her a six-month contract at $125 a week. The good news was followed by an invitation to come to America at her own expense.

As the wife of one of Austria's wealthiest men, she had presided over a luxurious ten-room apartment in Vienna and a castle in Salzburg, and had played hostess to such illustrious guests as Gustav Mahler and Franz Werfel. It had even been reported that she was a great favorite of Adolf Hitler and Benito Mussolini. But all she claimed to have salvaged from her marriage were "a fine wardrobe and a gold mine of determination." Even most of her fabulous jewelry collection was gone, sold to help finance her "escape" to Paris and London.

Mayer's behavior may not have offended her, but his offer certainly did. She turned him down flat. Speaking in her most precise broken English, which was horrendous at best, she refused to be intimidated or bamboo-zled into accepting "a cheap contract."

There was more to this girl than her lucious looks, Mayer had to admit. "You have spirit," he said playfully. "I like that." He would not accept her refusal.

Agent Ritchie met independently with Kiesler and Mayer to urge them to reconsider. By the following day, a more generous arrangement had been reached, one that included her paid passage to Hollywood.

Now, in the executive suite at MGM, a travel-weary Hedwig Kiesler faced the mighty Mayer as he groused over the most important decision of all—what to call his new star. "It's gotta sound good," he insisted. "It's gotta look good, like butter on hot corn."

"My name is Hedwig Kiesler," she sputtered. "Hedwig Eva Maria Kiesler."

"Eva Maria?" Mayer repeated incredulously. "Don't give me church songs."

Actually, he rather liked the shortened Hedwig—or Hedy. He felt it had an exotic quality, a certain mystique. But Kiesler? Never!

From the moment he had first set eyes on her, he had been reminded of another screen beauty, silent star Barbara LaMarr, "the girl who was too beautiful." Barbara was gone now, her young life snuffed out at the height of her career, in 1926, by a drug overdose. But another great beauty, perhaps the most beautiful of all, was standing before him—as if fate had led her his way. Surely he could take the slightest liberty with Barbara's name and call his new discovery Hedy Lamarr.

"Lamarr, Lamarr," the newly christened actress repeated. She shrug-ged her acceptance. At this point she would have agreed to almost anything. All she really craved—and requested— was time to relax, a moment's peace away from crowds and ponderous decisions.

Soon, the publicity man promised. There were other important people—future co-stars and co-workers—waiting to meet her, and an introductory tour of the lot had been arranged. After that, he said, she would have the balance of the day to herself. A private suite had been reserved at Chateau Marmont.

By the time Hedy Lamarr reached the Marmont, she appeared numb, or as one observor recalled, "rather befuddled." Her day had been unsettling and unaccustomedly rushed; from her arrival at the station to her first glimpse of MGM, from her reunion with Mayer to her new Hollywood home. In between she had assumed a new identity. Now she was being asked to sign one of the hotel's registration cards.

She shifted the wilting roses from one arm to another and reached for a pen. She started to write, then paused, her expression blank. She turned to the man from MGM, as if waiting for a cue, but none came. She lowered the pen once more, fixing her gaze on the small card at her fingertips. Then slowly, in childlike block letters, she painstakingly wrote for the very first time: H-E-D-Y L-A-M-A-R.

Louis B. Mayer had given her a new name, but he hadn't taught her how to spell it.

Hedy Lamarr's privacy was interrupted after a time, when MGM assigned her a roommate, the blonde and glamorous Hungarian singer-actress, Ilona Massey. The pairing, made in good faith by the studio to help its newcomers retain a touch of "home" while adjusting to unfamiliar surroundings and language barriers ("She buried the English language after I murdered it," Lamarr once remarked), seemed ideal from the start. Then trouble developed. To generate publicity for the two stars, Mayer directed a fictitious feud that cast them as film rivals. It wasn't long before they began taking their press clippings seriously. Unable to bear the presence of Massey another moment, Lamarr departed the Marmont for her very own bungalow apartment elsewhere in Hollywood.

Carole Lombard was introduced to guests at the Marmont by her new beau, Clark Gable.

Joan Blondell frequently played hostess at director Lloyd Bacon's penthouse parties.

# Chapter 3

## And The View Is Sensational

## The High Life

It took more than unsettling news from overseas and disappointing box-office receipts (the growing popularity of radio was creating a new and unwelcome competition) to dampen Hollywood's spirits.

The town loved a good party. If the studios weren't behind the latest razzle-dazzle celebration, the stars were. Any excuse would do, as long as it generated publicity.

In the mid-to-late Thirties, the most newsworthy invitations came from Hollywood's charmed couples. Joan Crawford and Franchot Tone were fast becoming the top-rated celebrity hosts; their mansion in Brentwood was the scene of one "how-do-they-keep-topping-themselves" extravaganza after another. A party at Pickfair was not to be missed, despite a change in husbands for Mary Pickford. The Goldwyns, Sam and Frances, rated high, as did Cary Grant and his blonde ex-model girlfriend, Phyllis ("Brooksie") Brooks. The gracious and elegant Countess Dorothy Di Frasso, a widow, even made the list. Filmland's royalty flocked to her magnificently rejuvenated palazzo in Beverly Hills where she entertained with great flair. Hostessing was just one of the Countess' talents. Earlier, for a time, she had miraculously transformed a Montana cowboy named Gary Cooper into a dashing, mannered boulevardier.

Not all of the parties made the columns. One of the hottest tickets in town was to the Marmont penthouse, where director Lloyd Bacon played host to movieland's liveliest crowds. The penthouse was his party place, his sumptuous in-town roost for wild weekends whenever his schedule permitted. Officially he lived with his toys—he had a priceless train collection—in a ranch house in the San Fernando Valley. He also owned a luxuriously appointed yacht, the *Cielito Lindo*, which he sailed between the mainland and Catalina Island.

Lloyd Bacon was second generation show business. He had originally hoped to follow in the footsteps of his acting father, Frank, but after a short stint on the legitimate stage, he turned to films, playing foils to Lloyd Hamilton and Charlie Chaplin in dozens of silent comedies. (Bacon's father became a celebrity of sorts for a remark he made on the opening night of his Broadway play, *Lightnin'*, in 1938. Arriving at the theater . . . past curtain time, he was met by the show's irate director, who barked, "For God's sake, Frank, we can't keep the audience waiting!" Nonplussed, the actor replied, "I've waited thirty years for a show like this. They can wait a few minutes for me!")

In 1921, seeking new challenges, Lloyd Bacon abandoned acting for directing. It took him seven years to earn his first major film credit; his big break came when Warner Bros. assigned him *The Singing Fool*, Al Jolson's follow-up to *The Jazz Singer*. Over the next few years he became one of the studio's most prolific and respected directors. His productions of *42nd Street*, *Footlight Parade*, *Wonder Bar*, and *Gold Diggers of 1937*, with choreography by the innovative Busby Berkeley, helped revive the sagging popularity of movie musicals.

Had Lloyd Bacon pursued an acting career, he doubtlessly would have become a matinee idol. Women were drawn to his elegant style, distinguished good looks, and splendid mane of graying hair (the envy of men as well). His manner of dress only enhanced the attraction. He had a passion for clothes; he could wear the gaudiest colors with more flair than many models gracing the pages of the latest fashion magazines. It was not unusual to see him decked out in white trousers, red jacket, blue shirt, and yellow tie.

As if looking sensational weren't enough, Bacon was also blessed with an ingratiating personality. That, more than anything, made him a popular host.

The parties in the penthouse began as private affairs; small, intimate shindigs where the director could hold court, while his friends and co-workers relaxed, away from the pressures of the studio. At the Marmont they would chat over drinks or lie in the sun on the immense terrace. The dizzying view was a tonic after days in windowless sound stages.

Joan Blondell, Warner's vivacious workhorse and one of Bacon's favorite stars, who had headlined six of his productions with more to come—was always on hand. Bright, winsome, and witty, she frequently took it upon herself to play hostess. Bacon was delighted. Her husband, who was far less gregarious, failed to share his host's enthusiasm.

When Joan Blondell first began attending the penthouse parties, she had been married for several years to cinematographer George Barnes. At Warner's they had worked together on several pictures, including *Footlight Parade*, and *Dames*. Professionally they had much in common; personally they were as different as night and day.

"Joanie was so outgoing and adorable," a friend at the studio recalled. "She loved being with people. George's idea of fun was a weekend in the mountains. He was a quiet, gentle man, whose only flaw was that he had no idea of the value of money, and he spent it like water. If George wanted something, he got it without thinking twice. One time, on a whim, he bought a huge camper, then took off into the hinterlands. That's one of the reasons Joanie left him. She couldn't take his undisciplined spending."

The break-up with George Barnes didn't leave Joan unattached for long. She soon began arriving for her Marmont weekends with a new man at her side. He was her five-time co-star and Warner's baby-faced crooner, Dick Powell. (Barnes didn't waste any time either. He'd had his eyes on dancer Betty Woods, a curvaceous blonde, who had won several beauty contests at Lake Arrowhead. Barnes and Blondell were both remarried in the same year, 1936.)

There were other familiar faces from the studio, stars and featured players, forming Lloyd Bacon's close-knit group: handsome leading men George Brent, Warren William, Richard Barthelmess, and Ricardo Cortez; Western heroes Johnny Mack Brown and Dick Foran; character actors Allen Jenkins, Guy Kibbee, the Williams Gargan and Gaxton; and wide-mouthed comedian Joe E. Brown. They were joined by actress Bebe Daniels and her actor-husband, Ben Lyon; actress-comedienne Winnie Lightner and her husband, director Roy Del Ruth; redheaded Peggy Shannon; the girl who had been brought to Hollywood as a possible successor to Clara Bow; and some of the shapeliest dancers from the chorus lines of Warner's toe-tapping musicals.

Surprisingly it took months for word of the informal gatherings to reach the lower floors of the Marmont. When finally it did, Lloyd Bacon found he had more "old friends" for neighbors than he realized. Up came Ned Sparks, Conrad Nagel, Lee Tracy, Dita Parlo, and the Ritz Brothers. Al was the first of the *freres* to appear, arriving alone as if to test the hospitality of the host. Finding an open door, he quickly summoned Jimmy and Harry. The trio soon became one of the most popular additions to the group, as they were willing to entertain at the clink of an ice cube. Stan Laurel, on the other hand, was simply tolerated. Week after week he stumbled into the penthouse only to head straight for the bar. More than once he had to be assisted, even carried, back to his own suite.

With the number of guests expanding rapidly, it was inevitable that outsiders would learn of the goings-on. Clark Gable, no stranger to the Marmont, began to show up with William Powell's ex-wife, Carole Lombard. (Somehow the rumor falsely began to circulate that they had been introduced in the penthouse.) The wild bunch from the Garden of Allah found the prospect of free drinks impossible to ignore. Thanks to Robert Benchley (whose fear of the traffic on Sunset prompted his legendary taxi rides from one side of the street to the other), Charlie Butterworth, Louis Calhern, Donald Ogden Stewart, and other mischief-makers, weekends at the Marmont were never quite the same.

Manager Ann Little, in later years, was fond of recalling the impeccable deportment of the guests during her time at the Marmont. "Everyone was high class, rather reserved," she would say. "I can't remember having problems with any of the guests, or even visitors. Of course they all knew we wouldn't put up with nonsense. They didn't stay if they caused trouble."

Either Ann Little had weekends off or she had closed her eyes and ears to the madness taking place on the sixth floor. Said one of the showgirls who had been a semi-regular over the years: "What started out as harmless, fun get-togethers for Lloyd's friends got out of hand real fast. Strangers began appearing with strangers—then *disappearing* with strangers. The place had more doors than the funhouse at Ocean Park pier. There were rooms, cubbyholes, and little niches at almost every turn. You never knew who you would find where, or with whom. It got so some of us were afraid to go into the bathroom for fear we would stumble across someone in the midst of a passionate affair." One celebrity *was* caught with his pants down. "It was George Brent," she admitted, "and seeing him gave me a start. That man had a ferocious temper. The suave gentleman he played in pictures was mostly an act, and I was afraid he would fly off the handle— maybe even make things rough for me at the studio. But he never did. Come to think of it, he probably didn't remember that night at all. He was more than a little high."

The fast times in the penthouse came to an abrupt halt in mid-1938 when

Lloyd Bacon informed the front desk that he was moving full time to the Valley. His place in the penthouse was taken by former Warner Bros. contractee John Wayne. The lanky ex-college football player had been tabbed as a star of the future as early as 1930, when his friend John Ford, for whom he had played bit parts in several films, had recommended him to director Raoul Walsh for the lead in *The Big Trail*. But the public failed to take special notice, and he was relegated to low-paying hero roles in scores of forgetable 'B pictures," primarily kiddie Westerns and serials. It was left to John Ford to hand Wayne his first major role in eight years by casting him as the Ringo Kid in the big-budget Western, *Stagecoach*.

The news had barely been made public when a jubilant John Wayne loped into the Marmont. "I'll take the best room in the house," he said approaching the front desk. The dark-haired beauty who stood beside him said he was celebrating, but Wayne wouldn't admit that. With the hint of a smile he alibied, "I just want to see how it feels to live like a star." And he did, for several weeks, before he was again on his way.

## Mr. Cohn's Guests

Hollywood's hands were tied. Even the most powerful studio chiefs—Mayer, Zanuck, Warner, Cohn, among them—were helpless to fight the dictums of censorship czar, Will H. Hays. It was Hays' unenviable task to clean up motion pictures, rid the industry of the slightest taint of unwholesomeness. Hollywood and sin had been synonymous for too long.

The earliest attempt to clamp down on Hollywood's evil doings came in the early 1920s, following a series of shocking revelations involving some of the brightest stars of the day. Olive Thomas, the exquisitely beautiful actress-wife of Jack Pickford, Mary's brother, died of a drug overdose in Paris at the height of her fame. Dashingly handsome Wallace Reid, clean-cut screen idol to millions, died an agonizing death in a Hollywood sanitarium while attempting to cure his addiction. Noted Director William Desmond Taylor was shot to death in his Hollywood mansion; Taylor's illicit affairs with popular leading ladies Mary Miles Minter and Mabel Normand were made public at the inquest, shattering their careers overnight. (Normand was further scandalized only months later when her chauffeur was found holding a pistol over the lifeless body of Hollywood millionaire, Cortland S. Hines.) Roscoe "Fatty" Arbuckle, America's adored rotund comedian, was charged with manslaughter following the death of starlet Virginia Rappe only days after he allegedly assaulted her sexually with a bottle during a wild San Francisco drinking party. Arbuckle was eventually acquitted of all wrongdoing—he even received a public apology from the jury for "the great injustice done him"—but audiences no longer found him adorable or remotely amusing.

The golden glow that had radiated from Hollywood quickly turned a dirty gray. Gods and goddesses of the silver screen, and the film industry in general, with its lustful cinematic themes, were suddenly being blamed for a decline in the nation's moral standards. Purge Hollywood of its unsavory elements, an outraged public demanded, or shut it down!

In panic, the movie colony turned to Washington, D.C., for its czar, a leader of undisputable strength and courage who could reassure America while establishing Hollywood as the leading producer of family entertainment. From the cabinet of President Warren G. Harding, the industry selected Will Hays, the country's clean-living, churchgoing Postmaster General. Hays willingly accepted Hollywood's offer and was appointed in 1922 as president of the newly formed Motion Picture Producers and Distributors of America, Incorporated. His first act was to banish "Fatty" Arbuckle from the screen.

From the start, Hays demanded that the studio heads show more responsibility. To discourage public scandals, morality clauses were inserted in every player's contract. Indiscretions that reached the newspapers meant instant cancellation and dismissal. Feudal obedience had come to Hollywood.

Cecil B. DeMille was one of the loudest defenders of the puritanical code, but he still found ways of showing sinful acts on the screen. So did other innovative filmmakers. In fact, movies became so subtly suggestive and violent that local censor boards began springing up all over the country, each with its own degree of prudery. Again Hollywood began to feel the pressures of an angry public.

The adoption of the Motion Picture Code in 1930, with its interminable list of rules and regulations governing everything, including sex, crime, violence, drugs, profanity, even *kissing*, did little to appease the nation's review boards. Religious groups were growing increasingly active, stirred by the sight of such stars as Jean Harlow in clinging, all-but-transparent satin and wispy creations of chiffon. Their strategic parts were covered, according to the Code, but little was left to viewers' imaginations. As a Decency Movement was mounted, Hays pledged to clean up "industry smut" once and for all. In July, 1934, a new Purity Seal was put into effect.

Films bearing the seal guaranteed the highest moral standards. Films without it could not be exhibited.

The discontented rumblings of distant voices began to fade as movies reflected a new innocence and wholesomeness. (Even Tarzan's loincloth took on added dimensions, rendering it less offensive.) Still, there were rumblings to be heard. The studio heads, bound by endless restrictions, did not look kindly upon their czar. In Will Hays they had created a tyrant, a monster worse than any seen on film. True, they had willingly surrendered much of their freedom and power to "Washington Will," but that was long ago. The fact that they did so to save their industry—and jobs—seemed incidental now.

The moguls weren't the only ones to feel a loss of freedom. It wasn't by choice that they found themselves increasingly involved in the private lives of their stars. Unsavory publicity or, God forbid, scandal could not only ruin a valuable property but severely damage a studio's reputation and profits.

Two of Hollywood's masterminds, MGM's Louis B. Mayer and Columbia's Harry Cohn, were particularly sensitive to their stars' wanderings. The most adventurous, or potentially troublesome, were directed to stage their romantic escapades out of the spotlight, behind closed doors and drawn shades. For that purpose, MGM rented a cluster of apartments in a quaint French Normandy "village" in the 10500 block of Santa Monica Boulevard in West Los Angeles. Columbia rented the small penthouse at Chateau Marmont

Harry Cohn, who was hardly a model of propriety, had long been Will Hays' most vociferous opponent, at times referring to him with strings of four-letter expletives in conversations with colleagues. Around the studio he was regarded as a despot, ruthless and vulgar. He deplored anyone meddling in his affairs and insisted that his authority in all matters be absolute. It was only natural that he earned the nickname, "Harry the horror."

It was rare for Harry Cohn to wander in and out of sound stages during filming, or even to stray from his office. He reportedly had his own methods for keeping a close check on everything from shooting schedules to the latest gossip involving his stars. What his network of informants failed to report he learned through an intricate spying system that included tapped phones, bugged sets and dressing rooms. There were times when he learned more than he wanted to know, particularly about his two most promising stars, William Holden and Glenn Ford.

Twenty-one-year-old Holden was a virtual unknown when Cohn

Harry Cohn's most promising young stars: Glenn Ford (*below left*) and William Holden (*below right*).

Erro! Flynn (*above right*) and Humphrey Bogart (*above left*) joined pals William Holden and Glenn Ford at the Marmont for "fun and games." (*Courtesy of Bison Archives*)

borrowed him from Paramount, where he had appeared briefly in only two films, to star as the boxer-violinist hero in Clifford Odets' *Golden Boy*. At Columbia, Holden received a big build-up. His winning smile and strong physique, coupled with an engaging innocence, made him an easy "sell." He dared not tell his mother, who lived in nearby South Pasadena, of his newfound popularity with the ladies—or of his delight in discovering an overabundance of readily available sexual partners. Earlier, in response to her pleas, he had promised that he would never succumb to Hollywood's loose ways.

The boyish and likeable Ford, appearing even younger than his twenty-two years, had been working in various West Coast stage productions when Columbia tested and signed him to a contract. Ford and Holden, the two newcomers, soon became fast friends. Their hot-blooded pursuits about town managed to raise Cohn's blood pressure to the danger point.

As Ford reminisced recently: "Harry really worried about Bill and me. He had put us under contract at approximately the same time, and we were constantly getting into trouble—going places where we shouldn't have gone and mixing with the wrong people. In his eyes, rather bad company. One day he sent for us and said, 'If you *must* get into trouble, go to the Marmont.' He made it clear that he had rented the small penthouse there just for us, to protect us. As upset and concerned as he was, he never raised his voice. But he made sure we got his point."

In early 1939, Harry Cohn turned the keys to suite 54—the small penthouse—at the Marmont over to his wayward young actors. He wanted to make certain that their wild behavior went no farther than the walls of the hotel, thereby protecting their clean-cut public image. The small penthouse became their personal playpen, and home away from home, for the next three years.

Throughout the spring and summer of 1939, Ford and Holden shared the suite with the roguish David Niven. Said Ford, "David was always calling to ask, in a desperate sort of way, 'Are you using it tonight?' He couldn't get over the fact that we didn't have to pay for the place. We told him we did, but he knew better. He was really impressed that we had this big spread all to ourselves. Everybody was."

"Everybody" also included their best pals, three of Hollywood's most notorious carousers:—Humphrey Bogart, Errol Flynn, and John Barrymore.

When Bogart began visiting the Marmont, he had been married just over a year to a hard-drinking, bosomy blonde named Mayo Methot. Like Mayo,

Bogart enjoyed a good argument; unlike Mayo, he was not violent. The daughter of a sea captain, she loved a slug-fest. He called her Sluggy. In her honor, he christened their boat—and their Scotty dog—Sluggy. Their small adobe house on Horn Avenue (in the shadow of the Marmont) became known as Sluggy Hollow. The "battling Bogarts" were the talk of Hollywood. To escape the too-frequent fireworks, he sought a hideaway. When the Beverly Wilshire Hotel refused to admit him, he turned to his young friends at Chateau Marmont.

Errol Flynn was also married. His wife, whom he referred to irreverently as "Tiger Lil," was the tempetuous French actress Lili Damita. The Flynns' homelife was reportedly even more volatile than the Bogarts'. At one point, the situation became so intense that Errol left Damita for a time to room with David Niven in a home owned by Rosalind Russell on Linden Drive in Beverly Hills. Niven later teased Flynn unmercifully about being so tight-fisted with money, but in truth, it was Flynn who paid the major share of household expenses. Niven never put up a fight. After all, he would explain wryly, he was earning considerably less money from this contract with Sam Goldwyn than Flynn was with his at Warner Bros. By the summer of 1939, however, Flynn and Lili Damita were back together again, having "patched things up for keeps." The reconciliation failed to interfere with the virile Flynn's visits to the Marmont.

The other member of the group, John Barrymore, was having marriage problems as well; he and his fourth wife, actress Elaine Barrie, were on the verge of divorce. Nearing sixty, the once-handsome actor, his appearance ravaged by the abuses of alcohol and reckless living, had become an embittered soul. As Ford remembered, "Barrymore would come over and sit outside on the terrace, wearing only a bathrobe and socks. He looked rather torn and tattered. He would stare ahead with a drink in his hand and sigh, 'Ah, Glenn, my boy....' I would say, 'Mr. Barrymore, may I get you some coffee?' and he would reply, 'You know, I have only two friends in this goddam town, and they're Haig and Haig.' Once in a while he would go off on binges reciting Shakespeare. When he was done, he would tell me never to try the classics. To Holden he would say, 'That goes for you too, cowboy.' "

Barrymore seldom remained long enough to enjoy "mornings after" or leisurely Sundays, which were reserved exclusively for Ford and Holden's cronies. The small penthouse contained two refrigerators and a freezer, which were kept well-stocked with items from Bee's, a nearby grocery store. Except for breakfasts at Schwab's, just a short stroll down Sunset from the Marmont, the actors and their guests generally stayed in the suite, preparing meals in the privacy of their kitchen. "We each had our own likes and dislikes," Ford said. "David was excellent at making omlettes, Bogart liked fruit with his scotch, and Flynn ate very little. Bill couldn't do much but cook hamburgers."

Despite the odd mix of personalities and temperaments, a surprising calm prevailed in suite 54. Even Niven and Flynn managed to control their emotions. That hadn't always been the case during their roommate days at the Russell house, where they had battled for the use of the master bedroom—the one with the double bed—"on state occasions," as Niven put in. At the Marmont, there were no such problems. The popular question, "Are you using it tonight?" brought one of two responses. The sought-after "no" guaranteed total exclusivity to the premises for the evening.

It did not take Glenn Ford and William Holden long to discover the main penthouse directly overhead. "Somehow we managed to get hold of a pass key," admitted Ford, "and whenever it was vacant—we always knew—we would go up and make ourselves at home. One night Bogart wandered in, and he sat with Bill and me on the big patio. As we looked out at the lights of the city, he told us, 'All this can be yours.' It sounded good, but we didn't say anything. We just kept looking." According to Ford, Bogart visited six or seven times. He would come over, have a few drinks, and fall asleep.

David Niven's visits to the Marmont ended September, 1939, when he became one of the first Hollywood stars to join the war effort, entering the British army as a lieutenant with the commandos. He would not return to the film capital for nearly six years.

In time, Bogart, Flynn, and Barrymore drifted away as well. Errol Flynn, following his divorce from Lili Damita, retreated to a mountaintop on Mulholland Drive, where a fast-fading John Barrymore took refuge during his final days. Flynn's new bachelor pad quickly became, in his own words, "the mecca of pimps, bums, gamblers, process servers, and phonies." It was also the scene of orgies and highly illegal cockfights.

William Holden and Glenn Ford remained at Chateau Marmont until their restless days and penchant for "bad company" had seemingly come to an end. Harry Cohn kept the doors open—just in case. As Ford noted, "He couldn't have been nicer about it. He told us we could stay as long as we were under contract."

The turnabout came in 1941, when Bill Holden married Brenda Marshall, then joined the Army. Not much later Glenn Ford joined the Marines, then married Eleanor Powell.

Throughout their years at Chateau Marmont, the reputations of Holden and Ford remained unblemished, thanks to the wily ways of Harry Cohn. In the eyes of the moviegoing public, they were clean-cut, boy-next- door nice, the epitome of young American manhood—their lives free of scandal, free of wrongful associations—as befitted the high moral standards of the times. "That was the wonderful thing about the Marmont," laughed Ford. "It was so very private. You would drive into the garage, get in the elevator, go upstairs, and nobody would see you. People would come and go, in and out, and no questions were asked." He didn't say it, but the implication was clear: for Glenn Ford and his close pal, William Holden, the Marmont was the perfect set-up.

Following World war II, new homes began to crowd the hillsides
surrounding Chateau Marmont (*right*), December 1945. (*Courtesy
of Jona Liebrecht*)

# PART II

# A HOME AWAY FROM HOME

As the economy grew and prospered, so did Chateau Marmont. In 1937, Albert Smith had acquired the adjoining property to the east. There was a large duplex dwelling on the property, which he remodeled to conform to the elegant style of the main building.

Improvements were made along Sunset Boulevard as well. Encouraged by the area's growing fame and popularity, the Sunset boosters cooperated with the Hollywood *Citizen News* in running a contest to name their meandering two-mile section of roadway. The competition generated enormous interest from miles around, stimulated to some degree by the $25 prize money. Entries poured in by the thousands, delighting the organizers and furrowing the brows of the judges:—actor-turned-interior decorator, Bill Haines; actress Lila Lee; developer Francis S. Montgomery; and the Marmont's Albert E. Smith. Disgusted with defamatory references to the area (such as No Man's Land), the panel bypassed submissions that sounded trite and meaningless in favor of one with substance and respectability: *The Sunset Eighties.* The name was highly appropriate, everyone agreed, as it referred to the majority of addresses—the numbers ranged from 8000 through 9200 —along the boulevard. Commented Albert Smith, "It tells people where we are—and it's catchy."

With the naming of The Sunset Eighties, the entire length of the boulevard was at last completely paved and widened.

In the best Hollywood tradition, the event did not pass unnoticed. A much publicized dedication ceremony attracted stars in fancy new cars and a daredevil pilot who thrilled the crowd with low-flying stunts, while scattering flower petals. Guests at the Marmont leaned from their balconies to watch the proceedings down the road.

Despite the hoopla, the prizewinning Sunset Eighties failed to find favor with the public. It was left to the county engineers, of all people, to come up with the name that finally caught on.

For years the county engineers had referred to the unincorporated stretch of Sunset Boulevard as "the county strip"—even, with an occasional slip of the tongue, as "the Sunset strip." They spoke of "the strip" not as a place but as a *thing* that needed repair, clean-up, or improvement. No one knows exactly when the term first came into use by the general public, but when it did, it stuck. And it took on an entirely new meaning.

As elegant shops, decorator salons, night spots, and theatrical offices replaced barren land and scattered fields of avocados and poinsettias, the *place* called The Sunset Strip began to attract even greater attention. At the gateway to this glamorous new midway for the rich and famous stood

Chateau Marmont. Just how closely their fortunes—and futures—would be intertwined no one dared imagine.

The development of the Sunset Strip opened new hunting grounds for Nellita Choate Thomsen. She covered all the popular haunts in her quest to ferret out the latest celebrity gossip for her column. In 1938, however, she found herself in the spotlight, and the object of reporters pointed questions—much to her horror. After seventeen years of marriage, her beloved husband Carl announced that he wished to marry his secretary. The unexpected news and the threat of scandal so unnerved Nellita that she had to be committed to an institution for psychiatric rehabilitation.

Nellita thought she had taken every possible precaution against scandal. When she began her career with the Hearst papers, it was considered highly improper for a woman of position to accept employment, so she had assumed a pseudonym—Pauline Payne—to guard her secret. Now divorce!

Nellita's departure from the Marmont had her missing such new arrivals as tall, husky, and perpetually tanned Greg Bautzer, whose growing reputation as a brilliant young motion picture attorney was occasionally overshadowed by his playboy image, as he vied for the favors of Hollywood's great beauties. (His latest was MGM's budding sweatergirl, Lana Turner.) Bautzer often shared his Marmont quarters with friends who had similar interests. One was infatuated with Milton Berle's wife, a lovely blonde he had known since high school, Paramount showgirl Joyce Mathews. Another was a strikingly handsome actor, temporarily in hiding from his future wife, French actress, Annabella.

Martha Scott came to Hollywood and the Marmont from Broadway, to test for the role of Melanie in *Gone with The Wind*. "David O. Selznick sent me home," she remembered. "He said I was terrible, so unphotogenic. He told me I'd never make it in films, and I agreed with him. Films weren't for me. So I headed back to the theater, with every intention of staying there." Early the following year, however, Scott was again signing in at the Marmont. This time Sol Lesser had brought her cross-country to test for the part of Emily Webb in his screen version of *Our Town*, a role she had created onstage. She not only got the part but was nominated for an Academy Award. Some months later, as Scott recalled, she ran into David O. Selznick at the studio. "I said, 'Good morning, Mr. Selznick,' but he wouldn't speak to me. I had done the unforgiveable.".

Also new to the Marmont during the late 1930s were aristocratic, white-maned conductor, Leopold Stokowski, who was appearing in films at

Paramount and Universal; concert pianist Jose Iturbi; bandleader Paul Whiteman; New York attorney L. Arnold Weissburger; actress Signe Hasso; the Joseph Cottons; director Rouben Mamoulian; and producer-director John Houseman, with his collaborating *wunderkind*, Orson Welles, whose daily breakfast of garden tomatoes was considered strange even at Chateau Marmont.

Welles was in Hollywood to embark on a film career, lured from New York by RKO, following his chilling, live radio dramatization of H. G. Wells' *The War of the Worlds*. The broadcast's all-too-realistic description of an invasion by space creatures had thousands of listeners, already edgy from the on-going news of Hitler's march across Europe, panic-stricken and fleeing their homes.

The war overseas actually seemed far away, yet the growing conflict could not be ignored. There were reminders everywhere. Banner headlines flashed reports from raging battlefields on virtually every streetcorner. Radio carried voices and sounds from strange places with strange names—Danzig, Dunkirk, Compiegne—along with the latest grim news. Defense plants were hiring all comers; army and navy camps were mushrooming. The sight of men and women in uniform wasn't at all unusual, and conversations often turned to such annoying possibilities as "the draft," shortages, and rationing. The confrontation in Europe was terrifying, everyone agreed, but America was at peace. Hollywood's favorite topic was still itself.

The surprise Japanese attack on Pearl Harbor in December, 1941, changed all that. Suddenly the United States was at war, and Hollywood—along with coastal Southern California—had the jitters. For good reasons. Just north of quiet residential Santa Barbara, a few hours' drive away, a Japanese submarine had been identified offshore after firing twenty-five shells into a strategic oil-field. Not much later, on the night of February 25, 1942, "fifteen enemy aircraft" were spotted over the skies of Los Angeles. Searchlights combed the darkness, as hundreds of rounds of high-explosives rocketed from huge artillery guns hidden in the hills. The mystery planes escaped without casualty, but their presence, however brief, left a lasting mark on even the staunchest of souls who had sworn "it can't happen here."

For nearly twelve years, Chateau Marmont had been a fortress of privacy, sheltering the rich and famous from the eyes and autograph books of inquisitive fans. Overnight, its heavy Gothic doors were thrown open to the public. Emergency bulletins mailed throughout the neighborhood announced to residents and merchants alike that the Marmont's cavernous underground garage, bound by concrete and steel, had been designated as the area's Official Air Raid Shelter. Signs were posted everywhere, along the streets, in shops and restaurants, pointing the way to safety, in the event of an enemy attack. The elegant salons and corridors of the Marmont were least spared.

At every turn, large squares of white cardboard with bold red and black printing and arrows aimed downward were taped to the walls. "It was so different," Ann Little recalled forty-two years later, shuddering at the memory. "We had become the bomb shelter for much of the Strip—a survival center for thousands of people. No sooner did the word get out than strangers began arriving in droves. They would wander in and out at will, wondering where to go and how to get there 'just in case.' There was nothing we could do but try to be helpful, at times at the expense of our guests. But few of the guests complained. There was such a spirit of togetherness." The majority of neighborhood visitors were genuinely concerned for their safety, Little said. Then there were those who were simply curious about the Marmont and "welcomed any excuse for a free tour."

There were other frightening reminders of the times. A remote corner of the garage became a depository for packaged foodstuffs, bottled waters, candles, and other emergency supplies. A small desk was manned by service personnel, installed in the main-floor drawing room, for armed forces registration and the sale of war bonds. Blackout shades became standard decor at every hotel window, large and small. Near the entrance to the garage driveway, a pole towered several stories high. It was capped with a siren that often sounded its screeching alarm in the dead of night. Surprise air-raid drills never failed to attract Civil Defense wardens, volunteers wearing regulation arm patches and hard hats, whose job was to make absolutely certain that blackout shades were drawn. "Even the flame from a match can be seen many miles at sea," they warned.

Strict wartime regulations and the Marmont's wartime look did little to discourage newcomers to the hotel. Many of the guests were service personnel, mainly high-ranking officers, along with the wives of servicemen who had traveled from all parts of the nation to visit their husbands at West Coast bases. There were a number of prominent guests as well, including Rita Johnson (working in *My Friend Flicka*) and her husband, Lt. Col. L. Stanley Kahn; Martha Scott (*Cheers for Miss Bishop* and *One Foot in Heaven*); Dorothy Arzner (while directing *First Comes Courage* and Women's Army Corps training films); Mrs. Hugh Marlow (Edith Atwater); *New York Times* caricaturist Al Hirschfeld; and Britishers Gertrude Lawrence, Ronald Colman, and Felix Aylmer.

Also signing their names to the registry were: Helen Traubel and her husband, William Bass; the Willard Parkers (Virginia Field) and Alan Curtises (Ilona Massey, back again after her earlier stay with Hedy Lamarr, this time with her *New Wine* co-star and husband); Audrey Totter; John Payne (*Hello, Frisco, Hello*); Minerva Pious (of the Fred Allen radio show); John Emery (recently divorced from Tallulah Bankhead, after touring together in *The Little Foxes*); Joan Caulfield (working on her first film, *Duffy's Tavern*) and her mother; Errol Flynn (returning to the Marmont as a *paying* guest, this time with his second wife, Nora Eddington); composers Hugh Martin and Ralph Blane (MGM's *Best Foot Forward*); Mrs. Talbot Jennings (wife of the noted screenwriter); Estelle Taylor; and the skating stars of Ice Follies.

Baroness Zina de Rosen became the Marmont's first wartime casualty. She had checked into the hotel in 1939, vowing to "stay forever." Her seventh floor suite was a showplace, filled with priceless furnishings shipped to the Marmont from her home in France. Foolishly she returned to Paris for a visit shortly before the German occupation. She did not get out in time. In July, 1940, the Baroness cabled Albert Smith:

UNABLE TO LEAVE. FUTURE UNCERTAIN. PLEASE TAKE MY PERSONAL POSSESSIONS FOR YOUR OWN. GOD BLESS YOU!

According to Smith's son, James Gordon, "Father left many of her valuable pieces at the hotel. Others he took home, including a magnificent antique mirrored French fireplace."

For respite from the depressing war news, visitors to the Marmont spent nights on the town at the Strip's glamorous celebrity hangouts. The major attractions were the Trocadero and the newly opened Mocambo, operated by Charlie Morrison. Ciro's, which debuted shortly after the Mocambo in 1939, struggled for several years until new owner Herman Hover took over. The early failure of Ciro's didn't discourage director-screenwriter Preston Sturges, however. On a vacant parcel of land just west of the Marmont, Sturges built The Players, one of the most innovative and classiest night spots along Sunset. Multi-level in concept, The Players boasted a revolving bandstand for continuous entertainment, moveable walls, swing-out tables, "the best food and drinks in town," and, for the convenience of those patrons too busy to bother with such things during daylight hours, a barber shop. Many guests from the Marmont made The Players their second home while in town. So did Walter Winchell, Humphrey Bogart,

Charlie Chaplin, Orson Welles, and Joel McCrea.

The war had no bearing on Albert Smith's decision to sell Chateau Marmont. The hotel, in mid-1942, was flourishing. Along with shortages of virtually everything came a paucity in housing. Guests were forced to book reservations months in advance, even for the most expensive suites. Smith kept his reasons for selling to himself, but it was no secret that he could no longer give the Marmont the personal attention he felt necessary for its success. He was nearing seventy and suffering from high blood pressure. Too, his children were older, with involvements of their own; sons Albert, Ronald, and James Gordon were in the service, and daughter Audrey was married, living in New Jersey. Sunday dinners in the main floor drawing room had become much less special.

Albert Smith's decision stunned his manager. The past years had not been easy ones for Ann Little. Her mother had been desperately ill and a constant concern demanding more of her time. "Everyone's heart went out to Ann," recalled a close friend at the Marmont. "She doted on her mother—sat with her, read to her, consoled her with prayer. Ann was so emotionally torn. She felt responsible for the hotel as well as her mother, and there were times when she didn't know which way to turn. She would be talking with a guest and have to run off, thinking she had heard her mother's cries. It was a blessing when the poor woman passed on."

The end came several weeks before Pearl Harbor. From that time on, Ann Little began thinking seriously about pursuing her longtime goal—delayed by her mother's lingering illness—of becoming a Christian Science practitioner. Out of loyalty to Albert Smith, however, she had remained at the Marmont. Now she submitted her resignation.

Representatives of the new owners, the Ajax Corporation, refused to let Ann Little go. They told her she *had* to stay, and promised her the moon. "It was made very clear to me that the Marmont would flounder if I walked away—that I was the only connecting link between the hotel's success and failure. I doubt that was true, but I believed them at the time. I simply couldn't leave." One of Ajax's promises was to hire an assistant manager to lighten Little's work-load. They brought in forty-eight year old Roy D'Arcy, a retired character actor with no hotel experience but a strong determination to learn. Fortunately for the guests, he had also retired his trademark villainous leer.

With more freedom, Ann Little began devoting more time to her religion. For the moment, she seemed content. But her days at the Marmont were numbered.

## Chateau Marmont

Orson Welles
NAME

322 East 57th Street
STREET

New York City
CITY AND STATE

Feb. 10, 1939
DATE

## Chateau Marmont

John Houseman
NAME

1730 Broadway
STREET

New York City
CITY AND STATE

July 21 - 39
DATE

# Chapter 4

## Refuge From The Storm

## Mrs. Cohn

Divorce had been unthinkable. For eighteen years Rose Barker Cohn had adored her Harry, at times with a love that bordered on the obsessive. Few women had ever loved more deeply, more completely; Harry had been Rose's life, her very reason for living. Yet on July 28, 1941, she found herself boarding a train for Los Angeles, after six weeks in Reno. Rose Barker Cohn knew only too well how her former husband manipulated peoples lives.

Rose had planned to return to her lovely porte-cochered mansion in Fremont Place, a private residential park in the mid-Wilshire district favored by Los Angeles society. But as the train neared the big city, she realized she could not do that. Not having Harry around didn't frighten her. She had managed without him before, recently for long periods. No matter how strained their relationship had become, she had never lost hope that they would again share the same roof, if not the same bed. Now all hope had vanished. The thought of living in the huge Fremont Place house as the *ex* Mrs. Harry Cohn suddenly devastated her.

Almost in desperation Rose directed her driver to Chateau Marmont. As she would later explain, "I really didn't know where to turn. For some odd reason, the words of a friend came back to me. She had told me, during a particularly dark stage with Mr. Cohn, that I must join her at the Chateau. At the time, I didn't give her offer a second thought." Rose's friend had been society matron (and Hearst reporter) Nellita Choate Thomsen.

The fact that Nellita, who was undergoing therapy for her own shattered marriage, was living elsewhere no longer mattered. Nellita would be back, Rose felt certain. But then she had felt the same way about Harry.

The last years of wedded life had not been happy ones for Rose Cohn. She knew of Harry's infidelities with ambitious young actresses, would-be stars, who inevitably found their way to the executive suite in search of their "big break." She knew of the passageway that led from Harry's private office into one of the ladies' dressing rooms. She knew of his passion for beautiful women. Harry demanded beauty, and Rose was painfully aware that she did not meet his high standards. It wasn't that Rose was unattractive. She was actually quite lovely, stylish and charming in her warm Italian way. At the Marmont, she was regarded as "a sweet, sweet woman, caring and considerate." None of these qualities impressed Harry as much as the "250,000 dowry she had brought to their union in 1923, money she had received as part of a settlement from her short-lived first marriage to a wealthy New York attorney. Harry promptly sank the capital into his newly formed Columbia Pictures.

The Cohns had their problems almost from the start. Rose could not provide Harry with the children he craved, which, in Harry's eyes, reflected upon his manhood. More and more, Rose found herself stranded at home, rather than accompanying her husband to industry functions. Harry made excuses. It was important for a rising Hollywood power to be seen with his stars, he said. He would not admit that he preferred more decorous company clinging to his arm. She would not admit that her marriage was in trouble.

The situation became increasingly tense over the next ten years, as Harry stretched his hours at the studio, leaving little time for Rose. He began to talk of a separation, even divorce, but she refused to listen. Never, *never* would she agree to such a thing. Unable to reason with Rose or function on a level at home, Harry left Fremont Place for the El Royale Apartments in Hollywood.

On one of Harry's frequent trips to New York, he met a young fashion model named Betty Miller. She captivated him; he found her to be incredibly beautiful. He offered Betty a contract, changed her name to Joan Perry, and brought her to Hollywood. As she worked her way through a succession of "B" movies, mainly who-done-its, she became the most important woman in Harry Cohn's life.

Rose remained undaunted, dismissing all talk of Harry and his mistress. She confronted her husband, only to tell him how empty her life had become, how lonely she felt without someone—or something—to fill her lonely days and nights. Harry responded with his favorite solution—divorce. Finding his words again falling on deaf ears, he flippantly proposed that she become a patroness of the arts.

Except for a fling at acting prior to her first marriage, Rose had never worked. She had even shied away from charitable activities. Part of the problem was her self-esteem, which Harry constantly challenged. While his latest suggestion, however insensitive, held little appeal for Rose, she refused to dismiss it. If kowtowing to Harry's wishes would make him look upon her more favorably, Rose figured, she had everything to gain. She steadfastly believed, despite all that had taken place between them, that Harry was not lost to her.

Through a friend at the hotel, Rose aligned herself with a small opera company dedicated to the presentation of regional productions. One of the group's members was a talented young Italian tenor who soon caught Rose's attention. When her professional interest in him blossomed, she adopted him as her protege. The two were together almost constantly, during and after rehearsals. Rose enjoyed the grateful singer's company. It had been a long time since a man had treated her with such kindness and consideration. Harry couldn't have been more pleased. Unknown to Rose, he had hired private detectives to follow her and her devoted young companion. The reports of their on-going togetherness made fascinating reading. Rose pleaded her innocence, but she was helpless against Harry's attack. Reluctantly, she at last agreed to a divorce. Within the month, she was on her way to Reno.

At the Marmont, Rose settled into a spacious suite on the third floor, joining such other guests as Russian composer Igor Stravinsky and his wife; actors Nils Asther, Ray Collins, and Everett Sloan; director Rouben Mamoulian; Countess de Sakhrioffsky; Mrs. Leslie Charteris (wife of "The Saint" creator) and their daughter; Swedish actress Signe Hasso (in Hollywood for her first American film, MGM's "Journey for Margaret"); and Eleanor Gehrig, whose husband, the famed Lou Gehrig of the New York Yankees, had only recently died. Rose made no attempt to acquaint herself with her celebrated neighbors.

Adjusting to her new surroundings wasn't easy for Rose. "She tried valiantly to put her past behind her," an acquaintence reported, "but all she could talk about was Mr. Cohn. Her thoughts were completely centered on 'my Harry,' as she called him. He was still so much a part of her."

Things got worse for Rose when she read the news of Harry's marriage to Joan Perry. The wedding had taken place at the St. Regis Hotel in New York, less than seventy-two hours after his divorce had been granted. There were photos of the groom and his beautiful new bride. One caption noted: "The new Mrs. Harry Cohn looked exquisite in her specially created gown by Columbia's top costume designer, Jean Louis."

According to a former Marmont staff member, Rose's attempts at independence were feeble at best. "She was so helpless, pitiful at times. There wasn't much of anything she could do. Of course, she had never had to bother before. She had always had someone at her beck and call." During Rose's first few weeks at the hotel, she attempted to prepare her own meals. A wretched cook (she once served ham to Harry's Jewish mother, who graciously commented how much it tasted like chicken), she was forced one evening to call on Golan Banks, the Marmont's chef, for help with the simplest menu. (She was tackling a small roast and one fresh vegetable.) The step-by-step instructions Golan provided did little good; the final result, after hours in front of her stove, was a disaster. In desperation, Rose hired a housekeeper, Mrs. Sullivan, not only to do her "kitchen chores" but to keep her company.

Throughout her years at the Marmont, Rose remained faithful to her "one and only love," the only man who truly mattered in her life, Harry Cohn. Surprisingly, Harry did not sever his ties with Rose after their divorce. In fact, their relationship actually began to improve, as Rose received more concerned attention from Harry than at any time since the earliest days of their marriage. He not only insisted on advising her on all money matters (once again she had received a sizeable settlement), but willingly provided her with the unlisted numbers to his private lines, both at home and at the studio. Only those people closest to Harry were so privileged.

A few minutes on the phone with Harry brightened Rose's outlook for days. But the sound of his voice was only minor consolation. In her heart she knew that Harry would never return to her; she had lost him to another woman. That thought would remain with her always.

# Two Gentlemen from Germany

It was early evening in November, 1943, when a taxi pulled up to the curb outside Chateau Marmont and two middle-aged men stepped out. One was tall and slender, with dark, close-cropped hair and a ruddy complexion. The other was extremely short, almost dwarflike, with rounded shoulders and a severely hunched spine. They were bundled in heavy woolen topcoats of the same cut and color, despite the balmy air.

The taller man stood momentarily looking up at the hotel, then turned sharply and walked toward the entrance, his heels pounding with authority on the tiles of the colonnaded walkway. The shorter man followed several paces behind.

The two men were entering the lobby when the taxi driver caught up with them to inquire, with unusual restraint, about the unpaid fare. The taller man continued, leaving his companion to settle the matter. With a look of resignation, the shorter man reached into his pocket and pulled out a roll of paper currency the size of a clenched fist. He left that untouched and dipped deep again, this time to retrieve a handful of loose change. Slowly, deliberately, he counted out the exact amount in pennies, nickles, and dimes, tipped his hat, and that was all. The cabbie glowered as he lowered his outstretched hand.

In the main-floor drawing room, a small gathering of guests watched the newcomers' arrival with some amusement. No one had the slightest idea who they were, although one viewer suggested innocently that they were an aspiring comedy team, possible successors to Laurel and Hardy or the currently popular Abbott and Costello. It came as a shock to discover their true identity.

"You may tell the person in charge that Dr. Brethauer has arrived," the taller man told the desk clerk, in a booming, heavily accented voice.

The clerk on duty, only recently hired, nodded and disappeared. She was back in seconds to apologize and offer whatever assistance she could provide. There was little else she could do. Ann Little was gone. At the time of Ajax's takeover, she had promised to stay one additional year— "not a moment longer"—and she had kept her word. Even the representatives from Ajax, who had assumed management duties on a rotating basis since Little's departure in August, were missing. No one had seen them for the past two days, not since they had left word at the desk that the Marmont had been sold. At the time, they had indicated only that "foreign interests" were involved. No specifics had been volunteered, not even a mention of the new owner's name: Edwin C. Brethauer.

It was left to Dr. Brethauer to break the news before a hastily assembled gathering of the night shift and a sprinkling of bystanders, who found the proceedings in the lobby intriguing. The moment was awkward. The staff listened in disbelief, but said nothing. No one rushed to congratulate him; there were no offers to shake his hand or to wish him well. "We were scared to death," one ex-employee remembers. "A German had taken over the Marmont and we were at war with Germany. We had been primed to hate these people. Everyone believed that Germans were evil, our enemy. How could we work for this man?"

As it turned out, the employees had more in common with Dr. Brethauer and his diminuative friend, who he introduced as Dr. Popper, than they realized. The two men shared their hatred for Hitler and Hitler's Germany. It was the mad dictator who had driven Dr. Brethauer's wife to suicide. It was Hitler's persecution of the Jews that had driven Dr. Brethauer and his friend, who were Jewish, from their once-beloved homeland. Somehow, miraculously, they had eluded the Gestapo, fleeing with only the clothes on their backs and one small suitcase. But the suitcase contained the key to their future in America—Dr. Brethauer's money, which amounted to a sizeable fortune.

It had been Dr. Popper's responsibility to guard the suitcase with his life during their escape, and it was never out of his protective clutches. His reward for loyal service to Dr. Brethauer was, in Dr. Popper's eyes, "eternal security." Soon after their arrival at Chateau Marmont, he became Dr. Brethauer's personal secretary. As such, he assumed the position of manager at the Marmont.

Dr. Brethauer's influence over Dr. Popper was absolute. When "Mister" Brethauer took on the self-appointed title of doctor upon arriving in America, believing it would gain him instant respectability, *Mister* Popper followed suit. When the newly decreed *Doctor* Brethauer converted to Catholicism, fearful that religious persecution might follow him across the Atlantic, so did the newly decreed *Doctor* Popper. When Dr. Brethauer lectured on the pitfalls of free and easy spending, Dr. Popper pinched pennies and knotted purse strings.

It didn't take long for the gentlemen from Germany to establish a reputation among the Marmont's working staff. The newcomers were described not only as "frugal," "penurious," and "cheap," but "stern and demanding." Dr. Popper, with a nod from Dr. Brethauer, ordered many of the services and niceties instigated by Albert Smith and Ann Little put to rest. No longer were fresh flowers awaiting incoming guests in their suites ("A waste of money," cried Dr. Popper). Catered meals became a thing of the past; the main kitchen was closed and Golan Banks was dismissed as "needless expenses."

Fortunately for the staff, only one of the "doctors" resided at Chateau Marmont. Unfortunately, it was Dr. Popper. The little man thrived on his newfound power; not a day passed that he wasn't overheard reminding subordinates of his position, usually in the course of issuing directives. His sixth floor suite (6G) became command head quarters, and a good deal more. Despite his physical deformity, Dr. Popper was enormously popular with the ladies. If days were devoted to bloating his ego, nights were for entertaining.

Dr. Brethauer's Hollywood home was far less active, mainly because his social life was more subdued. He prided himself on being a "one-woman man" and within six months of his arrival at the Marmont, he found her. Everyone at the hotel who came in contact with the new Mrs. Brethauer, a frail creature with penetrating eyes, agreed that she was "strange and moody," decidedly "peculiar."

Several nights a week, the Brethauers would dine at the Marmont with Dr. Popper and his lady-of-the-moment. Although the two men favored heavy German food, the menu frequently included American dishes in deference to the women. No matter what Dr. Popper served, however, Mrs. Brethauer refused to partake. She preferred only a lettuce leaf and one thin slice of tomato, which she would partially finish before excusing herself from the table. Just to see her nibbling gave Dr. Brethauer pleasure. At home or away she rarely ate at all.

Over the next few years, Mrs. Brethauer bore her husband two daughters. Her delivery days were occasions for great joy at the Marmont, for they signaled her return to some normalcy. Throughout both pregnancies, she spent most of her time in a lobby chair, glaring at the women employees. Mrs. Brethauer did not approve of working women. "Ladies never toil," she once remarked. "It is beneath their dignity."

With the owner and his aide wandering sternly about the Marmont, and a sporadically *schwanger* Mrs. Brethauer perched in the lobby, the staff had to stay on its collective toes. But guests saw only a delightful trio. Around them, Dr. Brethauer and Dr. Popper were the perfect hosts, mild and gracious, often affecting a royal manner. The sight of Mrs. Brethauer, patiently awaiting birth, lent a warm, domestic touch.

Following the war, the Marmont welcomed screenwriters Edward Anhalt (and his wife, Edna) and Leonard Spigelgass; *Life* magazine's Eliot Elisofon; the Bennett Cerfs; the James E. Doolittles; producer Edward Small; Paul Stewart (for the award-winning film, *Champion*); former silent screen star Jane Cowl and her maid, Priscilla Irens; the Norman Luboffs; Molly Mandaville (Darryl F. Zanuck's private secretary and a compulsive shopper, who rented two suites, one to live in, the other for her purchases); comedian

CHATEAU MARMONT

Prince ARTCHIL GOURIELLI
NAME

625 Park Aven
STREET

N. Y.
CITY AND STATE

Sept. 1st /45.
DATE

CHATEAU MARMONT

Ed. Wynn
NAME

325 Park Ave
STREET

N.Y.C., N.Y.
CITY AND STATE

8/22/47.
DATE

$12.00      50¢ garage      5 F

Phil Foster; playwright Mary D.Chase; the Jimmy Hatlos; Joan Caulfield; the Norman Mailers; Philip Bourneuf and his wife, actress Francis Reid; Jane Randolph; and Robert Hutton.

Also among the post-war guests was Gracie Fields. Probably England's most beloved wartime star, Fields wasn't quite as reserved as the "Brits" who had preceeded her. She could be outrageous without warning. It was not unusual to see her walk through the lobby and break into an impromptu dance step, accompanied by a line or two in song, as if she were on a music hall stage. Then she would turn sheepish and say, somewhat apologetically: "Underneath all the froth and bubble, I'm shy too!"

For the first time in six years, Nellita Choate Thomsen returned to the Marmont. She *had* to come back, she said, because the hotel and its stimulating clientele not only kept her young but constantly refreshed.

She moved into a second-floor suite and quietly resumed her place in society. Although she no longer had her daily column, she was not lacking in outlets to challenge her creativity. She became active in the Assistance League, joined the Nine O'Clock Players (supervising the casting of various productions, including her own playlets), and hosted extravagant dinner parties. "Los Angeles society is moving in a very beautiful way," she noted with great pleasure.

Nellita even found romance. The "young man" in her life, Stephen F. Whitman, was hardly that. An octagenarian, he was more than twice Nellita's age, but his still youthful enthusiasm and Victorian manner were irresistible. He was also, according to Nellita, a masterful writer; at one time he had been a regular contributor to *The Saturday Evening Post* .

Aside from Carl Thomsen and the Dr. Frank Barham, the Hearst publisher who had hired Nellita out of college, Stephen F. Whitman was the only person to know the true identity of Pauline Payne. Whitman was so touched to have Nellita confide in him that he began privately calling her "Polly" as a term of endearment. Even his love notes to her, which she kept in a scrapbook along with his yellowing *Post* articles, were addressed to "My dearest Polly" (and signed "Impatiently thine, Steve").

Nellita crowded her hours with charity work and, when her social calendar permitted, had time leftover for intimate dinners *a deux* with Stephen in her suite. But she still longed for the early days at the Marmont—the days of Carl Thomsen and Pauline Payne, of discovery and burning involvement.

With the lifting of travel restrictions came an increasing number of celebrity guests from wartorn Europe, many to start or resume their careers in American films. Among the first to arrive were Leo Genn (for *The Velvet*

*Touch* and *The Snake Pit*) and his wife; villainous character actor Victor Francen (for *The Beast with Five Fingers* ); Maurice Chevalier; the Alexander Salkinds; Barbara Laage (for *B.F.'s Daughter* with Barbara Stanwyck); Marta Toren (for her first American feature, *Casbah*); director Compton Bennett and his wife; Mady Christians (for *All My Sons* and *Letter from an Unknown Wife*); Greta Gynt; and the Prince and Princess Gourielli.

Gourielli, whose full name was Prince Artchil Gourielli-Tchkonia, was a White Russian from the region of Georgia. A large, handsome man, he had a warm, ready smile and a laugh that spread instant cheer. But it was his Polish-born wife who drew most of the attention at the Marmont. She had a high, high forehead and thinning jet black hair that was pulled back into a bulbous chignon. She wore enormous jewelry and billowing floor-length caftans that artfully camouflaged her ample form. Guests would comment how youthful she appeared, when, in fact, she was at least a decade older than her husband. At seventy-five, her face showed not a sign of aging; her pale, clear skin was still unlined, flawless.

Each morning Princess Gourielli swept through the lobby with a burst of energy, stopping only to greet friends and newcomers. Rarely would she ask a simple "How are you?" Her interest in people and life went far deeper. "Are you happy? Are you learning? Are you growing stronger?" she wanted to know.

The Princess would frequently end her busy days chatting in the main-floor drawing room with the Brethauers and Dr. Popper. She won Mrs. Brethauer over completely, despite the fact that she was a working woman, known far better by her maiden name, Helena Rubinstein. The moments of private conversation with one of the world's great authorities on beauty presented an opportunity Mrs. Brethauer could not let pass. "Do you have any special secrets for me?" she would ask the Princess time and again. One day, after several inquiries too many, the Princess confided, "Work, *hard work*. It keeps the wrinkles out of the mind and spirit. It keeps a woman young—and alive." Mrs. Brethauer smiled faintly. That was not the "secret" she longed to hear.

Fanny Brice came to the Marmont, not as a funny lady but as an interior designer. She put her considerable artistic talents to work in decorating Philip Weltman's fourth-floor suite (4H). Former staff members recall seeing Brice come in daily to check on the job in progress, then depart the hotel through a side door.

Ed Wynn, the dithery headliner of *Ziegfeld Follies* on Broadway (where he was billed as "The Perfect Fool") and radio's Texaco Fire Chief, registered at the Marmont on two occasions: in the fall of 1947 and again two years later. Wynn's first visit was uneventful; his second became historic. It was in 1949 that he was brought to Hollywood to headline the first CBS television comedy show originating from the West Coast.

Ed Wynn's producer-director on that live telecast was a bespectacled young man, transported from New York City, named Ralph Levy. Wynn and Levy came to the Marmont about the same time, but Levy stayed long after Wynn departed, to produce and direct the *Burns and Allen Show* , with George and Gracie, as well as the TV pilots for the landmark *I Love Lucy* and, later, *The Alan Young Show, Green Acres*, and *The Beverly Hillbillies*.

Of all their early guests, however, two expatriates became the favorites of Dr. Brethauer and Dr. Popper: Archduke Felix of Austria (the pretender to the throne) and Otto of Austria-Hungary. Whenever the men would meet at the Marmont, there was a resounding clicking of heels, a custom carried with them from another time and place. To the owner and his trusted aide, they were the most special of guests, so privileged that Dr. Brethauer personally underwrote their visits, a startling gesture, considering his frugal nature.

Dr. Brethauer and Dr. Popper were to govern Chateau Marmont for nearly twenty years, during which time the hotel took on a distinct European flavor. It would also mirror the tides of the motion picture industry. At the time of their arrival, in late 1943, movies were in the midst of a golden era. The Marmont would soon be entering one of its own.

Montgomery Clift disappeared from the set of *Red River* to visit Libby Holman at the Marmont.

# Chapter 5

## A Very Private Place

### Miss Holman

It was well past midnight when she checked into the penthouse that summer of 1946. She did not look well. Her face, with its poutish full lips, was deeply lined. Her once-flattering tan had faded to a pallor. Her dark, disheveled hair fell limply upon her shoulders, as lifeless as her cigarette-clouded expression. She made it clear, in a voice that no longer commanded attention, that her arrival was confidential. Guarding her secret would not be easy. The sixth-floor corridor outside her door was heavy with the overpowering fragrance of her Jungle Gardenia perfume.

Libby Holman's name still stirred memories, even though she had been out of the spotlight for years. She had first gained fame in the mid-1920s as a singer of smoldering torch songs, appearing in clubs and on Broadway, where she became a major star. Her throbbing, powerful voice had introduced songs by Rodgers and Hart, Cole Porter, and Howard Dietz and Arthur Schwartz. Her torrid solos of *Body and Soul*, *Moanin' Low*, *Something to Remember You By*, and *Can't We Be Friends?*, among others, were show-stoppers. But even greater fame—and notoriety—awaited her. It came with her storybook wedding to handsome twenty-year-old tobacco heir, Zachary Smith Reynolds.

On July 5, 1932, after only eight months of marriage, Libby's life turned sour overnight, when her robust young husband died of "mysterious circumstances," following a violent quarrel. She claimed that, in a despondent mood, he had put a gun to his temple, pulled the trigger, and fallen helplessly to the floor of their Winston-Salem estate. The Reynolds family claimed that she was after his thirty-million-dollar inheritance and charged her with murder.

The trial had been a tonic of sorts for a nation grown weary of reading the depressing news of the day. Certainly it offered something for nearly everyone, including sensational sexual elements and several bizarre twists. Zachary, one witness testified, had been driven to the brink of suicide on more than one occasion in the past, prompted by his latent homosexuality. Even Libby had to acknowledge that their marriage bed had been less than active. The family, stung by the startling disclosures and a lack of real evidence against Libby, reluctantly dropped its charges.

The trial had barely ended when Libby began appearing in public, wearing maternity clothes. Six months later, she gave birth to a two-pound boy. She named him Christopher Smith Reynolds and promptly returned to court. A long and bitterly contested estate battle resulted in an award of $750,000 to Libby and nearly seven-million to her son.

The scandalous trials of 1932 and 1933 had left Libby's reputation—and career—in shambles. She worked briefly in a 1934 Broadway show, *Revenge with Music* (in which she introduced *You and the Night and the Music,* before retreating to live in virtual seclusion. She bought a multi-acre estate outside Stamford, Connecticut, called Treetops, and with the help of a full staff, devoted her days to little Christopher. She was rarely seen without a drink in her hand. Alcohol—and there was talk of drugs—had begun to consume her life. More than once she had turned to specialists in the hope of finding a cure. She was also deep into analysis.

Another marriage had only fueled her problems. In 1939, she became the wife of Ralph Holmes, a pretty-faced, brooding actor who, at twenty-one, was twelve years Libby's junior. Like Zachary, Ralph's sexual preferences tended to stray from the norm. She seemed drawn to overly sensitive, troubled young men.

By the time Libby Holman arrived at Chateau Marmont in mid-1946, she was a tragic figure. Ralph was dead; an overdose of sleeping pills had ended his life during a lengthy separation, following several years of marriage. Ralph's brother, with whom she had had an earlier affair, had been killed in a plane crash. The twisted, frozen body of her beloved Christopher —so young, so intelligent, so handsome—had been found in a mountainside crevice; he had been on an unchaperoned winter excursion with school chums. Her son's inheritance, awarded to her, following another intense estate battle, was of little consolation. "I have nothing, no one," she had sobbed to reporters. "Everyone I've ever loved is gone."

That wasn't quite true. She had come to the Marmont to rendezvous with an exceedingly attractive twenty-five-year-old stage actor. His name was Montgomery Clift.

Libby Holman and Montgomery Clift had first met in early 1943, during rehearsals for an off-Broadway play, an experimental production of Ramon Naya's award-winning *Mexican Mural*. Clift had been cast in one of the sketches as a neurotic youth unable to cope with his squalid environment. Libby, hoping for a comeback, had been hired simply as a curiosity piece.

At the time of their meeting, Libby had only recently separated from Ralph Holmes. But she was immediately drawn to the youthful Clift, who embodied all she required in a man. He was movie-star handsome (some described him as 'beautiful'), sensitive, intense, and extremely talented. Her sensational past undoubtedly intrigued him.

Now, Clift had come to Hollywood for his first motion picture, Howard Hawks' production of *Red River*. The western was an odd choice for his movie debut. Indeed, even Clift had his doubts. He considered himself an unlikely cowboy; he was small-boned and slender, not rugged. He could barely sit on a horse, let alone ride one. He was far from expert with his fists, and his role called for a brutal confrontation with his co-star, John Wayne. But he longed to be in pictures, and he needed work. And he couldn't refuse the $60,000 Hawks had offered him.

Except for some interior scenes shot on the sound stages at United Artists studio, most of *Red River* was filmed on location between June and November. The company was transported to a remote area outside Tucson, Arizona, unspoiled wastelands, appropriately named Rain Valley. Storms continuously interrupted shooting, often for weeks at a time. There was nothing for the cast and crew to do except wait out the bad weather and try to enjoy one another's company. Many in the group came down with colds and dysentery. Montgomery Clift simply grew restless and depressed. He detested the "frontier conditions." He found it impossible to mix with his co-workers and play their rough 'n' tumble games; he was far from prudish, but their bawdy stories and dirty talk repelled him. There were even reports of a rift between Clift and John Wayne. It was said that Wayne's growing impatience with his "prima donna" co-star triggered repeated outbursts.

Crew members remember Clift secretly stealing away for days during the interminable rains. At first he sought relief with friends in Palm Springs. Then he turned to Libby Holman.

It isn't known who made the first contact, although it's unlikely that Libby called the Arizona location. More likely, Clift reached her at Treetops. At any rate, she was waiting at the Marmont when he needed her.

Montgomery Clift slipped into the hotel as stealthily as he slipped out of Arizona. If the lobby was busy, he entered through the garage. If the elevator was in use, he used the stairs. One quiet night, he roused Eddie, the elevator man, from the attentive stance Dr. Popper made him assume beside the lift's open door. "Mr. Clift came along so fast he surprised me," recalled Eddie. "Could be I was daydreaming, but all of a sudden he was in the elevator, wanting to go upstairs. He motioned for me to hurry, as if he had to get going before someone else came along. He got real nervous when a buzzer sounded from one of the other floors. He told me, 'Don't stop—keep going.' He acted like he was being pursued."

At the Marmont, Libby Holman provided more than a protective environment for Montgomery Clift. She offered warmth and compassion, and an endless supply of alcohol, to erase memories of people and places best forgotten. There were other benefits that only she could realize. Having the promising young actor all to herself for long periods was balm for her tortured soul. "In my lifetime," she had once remarked, "I want at least one great love—a man who has achieved something in the arts." She acted like she had found him in Clift.

Libby Holman was still at the Marmont when the *Red River* troupe returned to Hollywood from the rain-soaked Arizona location in December. Another month of shooting remained—interiors at the studio—and another month of entertaining her attentive Clift. Their secluded times together in the perfumed penthouse were the beginning of a long and strange relationship that would intensify over the coming years.

## Writers In Residence

At the Garden of Allah, noted resident writers F. Scott Fitzgerald, John O'Hara, Marc Connelly, Donald Ogden Stewart, and Robert Benchley were constantly in the columns, with their free-wheeling antics and drunken brawls. Across the street, Chateau Marmont had its own heavyweights and newsmakers.

Billy Wilder was the first of a long list of writers to call the Marmont home. He was soon joined by S.J.Perelman, humorist and screenwriter for two of the Marx Brothers' biggest films, *Monkey Business* and *Horse Feathers;* and playwright-screenwriter S. N. Behrman, who made no secret of his interest in a relatively unknown starlet named Lucille Ball.

Author-screen writer Corey Ford came to the Marmont to work on the script for *Topper Takes A Trip*, forsaking the company of his contemporaries at the Garden of Allah. The atmosphere there, he said, was "too noisy, too crazy to think."

Ford didn't count on the racket he would have to endure daily at the Marmont—or the view from the balcony of his top floor suite on the hotel's back side. "I seldom stepped out on it," he reminisced some years later. "There was nothing to see but a bare hillside, where bulldozers were gouging out new building sites, one drab excavation below another. Sandy rubble had spilled down from the successive terraces and was grown over with coarse trailing weeds. One night, Scott Fitzgerald arrived early to visit, and while I was pouring myself a highball, he wandered out onto the balcony. I joined him, prepared to apologize for the view, but his face was radiant. He pointed to the vine-covered terraces, bathed in moonlight. 'The hanging gardens of Babylon,' he said, and from then on my view was enchanted."

John Van Druten first arrived at the Marmont in 1935. He returned frequently in the years that followed—usually with his companion, Carter Lodge—to work on such screenplays as *Night Must Fall, Old Acquaintence, Gaslight,* and *The Voice of the Turtle.* Van Druten was often visited by Christopher Isherwood, whose stories of decadent Berlin prior to World War II formed the basis for Van Druten's dramatic stage success, *I Am A Camera,* and the musical, *Cabaret.*

In the 1940s, the Marmont also welcomed Ben Hecht and his favorite collaborator, Charles MacArthur; Aldous Huxley; Lillian Hellman; Sydney Box; and the dean of women screenwriters, Frances Marion, whose long and successful career included nearly 150 scenarios and original stories, and two Academy Awards (for *The Big House* and *The Champ)*.

Frances Marion, who had returned to Chateau Marmont following the suicide of her husband, director George Hill, in their Malibu home, was close to longtime Marmont resident, Anne Morrison Chapin. A onetime actress, Chapin had turned to writing in the early 1930s. She eventually signed a lucrative contract with MGM, where she turned out scripts for Judy Garland, June Allyson, Margaret O'Brien, and other top studio stars. Although Chapin was regarded as "a very pretty woman" and "a great friend of actors and actresses," she is best remembered at the hotel for her strange work habits.

She wrote propped up in bed, often while entertaining visitors; she encouraged drop-ins (Natalie Schaffer and Judith Anderson were her favorites) by leaving the door to her suite, 1A, partially open. Miriam Hopkins' boyfriend, another writer named Peterson, was less welcome, because he never left without "borrowing" cans of soup. "That man drove Miss Chapin crazy," her maid reported, "but she never let on to him. It wasn't what he took that annoyed her as much as having to keep restocking her pantry."

Despite Chapin's many friends, she was a lonely, unhappy woman. More and more she took to her bed. In time, it became her sanctuary.

When Dorothy Parker checked into the Marmont in 1948, she brought with her a little dog, but not her husband, Alan Campbell. They had recently separated, and Parker was attempting to carry on without him, bolstered by heavy sessions with a bottle in her suite, 4G. She was often so desperate for companionship that she would pick up the telephone and chat with the switchboard operator. It wasn't long before Parker began inviting her new-found friend to join her for drinks after work. "I would stay about a half hour, long enough for several cocktails," the operator recalled recently, "then scramble for the bus."

When the operator told her sister about her visits with the famous Dorothy Parker, the duo stretched into a threesome. The women would meet for lunch—and drinks, always—then adjourn to 4G, where they experimented with various hair-styles to try to brighten Parker's ever-gloomy mood.

One Sunday afternoon, following a get-together, the operator's sister phoned Parker in her suite to thank her for "a lovely time." Luckily, the third member of the trio had returned to her post at the switchboard. "It was a long conversation," she remembered, "or so it seemed. The board was very busy, and an hour had passed before I realized that the connection was still up. I don't know what possessed me, but I opened the key to make sure they were still talking. The only voice I heard was Miss Parker's, and she sounded far away, . . . crying for help. I called Gene Gordon, the garage man, and told him to hurry up to the fourth floor and see what was wrong."

Gordon found Dorothy Parker lying semi-conscious in her bathtub; she had slipped and fallen, hitting her head. An ambulance was quickly summoned, and Parker was rushed to the hospital, where she was examined and released, wrapped in bandages that all but covered her perky new hairdo.

The next day, the operator spotted Parker wandering through the lobby with her bandaged head. "I left the switch board and tried to console her, but she brushed me aside and kept on going." The operator was at a loss to explain Parker's sudden coolness, but then, there were other unanswered questions. In Parker's despondency, had her slip in the tub really been accidental? If so, why was she so angry with the person who had responded to her pleas? If not, why had she cried out? And why had she left her phone off the hook? There were insiders at the hotel who wondered if the mishap had been staged simply to gain attention and sympathy.

Throughout Dorothy Parker's stay at the Marmont, her mood never lightened. Only once did she have anything to say when she stopped at the front desk to pick up her mail, and that was to mutter, "Life would be a bed of roses if it weren't filled with pricks!"

# Mr. Cohen & The Upstairs Maid

Nothing seemed to bother Frieda. Of all the maids, and there were still nearly a dozen on staff, despite Dr. Popper's budget cuts, she was the Marmont's iron horse. Day after day she went about her duties—dusting, scrubbing, mopping, changing beds—systematically working from one end of the third floor to the other without the slightest complaint. Frieda was unflappable. Then she ran into Mr. Cohen.

Meyer "Mickey" Cohen had moved into the former Jean Harlow suite for a short stay. A squat, balding man in his mid-thirties with an outgoing personality and a glad-hand, he wore expensive clothes and diamonds on his fingers. He had introduced himself to Dr. Popper as a haberdasher. No one at the Marmont dared mention his other occupation as one of the West Coast's leading racketeers.

One afternoon, Frieda approached the Cohen suite with a supply of fresh towels neatly looped over an arm. She knocked on the door, then stood awaiting a response, as all the maids had been instructed to do. Getting none, she knocked once more. When no one answered, she reached into the pocket of her pale blue uniform, pulled out a pass key and went inside, leaving the door partially open behind her.

She had been inside only moments when an ear-piercing shriek echoed through the tranquil corridors of the Marmont. Seconds later Frieda reappeared. Her face was flushed; her ample chest heaved as she gasped for breath. She paused briefly before bolting down the stairway to the lobby, leaving a path of rumpled white terry cloth in her wake. She wailed all the way.

By the time Frieda reached the front desk, her legs had turned to rubber; her body was trembling so violently that she could barely stand. The desk clerk grabbed her arm. The telephone operator rushed to her side. Frieda covered her face and burst into tears. "I won't ever go in that suite again," she cried. "Never, never, *never!*"

It took several minutes for Frieda to regain her composure. Even then she couldn't stop shaking, and she refused to talk. The desk clerk begged her, the telephone operator pleaded with her. "What's wrong?" they asked in unison. "Tell us what happened."

Frieda rolled her eyes then buried her face again. "I'm too embarrassed," she said in muffled voice. Then she started blubbering all over again.

"Embarrassed about what?"

"I can't say," Frieda sobbed. "It was too terrible."

"If somebody did something to you, Dr. Popper should know about it," the desk clerk said.

Frieda looked up quickly. "Oh, no, don't tell *him.* Don't tell *anybody.*"

"Then what is it?"

"Well.", Frieda started. She stopped, sighed, drew in a deep breath, then blurted, "I saw Mr. Cohen."

"So?"

"He was lying in bed. *Naked.*"

"Is that all?"

"There was a woman with him, and *she* was naked. He was lying on top of her and they were . . . they were . . . " Frieda's face turned crimson.

"Go on."

*"Mr. Cohen saw me!"*

"Oh? And?"

"And nothing. He didn't say a word. He just smiled and kept on doing it . . . , right in front of me!" She sighed again, then moaned, "How can I go in that suite again? How can I face that man? What would I say?" Frieda wiped her eyes with a borrowed handkerchief and whimpered, "What am I going to do?"

Only Dr. Popper could answer that question, as Frieda knew all too well. But having to confront him suddenly seemed less terrifying. "What have you to fear?" the telephone operator asked. "It wasn't your fault. You didn't do anything wrong."

Dr. Popper had to know everything, from the moment Frieda approached the door to the Cohen suite to her hasty retreat. He even asked questions.

For some reason he was overly inquisitive about the bedded mystery woman.

Reliving the incident wasn't easy for Frieda. By the time the interrogation ended, she was teary-eyed, red-faced, and slump-shouldered.

"You will continue working as if nothing has happened," Dr. Popper advised, adding with a rare show of compassion, "only you will trade floors with one of the other girls until Mr. Cohen ends his visit."

Frieda's face brightened at the happy news. She leaned over to thank Dr. Popper, then stood straight, her shoulders squared. The iron horse had returned to the Marmont. Her rust spots weren't even visible.

Howard Hughes—an absolute night person with a passion for privacy.

# Chapter 6

## Wanderlust

## Mr. Hughes

For years, stories circulated around the Marmont about a passionate affair "under the gables" between two of the hotel's most prominent guests: Jean Harlow and her *Hell's Angels* producer-director Howard Hughes. None of them were true, but they made good listening.

According to the most reliable accounts, Hughes never set foot inside the hotel during Harlow's turbulent honeymoon stay. At that time, she was under contract to MGM; her ties to Hughes had been severed for over a year. In fact, the Hughes legend at the Marmont didn't begin for more than a decade after Harlow's untimely death in 1937. Even then, it's doubtful Hughes would have been drawn to the hotel had it not been for yet another of his fabled "discoveries."

For two decades, Howard Hughes had been one of Hollywood's most eligible bachelors and resident studs. He was tall (6 foot, 3 1/2 inches), lean, and lanky, in the Gary Cooper mold. He spoke softly with a disarming Texas drawl. He was enormously wealthy and involved in broadly diversified activities. He made motion pictures; he designed and flew aircraft, setting speed records and winning honors along the way. He was a hero, a crusader, a mechanical genius, and a womanizer. His date list of screen beauties read like a who's who, everyone from Katharine Hepburn, Carole Lombard, Ava Gardner, Lana Turner, Dorothy Lamour, Ginger Rogers, Hedy Lamarr, Polly Bergen, Judy Garland, and Janet Leigh to practically the entire Fox stable of youthful stars—Linda Darnell, Gene Tierney, Susan

Hayward, Debra Paget, Jean Peters, and Terry Moore.

Noted Hollywood photographer, Wally Seawell, was the person responsible for bringing Hughes to the Marmont. An associate of the famed Paul Hesse, whose magnificent color portraits of stars first graced the covers of *Photoplay* magazine, Seawell had been asked to shoot a series of glamor portraits for his latest protegee, an unknown but promising teenage dancer-singer named Mitzi Gaynor.

According to Seawell, the Gaynor assignment was one of his most difficult, even more challenging than his sessions with Hughes'discovery, Faith Domergue. ("We took a million pictures of her, and nothing happened.")

"When Mitzi first came in," Seawell says, "she was so unattractive. We finally had to call in hair stylist Larry Germaine, who completely did her over, creating an entirely new look for her. It took three days to get her ready to shoot, but we got some marvelous shots."

During the lengthy and arduous "shoot" Seawell learned that Hughes intended to set Gaynor and her mother up in an apartment at Sunset Tower, but it first had to be redecorated. He contacted Walter Kane, Hughes' right-hand man, to tell him that the penthouse at the Marmont was not only vacant but available for far less than Sunset Tower was asking. Best of all, the penthouse had just been redone by celebrated fashion and interior designer, Don Loper, who had incorporated a number of his own luxurious touches, such as black-and-white harlequin tiles in the entry hall and floor-to-ceiling antique mirrors encasing the fireplace.

Kane called the Marmont immediately and secured the penthouse. When Gaynor arrived with her mother, she was overheard to remark, "Won't it be wonderful? When I sit on the john, I'll be able to see all of Hollywood!"

Mitzi Gaynor remained at the Marmont until Hughes discovered he wasn't the only man in her life. As Seawell remembers, "She was also seeing [talent agent] Jack Bean on the sly at night—after she had been out with Howard. When Howard learned about that, he dumped her."

The penthouse didn't remain empty for long. Singer Tony Martin, who once vied with Hughes for the afffections of Cyd Charisse (Hughes lost), told in his dual autobiography (with Charisse) of an incident that occurred following a luncheon with Walter Kane at the RKO commissary. What made the occasion memorable was a magazine Kane had spotted at the commissary stand; on the cover was an illustration of an exceptionally lovely, unidentified girl. Kane was so impressed with her beauty that he bought a copy for his boss, believing that "she was the kind of girl Hughes would appreciate."

She was. "Find her," Hughes told his aide. "Bring her here."

Kane's search for the mystery cover girl led him to Italy, where she lived with her husband. The fact that she couldn't speak English didn't matter; Hughes wanted her in Hollywood, and Kane delivered.

She arrived with her sister, a child, and a nurse, and was taken to Chateau Marmont. Not only were her expenses paid, but she was put on salary at $300 a week.

According to Martin, Hughes then forgot about her. Six months later, he inquired of Kane, "What happened to that Italian girl?"

"She's learning English," Kane replied.

"Well, she's been here long enough," Hughes reportedly said. "Send her home."

It is doubtful Hughes ever had direct contact with the girl.

Terry Moore, in recounting her life with Hughes, tells of a similar incident. The "girl" in her story was Gina Lollobridgida.

When the penthouse wasn't occupied with "Howard's girls," Hughes himself was often secreted there for weeks at a time. It was a natural hideaway. The center for his manifold enterprises, the greenish-gray stucco building at 7000 Romaine, was only a few miles away. Even closer was the office he kept at Goldwyn Studios. (Curiously, he never maintained an office at RKO during his tenure.) Aside from Walter Kane and Johnny Meyer, another Hughes aide, few people in or out of Hughes' circle knew where he was. There were exceptions, of course, particularly on the Marmont's sixth floor. At the slightest sound, guests in surrounding suites would crack their doors in the hope of catching a glimpse of the increasingly reclusive millionaire.

Hughes hadn't always been a mystery man. Prior to 1946, he was one of Hollywood's most visible personalities, a flamboyant, nightclub-hopping playboy. But in July of that year, while test-flying an experimental XF-11 photo-reconnaissance plane over Beverly Hills, he was forced to crash-land. The plane burst into flames, and Hughes was severely injured. His chest was crushed, nine ribs were broken; he suffered a collapsed lung, a lascerated skull, facial burns and cuts, and more. He was not expected to live. Miraculously, he recovered—but he was a changed man.

At the Marmont, Hughes was regarded as "an absolute night person with a passion for privacy." He would leave the penthouse late at night, "dressed in the worst-looking get-ups"—usually baggy knockabout clothing, with rolled up shirtsleeves and pants cuffs that drew attention to his skinny legs and scruffy tennis shoes—and take off in his battered, unwashed Chevy for an out-of-the-way steak house on Pico Boulevard. There, long after the dinner hour had passed, he would sit alone in the near-empty dining room, out of the limelight, enjoying his standard fare—butterfly steak and baby peas. (He once confessed to cutting the meat into miniscule pieces for fear his delicate digestive system would reject larger bites.) Following dinner, he would return directly to the Marmont for dessert. He craved ice cream, and he made certain that the hotel's kitchen freezer was kept well-stocked just for him.

Day by day, Hughes' other eccentricities began to surface. At some point, as one of his aides admitted later, he had developed an extreme suspicion of minorities. "Howard was a devout bigot, especially when it came to black people. He had an insane belief that blacks were bent on destroying everything he had accomplished. His paranoia—about blacks in particular—ultimately became so intense that he secretly waged a personal war against them."

It's possible that Hughes' "paranoia" was in its formative stage during his off and on stay at the Marmont, for his behavior was never insidious. Still, there were signs of prejudice that could not be ignored. Two of the hotel's most popular and affable employees, who were black, terrified him. Scotty headed the garage staff; Eddie manned the elevator. Hughes purposely went out of his way to avoid both of them. Whenever Scotty and Eddie were on duty, he would park his car on a side street, then climb six flights of stairs to his suite.

Hughes' bigotry became a real concern, but none of the employees dared put their feelings into words, not even among themselves. The point wasn't even whispered to reporters who were constantly on the prowl for inside information about the millionaire playboy. Their secrecy wasn't so much to guard Hughes' privacy (his "weirdness," as one staff member put it) as to protect a number of other guests. In those days, the Marmont was one of the few hotels to admit minorities. "We have no color barrier," Dr. Brethauer made a point of saying, his eyes haunted by reminders of persecution. Had Howard Hughes known that he was at times sharing the same roof with Diahann Carroll, Della Reese, Erroll Garner, Sidney Poitier, Duke Ellington, Archie Moore, Pearl Bailey, Eartha Kitt, and Althea Gibson, his stay would have ended long before it did.

There were other signs of odd behavior. Since his accident, Hughes had lived in constant fear of infection (though no one would have guessed by his generally unkempt appearance—he often went unshaven for days at a time —and his unwashed car). His fetish for hygiene was made clear from the start. He not only instructed the housekeeper to make certain that the penthouse was scoured and disinfected on a daily basis, but he constantly harped at the maids, while following them from room to room. The sight of a fly or gnat would start him whimpering, they reported, and the mere mention of germs all but reduced him to a state of catatonia. "They are mankind's greatest enemy," he volunteered one day, shrinking at the thought. He was certain they would kill him and the rest of the world.

The enigmatic Hughes was a study in contrasts, often shifting from one extreme to the other in the blink of an eye. Craving his privacy, he would slip in and out of the Marmont like a fugitive, then he would open his door to strangers. Several times a week, at least, he entertained "the most beautiful young girls in Hollywood," newcomers to movieland who came to the hotel dressed to impress, believing that an audience with the rich and powerful Hughes would lead to their big break—if not a chance at stardom, then surely a role in one of his productions.

One evening a very attractive, fresh-faced young lady arrived at the front desk, eager to be announced. She had "an appointment with Mr. Hughes," she said blithely. But only minutes after entering the penthouse, she was seen running out in tears. She didn't get far. At the elevator she was in- tercepted by "a rather formidable-looking woman, a matron type," who led her back inside, but not without a struggle. The girl was not seen again for nearly an hour.

Of Hughes and his young, hopeful hotel guests, one reporter later com- mented: "Although he could have most any woman for nothing, he found pleasure in buying sex on occasion to appease his high sexual appetite. He knew he could get anything he wanted for money—if the price was right. But once he got it, that was it; he never dallied after sex. He was afraid, that, if he expended too much energy, he would become tired, lowering his resistance, and catch something."

Dr. Popper looked upon Hughes' young visitors with a wary eye. "He's up to no good up there, leading those poor girls on," he would say dimly. But he couldn't explain the matron. Other than speculate that the woman served as Hughes' "greeter," imparting an initial aura of respectability to the proceedings, as well as a strong arm for uncooperative victims, no one could explain her presence. In fact, no one ever saw her entering or leav- ing the Marmont. She seemed to be ever present, however, whenever Hughes "entertained."

Dr. Popper also took a dark view of Johnny Meyers, who resided in the penthouse in Hughes' absence. Not only did Meyers sleep with a loaded pistol under his pillow (the gun was discovered by one of the maids), he also took to bringing cocktails to the night shift working the front desk. Though hardly a teetotaler, Dr. Popper could not condone drinking on the job. But he did not have the nerve to confront Meyers or his boss. It was therefore understandable when Hughes gave up his hold on the penthouse in the late 1950s that no attempts were made to persuade him to stay.

# Miss Kelly

Several weeks before Christmas of 1950, writer-producer Gant Gaither registered at Chateau Marmont. At the time, he had no way of knowing that one of New York's loveliest models and an aspiring actress would one day soon be coming to the hotel for an extended stay. Nor could it have been within his wildest imagination that they would ultimately become such close friends that he would be entrusted with the writing of her first official biography.

Gaither's story of the well-bred beauty, whose spectacular but brief film career ended with Hollywood's first royal wedding since "love goddess" Rita Hayworth married Prince Aly Kahn in 1949, told her adoring fans exactly what they wanted to know—and believe. Had Gaither been at the Marmont during her stay, however, his revelations might have taken on a slightly different tone, one offering a less reverential portrait of America's newest fairytale princess. Certainly he would have discovered a far different girl from the one he thought he knew so well.

No one at the Marmont had even heard of twenty-two-year-old Grace Kelly when she checked in on August 19, 1951. She was unknown, even though she had appeared on the covers of *Cosmopolitan, Redbook,* and *True Romance,* had been seen in dozens of ads (everything from vacuum cleaners and soap to cigarettes), and had made her film debut in the suspenseful *Fourteen Hours* only months earlier. Though more beautiful and polished than most newcomers, there seemed little else to distinguish her from the long line of Marmont blondes that began with the legendary Jean Harlow. Now she was in Hollywood to appear in her first major motion picture, as Gary Cooper's young Quaker wife in *High Noon* .

There were no photographers or studio press agents awaiting Grace Kelly's arrival at Chateau Marmont. She had only her younger sister, Lizanne, an amazing look-alike, with refined, delicate features and even blonder hair, for support. Grace didn't seem to notice the lack of a welcoming committee. She calmly approached the front desk, pulled her dark-rimmed glasses from her purse, and signed a guest registration card, listing the newly opened Manhattan House on New York's 66th Street as her permanent residence.

"There'll be one more of us," Grace informed the desk clerk in a rather refined voice. Her older sister, Peggy, would be arriving the following day, she said.

Grace admitted that her parents did not want her living alone in Hollywood. In fact, she confided, they had insisted that Lizanne and Peggy be with her. At first, her remark sounded so harmless that no one at the Marmont gave it a second thought.

As the daughters of a wealthy Philadelphia family, money had never been a concern for the Kelly girls. Grace's move to New York several years earlier had hardly put a crimp in her style of living. Frequent modeling assignments and occasional roles in stage productions had brought in steady earnings, which enabled her to furnish her Manhattan apartment in high style.

For some reason, Grace and her sisters were content to live in one of the hotel's smallest, least expensive suites, a "single" that owed much of its charm to a sweeping view and a larger than average kitchen. The kitchen, however, held little attraction for Grace. Waiting for dishes to "be done," as she put it, made her restless, and she all too willingly confessed that preparing anything other than snacks ended in disaster.

Breakfasts never seemed to be a problem. Grace and her sisters were awakened promptly each weekday morning at six, in time to catch a fast bite before dashing to the studio, where Grace had a six- thirty makeup call. The sisters returned to the studio later in the afternoon. They would meet Grace, bring her back to the Chateau, and make plans for dinner.

For a time, the girls would join some of Grace's male classmates from New York's American Academy of Dramatic Arts, where she had briefly been a student, at one of the inexpensive restaurants neighboring the Marmont. The Kellys could afford better, but the young men, aspiring actors all, were on an exceedingly slim budget. More than once, the sisters surprised their dinner companions by picking up the tab.

Those evenings among old friends must have been good therapy for Grace, especially during her early days on *High Noon,* for there were times when she would return from the studio looking rather distraught, not the "cool, classy beauty" that publicity handouts were beginning to describe. One day while passing through the lobby, she was overheard to say, "I wonder

Grace Kelly never went calling without her little white gloves.

if I'm going to be any good."

Sanford Meisner, the noted drama coach, called Grace a "thinking and feeling actress by nature, without having to be taught." He also admitted that Grace was not blessed with a photographic memory, which made learning dialogue difficult for her. Only when she could get up on her feet, Meisner said, and begin to walk through the part, identifying the business or action with the dialogue, did she become an infallible performer.

Whatever doubts Grace may have had about her abilities as an actress she tried to overcome with preparation. Each night following dinner, she set aside a specific time to study her lines so that she would be word-perfect before the cameras. She would repeat them over and over, often with such fervor that she could be heard in the corridor outside her door. The sound of her voice, growing more shrill as it reached emotional highs, brought smiles rather than nods of approval from passersby.

But rehearsing filled only a portion of Grace's after-dinner hours. At the Marmont, she is remembered not for her disciplined study and dedication to her craft but for her rather startling and seemingly uncharacteristic behavior.

The first indication of a "different" Grace Kelly came years later from her old friend, Gant Gaither. Upon leaving the Marmont in late 1950, he returned to the East Coast to produce the tryout of a new play, *Alexander*. Grace had a featured role of a society-girl-turned-singer, which she had accepted, she said, to help broaden her acting range. Most everyone in the cast felt she was wrong for the part, and limited as an actress. She was "too cool, too reserved," they felt, to ever really be successful.

At a cast party, however, Grace startled everyone. Said her friend, "Grace suddenly leaped up and started dancing to the electric guitar one of the actors was playing. It wasn't long before she threw off her high-heeled pumps and danced barefoot. She had on a full skirt, but her hair was still up in a chignon from the performance. All at once, she ran her hands through her hair, and as it fell to her shoulders, the pins flew in all directions. If she had been raven-haired instead of platinum, she could easily have been a gypsy—especially when her hair began to sway with her body as she danced."

"There's fire beneath that surface of ice!" production stage manager Ernestine Perrie was heard to remark.

It was from *Alexander* that Grace Kelly was summoned to Hollywood for *High Noon*. The girl with the elegant style and patrician looks may have been unknown when she arrived at the Marmont, but she quickly made her presence felt. Men found her fascinating, aloof yet approachable, cool yet sensuously steamy.

Both Grace's director, Fred Zinnemann, and her co-star, Gary Cooper, fell under her spell early on. Word filtered back to the hotel from the set that Zinnemann was allowing the camera to linger much too long on Grace's fabulous face. Columnist James Bacon made it public when he reported Zinnemann was shooting more than the necessary number of "loving close-ups of his ravishing new star." (Film editor Elmo Williams left much of Grace's footage on the cutting room floor after the disastrous sneak preview.)

The fifty-year-old Cooper was wildly attracted to Grace, despite his off-and-on marriage and a much-publicized involvement with actress Patricia Neal. The strong sexual vibrations he felt from his leading lady led him to comment, "She gave the impression that she could be a cold dish until you get her pants down—and then she would explode."

Grace's detached attitude rubbed many people in Hollywood the wrong way, giving rise to the claim that "she looked as though butter wouldn't melt in her mouth—or anywhere else." She was earning a nickname, "Miss Refrigerator," as rumors began to surface that she was incapable of having children. But Gary Cooper seemed oblivious to the sniping criticism coming Grace's way; the long hours he spent with her each day only whetted his appetite for more. If being with Grace at night was impossible, as it often was with her living arrangements, he made certain to contact her by phone.

The telephone calls to Grace's suite at the Marmont were constant, but Cooper was not alone in wanting to talk with her. There were calls from an internationally famous fashion designer whom Grace had known during her modeling days in New York, a prominent Hollywood producer, and a noted film director. Said one of the switchboard operators: "It seemed Miss Kelly's line was always lit up. But it was her director friend who kept her line burning, and their conversations often got pretty spicy. That double-entendre dialogue Mr. Hitchcock had her recite in some of his films was more Grace Kelly than most people realized. Like her remark during the picnic scene in *To Catch a Thief* when she asked Cary Grant if he would care for 'a breast or a leg.' The subject was chicken, but everyone knew what she *really* meant. Miss Kelly could get away with those lines because of her saintly image, but, believe me, she was no saint!"

"She sought the company of men," said another insider. "All that talk about her being so shy. It just wasn't true. If she showed interest in a man staying at the Marmont, she inquired as to his whereabouts and went calling. But she never made her way through the halls without wearing her little white gloves. She must have felt they made her look prim and proper, quite the lady."

Grace was frequently seen wandering the corridors, checking room numbers, as if she had lost her way to her own room. "She wasn't the same girl we would see in the mornings," a maid reported. "She never dressed up for the studio. She would wear the plainest clothes to work—old sweaters, slacks, sneakers, or English walking shoes, and her honey-blonde hair pulled straight back. But at night she looked like a fashion plate come to life. Gorgeous full-skirted dresses, with high-heeled pumps, pearl earrings, and her hair hanging soft and loose. And, yes, she always had on little white gloves."

Grace's escapades nearly backfired one evening, when one of her male admirers turned the tables and called on her. It's not known whether he was among her hotel beaus or if he came from the outside, but his desperate pounding on her door was so loud it could be heard all the way to the lobby. "I'm sure Miss Kelly was inside," the manager reported, "but she probably was afraid to answer, especially if her sisters were there. Oh, the commotion that man made! But then it stopped as quickly as it started. He must have gotten discouraged and left."

Grace Kelly departed the Marmont in late September, but she returned to Hollywood many times over the next few years, only to be linked with other men, including several of her co-stars. There was talk of liaisons with Bing Crosby, Frank Sinatra, and William Holden.

Holden, for one, was not taken by Grace's aggressiveness. When she appeared at his dressing room door during the filming of *The Country Girl*, he told her in a voice loud enough for others to hear, "Baby, when I want somebody, I go to them!"

The people who knew Grace best at the Marmont weren't in the least surprised to learn of the tension on *The Country Girl* set. Or of William Holden's remark.

## Mrs. Ducos

Dr. Popper had paced the lobby for nearly fifteen minutes before taking to the drawing room, breaking his short, erratic steps only to rush to the closest window at the sound of an on-coming car. He wore his best dark blue suit with a flower, freshly plucked from the garden, in his lapel. He talked to no one; he had left orders to take messages from guests and waved off all questions from the staff. He had even rescheduled a long-standing doctor's appointment at the last minute. This day was much too important to be away. Nothing could keep him from welcoming Edith Piaf to the Marmont.

It was approaching noon when her taxi slowed to a stop outside the main entrance. Dr. Popper watched incredulously as the great French *chanteuse,* her tiny body garbed in black as always, stepped cautiously to the curb and made her way toward the hotel's open front door. "She looked so fragile, so inconsequential," he commented later. "It seemed impossible that such a creature could contain a voice so strong and mesmerizing. I had to remind myself who she was."

Piaf was not alone. She was accompanied by a striking older man, Rene Ducos, whom she introduced as her husband. They had been married in Paris several months earlier—on July 29, 1952—at a quiet town hall ceremony. It was the thirty-seven-year-old Piaf's first marriage, following years of ill-fated relationships with a seemingly endless variety of men, including her one-time protege, a young cabaret singer named Yves Montand. Her stormy love affairs and interminable personal problems (blindness as a child, abandonment, singing for handouts on streetcorners, a debilitating series of accidents and illnesses) had earned her an international reputation as a tragic figure. Howard Taubman, the esteemed New York Times critic, had adoringly christened her "the High Priestess of Agony."

Her simple town-hall marriage ceremony had not pleased Piaf. "It was a rush job. We did it on the run," she told Dr. Popper. "I couldn't feel really married till we had said our vows in front of a priest. You can't cheat with God." She had even refused to wear her wedding ring until it had been blessed.

Only days before arriving at the Marmont in late September, Piaf and Rene Ducos had repeated their vows before a large gathering of notables at New York's Saint Vincent de Paul's Cathedral. She wore pale blue and carried a bridal bouquet. Marlene Dietrich was one of her attendants. Bells rang and organ music filled the hugh church. It was a dream come true. She was thrilled—yet terrified. She tried to bolster her frayed nerves with drinks and her customary "shot of medication." One report had her hand trembling during the exchange of rings, "not only from emotion but alcohol and drugs."

Dr. Popper was not alone in observing Piaf's frail appearance the morning of her arrival to the hotel. Bystanders in the lobby took note of her "odd pallor" and "the dark look about her eyes." There was reason for concern. No sooner did she check into her suite than she collapsed. Her husband tried to calm everyone's fears by claiming "Edith is merely exhausted."

Piaf and her husband, a singer-songwriter (known professionally in America as Jacques Peals), were in Hollywood on a working honeymoon that would also take them to San Francisco, Las Vegas, and Miami. Audiences would see "the great Piaf," no matter how poorly she looked or felt. A forgotten lyric, an off-key note, the unsure stance and faraway gaze were all part of the raw, mournful mystique that Jean Cocteau likened to "a terrified little sleepwalker who sings her dreams to the air on the edge of a roof."

A surprise was awaiting Piaf on her first night in Hollywood. Charlie Chaplin had come to hear her sing. She worshipped Chaplin. She called him "the greatest..., a genius." When word of his arrival reached her dressing room prior to the opening curtain, she froze. "I was scared stiff," she said. "I had such stage fright I almost couldn't open my mouth!" But she did—and she sang gloriously. Chaplin was so taken by her performance that he invited her to his home the following day.

The visit to Chaplin's Beverly Hills estate filled Piaf with awe, and for days she spoke of little else around the Marmont. She had never seen a house as lovely or as immaculate, she said, comparing it to "a set for an American movie in Technicolor—you would think they repainted it every day!" But it was Chaplin, the man, who truly impressed her. She talked of his beautiful eyes and thick lashes, his silvery hair and his flashing smile, his gentle demeanor, and his talent as a musician and songwriter. "When I left," she reflected warmly, "he promised to write me a song. Words and music just for me. Imagine!" Piaf's private meeting with Charlie Chaplin was the highlight of her 1952 Hollywood visit.

Four years later, her return to Chateau Marmont was marked by events far less heartening. Once again she was in Hollywood on tour, but this time her one-woman show—scheduled over a period of eleven months—would take her from coast to coast and back again. Never had she committed to so many performances over so long a period. But the money was irresistible. It would make her one of the highest paid stars in the world. Only Bing Crosby and Frank Sinatra commanded greater fees.

When Piaf checked into the Marmont on December 10, 1956, she was on the first leg of her tour—and she was without Rene Ducos, who had left her. Alone and filled with despair, she tried desperately to mask her fears with bravado. "Americans give me strength," she told an acquaintance in the lobby. "They are my pals." She needed all the support she could muster. Several months earlier she had been hospitalized for alcohol addiction, following a breakdown.

Unfortunately, Piaf's spirited remarks were only wishful thinking. One afternoon, she was found lying limply in bed staring into space, her short dark hair matted with perspiration that ran from her strangely bloated face, neck, and arms onto the tangled sheets that surrounded her. Empty bottles of beer and containers of pills crowded her bedstand. She had been discovered by one of the maids, whose raps on her door had gone unheeded, and probably unheard.

There were times too when, unable to find a drink at the Marmont following an evening performance, she would wander across the street to the bar at the Garden of Allah. She would exit the hotel through the garage, wearing an old coat over her nightgown and a pair of dirty slippers on her feet. After several hours, she would return, clutching the arm of some male, whose steps were only slightly less staggering than hers. Later, she admitted that the nights made her lonely; she needed a man.

Seven months later, on July 18, 1957, Edith Piaf was back at the Marmont. She appeared to be a different woman—more relaxed, spirited, and in better health—even though her non-stop schedule had been rigorous.

At the time, the hotel was playing host to such celebrity guests as Shirley Booth, Walter Matthau, Carroll Baker, Josephine Premise, Mildred Dunnock, Staats Cotsworth, Dina Merrill, Valerie Fabrizzi (Miss Italy), Tina Louise, Conrad Janis, Robert Goulet, Farley Granger, and Maurice Chevalier. Piaf was particularly pleased to know that Chevalier, her close friend and countryman, was her neighbor. Although their schedules did not permit more than a fleeting visit (he was filming *Gigi*), she occasionally found a free evening to entertain and display her expertise in the kitchen. Ginger Rogers, a guest at one of Piaf's small gatherings, recalled recently:

"Edith had invited me to her suite for a real French dinner—and that it was! First she prepared a green salad *a la* the French method—oil, vinegar, salt and pepper—which we ate as we watched an electric spit turn her favorite meat, leg of lamb. While it completed its cooking, she dropped thin-sliced white potatoes into hot oil for our next real French treat, *pommes frites.* Never have I tasted a better slice of lamb than the one Edith Piaf prepared—or better French fries. And never had I enjoyed her bubbling personality more than when she was preparing her favorite meal for friends."

According to Rogers, Piaf was no longer without male companionship, which may have contributed to her sharp change in moods. As Ginger Rogers remembers: "Her gentleman friend played his guitar all through the preparation [of the meal], giving her hungry guests an earful of music while we waited."

Piaf departed the Marmont at the close of her Hollywood engagement, vowing to return "one day soon." She never did. Between several automobile accidents, various drug cures, an attempted suicide, fits of delirium tremors, bouts with bronchial pneumonia, a pulmonary edema, and hepatic comas, she found a moment of happiness with a young, aspiring Greek singer, Theophanis Lamboukas. She gave him a new name, Theo Sarapo (*"I love you"* in Greek), and launched his career. They were married in October, 1962. She died the following year.

The castle on the hill, Chateau Marmont, rises above the Sunset Strip, 1950. (*Courtesy of Bison Archives*)

# PART III

# THE GOLDEN YEARS

It seemed that Hollywood was riding into the Fifties on the crest of a gold-plated wave. The war years had firmly established Hollywood as the world's greatest film factory. Whatever the studios churned out had made money, thanks to a public that was hungry for escapist entertainment. The post-war years had been equally prosperous. Buoyed by the return to the screen of ex-servicemen such as Tyrone Power, Clark Gable, Robert Montgomery, James Stewart, Robert Taylor, and Glenn Ford, as well as the emergence of promising newcomers such as Marilyn Monroe, Tony Curtis, Debbie Reynolds, Rock Hudson, Dean Martin, and Jerry Lewis, box-office receipts reached a high of close to two-billion dollars in 1949. Hollywood had become the land of milk and honey, the end of the rainbow. With the future appearing so bright, it was almost impossible for anyone to predict that the honeymoon would soon be over.

The first of Hollywood's problems had surfaced as early as 1946, when independent theater owners filed an antitrust suit against the studios. The government ruled in favor of the theater owners, forcing the major studios to divest themselves of their chains of motion picture houses, through which they normally released their productions. At a time of rising inflation, which spelled higher production costs, salaries, and taxes, Hollywood was suddenly without its built-in channels of distribution.

There were other threats to Hollywood's continued well-being: industry strikes, and the end of "block-booking" (the Department of Justice ruled that studios could no longer force distributors to accept films of lesser quality along with big name, class "A" releases), and the most potentially troublesome problem of all, television.

For nearly a decade, starting in 1939, film industry leaders had been dreading the arrival of television. Wartime restrictions had stalled its development, but only for a time. By 1948, television was being hailed as "the new miracle home entertainment." The programs being shown weren't too good—mostly travelogues and resurrected vaudeville routines— but they were getting better. And they were *free*.

Hollywood quickly banned its stars from appearing on television shows, then trotted out a few "miracles" of its own as competition. Lavish epics and adult dramas began to appear in spectacular new widescreen processes and eye-blinking 3-D, with booming, wraparound stereophonic sound. How could anyone remain in their homes watching snowy black-and-white images on twelve-inch picture tubes when movie theaters offered splashy, star-studded, wall-to-wall entertainment? As far as Hollywood was concerned, movies were better than ever.

Maybe so, but the public was nevertheless fascinated with the novelty of television. Less than four-million homes had sets in 1950, but that figure in no way represented the number of nightly viewers. Families fortunate enough to own a set invited friends and neighbors in to view the latest programs, while mesmerized onlookers clustered on sidewalks before showroom windows. America's love affair with television was on. Much to Hollywood's alarm, sales of sets were expected to triple annually.

Even the Marmont, of all places, succumbed to the miracle of television. In 1949, as Hollywood planned its strategy to combat the menacing new medium, Dr. Brethauer surprisingly unknotted his purse strings and bought a small-screen set. He had Dr. Popper install it in the main-floor drawing room, just off the lobby, where guests could relax while enjoying the work of such Marmont regulars as Ed Wynn and Ralph Levy. Dr. Brethauer was not being generous. To watch the contraption, a quarter had to be inserted every half hour. No one complained.

There were other additions to the hotel during this period, namely two important new staff members, Corinne Patten and Meemi Ferguson.

Corinne Patten was forty-eight years old when she arrived at the Marmont in 1950, following her divorce from her second husband. In those days, she was known as Mrs. Jameson, but she shed her married name, and a flashy diamond solitaire given to her by husband number one, when she discovered that they had a negative influence on the size of her tips.

The stylish, slender Patten was the Marmont's jack-of-all-trades. She worked the front desk, filled in at the switchboard, handled the bookkeeping, and "kept her eyes on things." In addition to her appointed duties and religious interests (she would pass out copies of *Daily Word* at will), she eagerly answered inquiries about the hotel's past and present. Unofficially, she assumed the role of "Official Historian." Among her most cherished possessions were her autographed photos of current and former guests, which she kept preserved between glassine sleeves in two giant albums.

From the start, Corinne loved to chat about the stars she met at the Marmont. She would open with stories about Maurice Evans, Joe E. Lewis, and Tom Ewell, then continue with Mel Brooks, Jack Lemmon, Miriam Hopkins, and Lillian Roth. From time to time, she would stop to ask, tauntingly, "Want some more?" Corinne always had plenty to tell.

Scarcely a day passed that Corinne didn't record an entry in her "Marmont Journal," a dime-store scrapbook crammed with anecdotes that she had either witnessed first hand or gleaned from others. Over the years, she jotted down such happenings as:

"Paul Newman had his picture taken with Joanne Woodward at the desk. Then he jumped up on the counter and reached over my head to get the mail out of his box. I must remind him not to hang his socks out to dry on a string across his balcony."

"Mr. Walt Disney came to visit Errol Flynn. They met in the lobby and had a long, long talk. It must have been fascinating, judging from the expressions on their faces. What an unlikely pair!"

"Tony Curtis, one of my four famous Tonys [along with Franciosa, Randall, and Perkins] called on Christine Kauffmann in her bungalow today. On his way in, he stopped at the front desk to present me with a lovely arrangement of flowers."

Mildred "Meemi" Ferguson joined Corinne Patten and Carmel Volti at the Marmont when she was hired as housekeeper in 1953, after having worked in a similar capacity at the Montecito and Ravenswood, two of Los Angeles' top apartment houses. Within two years, she was promoted to manager.

Tall (5 foot 8 1/2 inches), elegant, and very proper (her upper-class Boston breeding left her with a slight Victorian air, but prudish she was not), Meemi had more than sound credentials in her favor. She was also well-connected on both coasts, related to the great stage and silent screen star, Elsie Ferguson (who, coincidentally, was discovered by Albert E. Smith for his Vitagraph Films), and was a longtime friend of the Kennedy family.

Few questions rattled Meemi more than those concerning her age, which she absolutely refused to discuss. No one knew how old Meemi really was. (Guesstimates ranged from "fortyish" to "sixtyish.") Anyone who dared ask was met with the simple reply, "A woman who tells her age will tell anything," a phrase she had borrowed from her friend, Lillian Gish—with a nod to Oscar Wilde. Meemi went to extremes to hide her years. She even led intimates to believe that her two visiting grandchildren were her son and daughter.

Meemi's preoccupation with age had her spending an inordinate amount of time before her mirror. An oft-told story around the Marmont, one that began tragically with the suicide of a terminally ill guest, best illustrates that point. As syndicated columnist Jill Jackson, who was living in the hotel at the time, remembered:

"I had just gotten up to get a glass of water, and was getting back in bed—it was early one Sunday morning, around 6:30 or 7:00—when this thing hurled past my window. Then I heard a plop. I went to see what it was and found the most ghastly sight lying on the sidewalk. Carmel was on the board when I called downstairs. 'Something terrible had happened,' I told her. 'Somebody either jumped or fell out of a window.' "

" 'Oh, don't be silly, Jill,' she replied in her soothing way. "I heard a noise too, but it was little Arnella coming in to get the paper.' Arnella was Errol Flynn's lovely six-year-old daughter who lived with her mother, Patrice Wymore, in one of the bungalows.

"You'd better go look,' I told Carmel. She did, and you could hear her shriek up into the canyons. Next thing I knew she had called the sheriff, and everybody was up in my suite, since I was the one who had reported the accident. Then we waited for Meemi Ferguson. I'm not exaggerating when I say that it took her two-and-a-half hours to fix her honey-blonde hair to perfection, put on her make-up, false eyelashes, designer jump-suit, and jewelry. She wasn't about to appear until she looked *absolutely gorgeous*. She figured the place would be crawling with photographers— and she was right!"

Meemi was probably privy to more Hollywood gossip than either Hedda or Louella. Her sources were impeccable, and she kept in constant touch with each of them. Once a month, at least, she and her former colleagues from the Montecito and Ravenswood would join forces with women from movieland's other star-infested havens, such as the Fontanoy and Bel-Air Hotels, and trade "items" over dinner and cocktails. Meemi's grand-daughter, Connie reported a typical get-together:

"One year Meemi gave a St. Patrick's Day dinner at the Marmont for her cronies. These ladies, all leading hotel women of the day—Edgar Bergen's mother-in-law was one—had known each other for years, ever since they were housekeepers and coming up in the business forty years earlier. Whenever it was Meemi's turn to entertain, she would have me cook for the gang. It wasn't that she didn't want to do it, she didn't know how.

"For St. Patrick's Day, she decided to serve gimlets—the ladies *loved* gimlets—with green food coloring added—beef Bourguignon, parsley, and a lot of little green touches. I got everything ready—the green gimlets and dinner—set the table, gave them each a drink, and left. When I called around midnight to see how things were going, nobody answered. Meemi later told me that she had passed out at the top of the stairs—just after one of her guests had left, wearing someone else's shoes and complaining that her feet were killing her, while still another had fallen into a hedge near the front entrance and had to be rescued by a passerby. Meemi didn't say anything unusual had happened that evening. She just smiled and said, 'We all had a wonderful time.' "

Meemi's "grandchildren," Connie and Lee, were seldom without playmates when they came to visit. At times, the Marmont register listed the names of more children than a day-care center. For starters there were Imogene Coca and King Donovan's youngsters; Dave Brubeck's five toddlers; Ken Murray's two sons; Robert Middleton's son; and the daughter of Leslie Charteris.

From an adult's viewpoint, the Marmont wasn't an ideal setting for children. The kids looked at it differently. There were secret hiding places and shiny banisters, mountains of stairs and raceway corridors, winding trails, and grassy slopes. Best of all, it had the look of a storybook castle. What better place to live!

Then there were the youngsters "down under"—the garage boys.

Maintaining a semblance of order and flow within the garage's columned interior, especially during morning and evening rush periods, has to be like choreographing a mob scene for the movies. One out-of-place car, or a stalled engine, and there is chaos. In *Slow Days, Fast Company,* Hollywood-born writer Eve Babitz described the garage as " . . . impossible. Even sober. It's no mean feat to negotiate, with its gigantic pillars everywhere . . . " The pillars do serve a purpose, however. As Babitz explained, "[they] support the past."

To keep things running as smoothly as possible in the garage, the hotel has hired its share of gifted "traffic engineers" over the years. None is remembered more fondly than Scotty Thompson.

No one recalls exactly when Scotty came to the Marmont, only that it was "sometime around 1952." Scotty was dedicated to his work. Although he had a wife and daughter across town in Watts, he seldom left the hotel, even during his off hours. Rather than going home between shifts, he would bed down in the garage, usually in the back seat of a parked Rolls Royce.

Scotty had an assistant named Gene Gordon and, for nearly five years starting in 1956, the help of a group of neighborhood teenage boys—more "high-potential low-achievers" than juvenile delinquents—who not only worshipped Scotty but thought of him as a surrogate father. One of the gang, Tom Wheat, reported, "It didn't matter if we had run away from home or had a fight with our parents, Scotty would take us in. We were hanging out more than hiding out. Our parents always knew where to find us—if they needed us."

It was Morgan Cavett who brought the boys to the Marmont. Regarded as "the meanest and baddest" of the group, Morgan lived in a house directly behind the hotel. His father, Frank, was a successful screenwriter who had won an Oscar for his screenplay of *Going My Way.* His Godmother was off-and-on Marmont guest Dorothy Parker; she and Frank Cavett had collaborated on the screenplay of *Smash-Up—The Story of a Woman,* which brought them, and actress Susan Hayward, Academy Award nominations in 1947.

Morgan was a familiar face around the Marmont for several years before he started hiding out in the garage. One day in 1950, while returning to his family home on Monteel Road, he accidentally set fire to the rough framework of the new bungalows under construction, adjacent to the hotel property. "The fire started out small," Cavett revealed, "and I thought I could put it out with a little water. So I got an empty Coke bottle and began running back and forth with water from my house. But the flames kept spreading!"

At that point, the construction foreman arrived. "He parked his truck down below on Sunset. Another man was with him—I guess he wanted to show off the progress that was being made—and, when they looked up, all they could see was smoke. Nobody knew how the fire started, and I wasn't talking. But some people had seen me running frantically with my little Coke bottle trying to put it out. I became a hero around the hotel!"

Besides Tom Wheat and Morgan Cavett, there were Ken Schwarz, "the little shrimp," whose greatest accomplishment had been to grow from five-foot-six to six-foot-two in one year; and Pete Dickel.

"The Marmont was our second home," said Wheat. He admitted that he and his friends often slept overnight in the garage, then played hookey from school the following day. The boys were students at Hollywood High, but they never got caught cutting classes. One of them had worked in the school's administration office and had learned how to forge the truant officer's signature.

Scotty's loyal helpers like to think of themselves as "an unsavory bunch." They weren't really, but they had their moments—like the times Pete Dickel "borrowed" Dennis Hopper's car (among others) from the garage for joy rides. One day he went zooming into the hills with Hopper's car and blew two tires. "Pete had to steal the tires off another car to get back," remembered one of his cohorts. "If Dennis found out, he didn't seem to care. He was one of the boys too."

Then there were the packages of cigarettes they stole for Scotty from the parked cars. Scotty wouldn't tolerate that. (He didn't mind when they stole his brand, Pall Mall, out of the Marmont vending machine, however.) Scotty was a chain smoker. During slow periods, he would sit in clouds

(*Above*) Former manager Meemi Ferguson stands before mirrored fireplace in the Don Loper-decorated penthouse, late 1950s. (*Courtesy of Connie Nelson*)

(*Above Right*) Birthday party at the Marmont, early 1950s. Among the young guests were the children of Irish actor Cyril Cusack and Carmel Volti's son, Rudi.

(*Bottom Right*) George Stevens, Jr., plays with his little friend, Blanche, the daughter of Carroll Baker and Jack Garfein, in the garden of the Garfein bungalow, 1958. (*Courtesy of Steffi Sidney*)

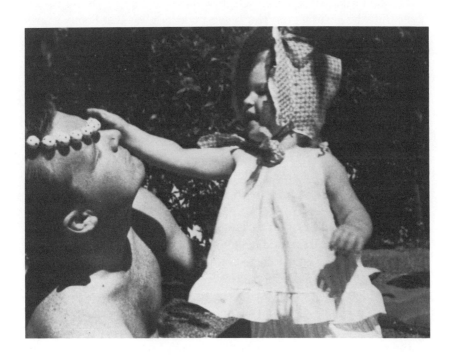

of smoke as he fascinated his young listeners with grisly tales of black magic and outrageous predictions based on astrology. Scotty fancied himself as an expert. He happily charted the future for anyone interested, guests included.

The boys were all too willing to earn some spending money by helping Scotty park and wash cars, cart groceries upstairs, and walk dogs. As unofficial staff members, they didn't receive a salary, but frequent tips kept their pockets jangling.

There were other incentives, particularly the "Sin Bin," a dimly lit area in the garage's southwest corner, where the boys lured their dates. Hidden by rows of parked cars and columns, it was ideal for anytime action. (One of the boys admits to having discovered sex in the Marmont's underground.) The only drawback was Red, the hotel's mechanic, and, according to all sources, "a raging alcoholic and real scuzzy guy." Red had a short fuse. He was extremely touchy about the Sin Bin, because it overlapped "the repair corner." Red would turn mean to protect "his turf."

It's doubtful that Meemi Ferguson knew about the goings-on in the garage. If she did, she never let on. Her biggest concern was that Scotty's boys behave themselves in front of the guests, and she insisted that they act politely and maintain silence. Especially silence. The garage, as Meemi made clear, was the Marmont's focal point of entry and departure for guests and visitors; more people—*important* people—made, their way through the garage than the hotel's front door. "Most of our guests come and go by car," she would emphasize. "They take the elevator from the garage directly to their suites or bungalows and back again. There are stars who seldom come to the lobby."

"Meemi was intensely loyal to the Marmont," recalled Tom Wheat. "She told us we would see and hear a lot of things that weren't to be repeated. 'If you want to work here,' she would say, you'll have to keep your mouths shut.'"

That wasn't always easy for the garage boys. Not when they would catch an odd twosome like Charles Laughton and Dame Judith Anderson engaged in more than talk in one of the parked cars. Dame Judith, it was noted, "appeared embarrassed as they drove off."

Archie Moore, the world-famous boxer, liked to park his own car, but he was so easy-going, according to one of the boys, that he would nod off behind the wheel before he could get out. "Archie was a super sweetheart— nothing seemed to faze him. He could fall asleep while his car was being washed, even with the top down."

The Marmont's garage was often crowded with many rare and classic cars—Bentleys, Rolls Royces, Reos—some dating back to the 1920s. Most were sitting idle in storage, including Burl Ives' enormous Packard convertible touring car, which he had nicknamed "Fosdick." Then there was the "just postwar" 1948 Chevy Paul Newman was driving. It was a studio car that had been modified for hand operation by paraplegics, and was supposedly being used in a picture Newman was filming.

Tom Wheat had a crush on luscious Joan Collins when she first came to the Marmont. She was a rising young star, but, according to one early Collins observor, few of the guests paid much attention to her, "Both Joan and her sister, Jackie, were very distant, a little on the haughty side, which made for some bad feelings. It was as if everyone thought, 'Those two girls are here,' and no one cared. Besides, Joan was being unfairly compared to another of the Fox girls, Terry Moore. 'She's another Terry Moore,' people would say. At the time, one was enough."

Joan Collins, and Scotty never got along very well. Scotty didn't care for Joan's attitude; he felt that she was "a little too uppity." His opinion might have changed had she been more generous. Joan and her sister Jackie were in that minority known as Low Tippers. "They must have taken lessons from Eartha Kitt," Scotty groused one day.

Big tips or small, the Marmont garage was an exciting place to while away the hours for Scotty and his boys. Where else could they trade gossip with Pearl Bailey and Hermione Gingold, and meet some of the greatest names in show business —everyone from Duke Ellington, Helen Hayes, and Sophia Loren to Carol Channing, Patricia Neal, and Sidney Poitier? Every day was like a premiere.

The guests who came to the Marmont during the Fifties were, for the most part, from an era in motion pictures often described as golden. Behind the scenes, Hollywood was still in turmoil, but audiences continued to flock to films and cheer their stars like royalty. Looking back, these were indeed golden years at the Marmont. And that is how they are remembered.

Natalie Wood and Nicholas Ray (*right*) chat with Steffi Sidney and Clifford Odets in the foyer of Ray's Marmont bungalow. (*Courtesy of Steffi Sidney*)

*Rebel Without a Cause* cast members study scripts in director Nicholas Ray's Marmont bungalow. Clockwise: Ray (with cigarette), scriptwriter Stewart Stern, Irving Shulman, James Dean, Jack Simmons, Jim Backus, Natalie Wood, Nick Adams, Mitzie McCall, Frank Mazzola, Jack Grinnage, Beverly Long, and photographer Dennis Stock. (*Courtesy of Steffi Sidney*)

# Chapter 7

## East Meets West

## The Strasberg Connection

The Marmont has been Hollywood headquarters for so many New Yorkers over the years that it was once dubbed "Sardi's with beds." The large contingent from "the big apple" was made up of Madison Avenue advertising executives and network television teams; publishers, editors, writers, and photographers; and Broadway producers, directors, choreographers, set and costume designers, in Hollywood to oversee road companies of their productions.

Throughout the 1950s and 1960s, the Marmont guest list read like the Manhattan phone directory. But the majority of New Yorkers were from the theater, actors who had more in common than their profession. They were students, alumni, or friends of Lee Strasberg, artistic director of the famed Actors Studio. Among them were John Garfield, Montgomery Clift, Rod Steiger and Claire Bloom, Mildred Dunnock, Julie Harris, Jo Van Fleet, Burgess Meredith, Kim Stanley, Eli Wallach and Anne Jackson, David Wayne, Lee Remick, Geraldine Page and Rip Torn, Marlon Brando, Elia Kazan, Shelley Winters and Anthony Franciosa, Franchot Tone, George Grizzard, Carroll Baker, George Peppard, Ben Gazzara, Marilyn Monroe, Paul Newman, and Joanne Woodward.

Few of Strasberg's followers were established stars when they first arrived at the Marmont. Many were known only within Broadway's inner circle; their finest work and national recognition were still to come. There were several exceptions, however.

John Garfield, the first actor to establish the Strasberg connection at the Marmont, had reached his peak during the 1940s with a series of dynamic screen roles, portraying tough,defiant young men at odds with society. His hot-blooded characterizations in such films as *Humoresque* and *Force of Evil* had earned him a tremendous following. He was early James Dean, early Brando. By the end of the decade, his best years were behind him. Still, he kept busy.

Garfield's success came long before the establishment of the Actors Studio in 1947. But as his career began to slide, he sought help to redevelop his craft. He worked with a number of coaches before turning, finally, to Lee Strasberg. At times, he pushed himself with the dedication of an athlete half his age. At thirty-six, he wasn't that strong, as he would soon find out.

In early 1950, Twentieth Century-Fox offered Garfield the lead in *Under My Skin*, a film based on Ernest Hemingway's *My Old Man.* He returned to Hollywood for the first time in two years, leaving his wife and children in their Central Park West apartment, and checked into 5D at the Marmont. He was rarely there.

In many respects, Garfield's personal life paralleled the tumultuous characters he played in films. Like his screen counterparts, he was restless, rough-edged, and boyishly virile; women fascinated him. During the filming of *Under My Skin,* rumors persisted of an affair with his leading lady, Micheline Prelle.

He could not have prepared for the emergency that came. He was on a court at the Beverly Hills Tennis Club when he complained of feeling dizzy. As he walked to the sidelines, he collapsed. At Cedars of Lebanon Hospital, his condition was diagnosed as myocarditis, an inflammation of the heart muscle. Avoid all exercise and exertion, he was told, or else!

The studio closed down production on *Under My Skin* for four weeks, while John Garfield recuperated, but he spent precious little time in bed at the Marmont. Several days of "rest," with a telephone constantly at his ear, and he was up and active again. He was even back at the club, playing tennis. There he met singing star Margaret Whiting. An intimate relationship developed. The only visible change in his lifestyle was the addition of an entourage that seemed to follow him everywhere.

After his stint at Fox, he returned to his old home studio, Warner Bros., for a remake of *To Have and Have Not,* the Hemingway story that had brought Bogart and Bacall together only six years earlier, retitled *The Breaking Point.* He remained at the hotel throughout the filming, then headed east.

When he next appeared at the Marmont on October 16 (to start production on *He Ran All the Way,* a low-budget "quickie," co-starring Shelley Winters and Wallace Ford), he was a changed man, devastated by events that had taken place during the summer. The movie industry was under investigation by the House Un-American Activities Committee, and he was one of ten top Hollywood personalities suspected of left-wing sympathies. He denied the allegations and refused to name friends as Communists.

Garfield completed *He Ran All the Way,* then waited for new offers. None came; Hollywood had closed the door. He grew more distressed. Less than two years later, his heart failed him.

Shelley Winters was a svelte glamor girl when she first visited the Marmont in the mid-1950s. In the following years, she returned many times (somewhat plumper and more mature), to the delight of the staff, who discovered that she not only had a good sense of humor but "a great set of pipes," which she tested more than once.

"One evening, shortly after she moved in 1B," Corinne noted in her journal, "she came walking down the tile steps into the lobby, holding a large box. All of a sudden I heard her shriek. The box had slipped out of her hands and landed on the floor, scattering jewels everywhere. There were diamond rings, strings of pearls, *more* pearls, emeralds, bracelets—a fortune in jewels—all bouncing around like hailstones. Shelley froze, then *really* started screaming. Carmel called the houseboy, who came running, and we all helped retrieve the sparkling treasures. Shelley eventually calmed down, even made fun of herself, before she went happily on her way."

It took Shelley longer to regain her composure on another occasion. She was then living in 3E with her new husband, Anthony Franciosa, who was appearing in Hal Wallis' production of *Wild Is the Wind* for Paramount. Franciosa's co-star, Italian actress Anna Magnani, was also staying at the Marmont, three flights up. According to the best hotel sources, the trouble began when Franciosa started visiting Magnani in her suite.

Anna Magnani was a short, stocky, rather dowdy woman in her early fifties, who wore only black dresses, black stockings, and black shoes. Despite her unglamorous appearance, she projected a sensuality that made men take notice—and women burn with envy. Jean Renoir once called her "the complete animal." Shelley Winters probably had another description in mind when she took off in a rage to track down her husband.

If Shelley didn't know where the pair was sequestered, it didn't take her long to find out. The garage man reported that she had coaxed one of his helpers into giving her Magnani's suite number (why she didn't get it from the desk—or follow the heavy aroma of garlic that came from the cookpot in Magnani's kitchen—no one knows), then departed in a rush. The next thing anyone remembers is hearing "the worst God-awful racket coming from the sixth floor. Such yelling and screaming, you would have thought a pack of banshees was on the prowl!"

Dr. Popper, just down the hall in 6G, admitted later that visions of Gestapo Germany flashed through his mind. In panic, he reached for the phone and told the switchboard to call the police. A moment later he rescinded his order. "Never mind the police," he said, "but find out what's going on."

By this time the switchboard operator had some idea, thanks to calls from frantic guests offering bits of information. "There's a problem in Miss Magnani's suite," she told him. "It seems Miss Winters is trying to get in."

Dr. Popper put down the receiver and went to his door, cracking it just wide enough to get a view of Anna Magnani's door. There he found Shelley Winters in "a warlike stance, pounding with her fist and clamoring, 'I'm going to kill you!'" He claimed that her other hand held a knife.

When the door to Magnani's suite at last opened, the shrieking hit a new high. (Magnani, it was said, could also break glass with her voice when provoked.) Then, just as quickly, all was calm again. "That Shelley," Dr. Popper sighed, with a shake of his head, "a nice talented girl, but such a terror."

One of Lee Strasberg's most promising pupils was an intense, hirsute young stage actor who, in the early 1960s, was starting to attract widespread attention in motion pictures. He wasn't doing badly off the screen either. He had a wife in New York and whomever he wanted in Hollywood.

The young actor (who shall remain unnamed) had met "Frankie" at the Marmont, where they were both living while on film assignments. Frankie was a lovely Canadian girl,who had worked with the Abbey Players in Ireland. When Paramount first brought her to Hollywood, she lived at the Studio Club; her next door neighbor was Marilyn Monroe. Frankie never revealed her beauty secrets, but, like Monroe, she had extraordinary skin. Friends say Frankie was "always creaming her body."

Frankie never made it in films, because she refused to take her work seriously. She found parties much more fulfilling than studying lines; she loved a few drinks and a good time.

One evening, fun-loving Frankie had a surprise for the new man in her life, the ruggedly handsome student of Strasberg. Arriving at the Marmont after a long day before the cameras, he found Frankie waiting for him in his suite. More precisely, she was stretched out languorously in his bed, wearing one of his jock straps, and nothing more. He had a surprise for Frankie as well. His latest "catch" was clinging to his arm.

Before Frankie could explain, she found her bejocked self standing in the hallway, facing a locked door. Her clothes and room key did not travel with her. Shivering, and a little stunned, Frankie didn't know where to turn. In her state of undress, she couldn't chance dashing across the lobby to the front desk. And there wasn't a phone or maid in sight. So she did the next best thing. She began wandering the corridor.

As luck would have it, as Frankie approached suite 2H, the door opened. There stood Shirley Booth. "Oh, my dear," Booth said, looking rather nonplussed, "what are you doing out there like *that?*" Frankie fumbled for words, but, at the moment, Booth wasn't interested. "Come on in," she said, opening the door wide. The next thing Frankie knew, Booth was wrapping a coat around her and they were having a nice chat.

Frankie didn't pursue her relationship with the man from the Actors Studio. She was more interested in having a good time, and he turned out to be not much fun.

Long before Lee Strasberg's involvement with the Actors Studio, he helped found New York's renowned Group Theater. It was during those early years of the 1930s that Franchot Tone became one of Strasberg's original believers and a crusader for "Lee's wonderful new way of working." Eventually, the two men became such close friends that Tone became godfather to Strasberg's son, Johnny.

The debonnaire and smoothly handsome Franchot Tone was a guest at the Marmont for the better part of a decade, starting in 1956. For three of those years (1956-1959), he was married to his fourth wife, actress Dolores Dorn-Heft; for another two (1965-1966) he costarred in television's highly successful doctor series, *Ben Casey.* In between he worked in motion pictures and on Broadway.

At the Marmont, Tone was "very much the gentleman." He would not think of departing the hotel, if only for a few days, without tucking a hundred-dollar bill in an envelope for the employees.

The staff adored Franchot Tone—most of the time. When he was sober, "no one was more thoughtful and considerate." When he drank, which he reportedly did with increasing regularity, he became "feisty and obnoxious," even destructive. The housekeeper, an eighty-year-old woman named Mrs. Grossen, used to complain about the extra work he made for the maids. "Come look at this!" she would tell Dr. Popper, leading him to Tone's third-floor suite. There she would point to a broken lamp or two, ashtrays and dishes that had been flung at who-knows-what.

Tone wasn't always so fond of Mrs. Grossen either. He resented the disgusted sidelong glances she gave him on occasion, usually the morning after. One day, still feeling the effects of the night before, he called her aside and said, "You're too old to be working. Why don't you quit?" A woman with half her stamina (not to mention years) might have folded, but not Mrs. Grossen. Insiders called her "a tough old bird," and that she was. She simply turned her back on Tone, made her way to the linen room, where she downed a can of cold spaghetti, and went back to work.

Corinne Patten was fond of telling visitors that the Marmont was a romantic place. She had a list of favorite couples, but closest to her heart were Joanne Woodward and Paul Newman. "They first started coming to the hotel around 1955," she once told a reporter, over coffee and cigarettes. "They weren't married to each other then, and nobody really knew who they were. Paul had just come from New York, where he had studied with the Actors Studio and had appeared on Broadway in *Picnic.* Joanne had arrived from Broadway, too, but they were having such a difficult time making names for themselves in films. All that changed within a few short years. Joanne won the Academy Award as best actress (in 1957) for *The Three Faces of Eve,* and, the following year, Paul was nominated best actor for *Cat on a Hot Tin Roof.* From then on, they were on their way."

The sudden turnabout in the careers of Paul Newman and Joanne Woodward thrilled Corinne, but not nearly as much as watching their romance blossom. "It seems that Paul and Joanne have been together as long as I can remember," she told the reporter, "but that isn't so. When they first checked into the Marmont, they hadn't even been introduced to one another. Joanne swears that she met Paul here at the hotel. And, of course, this is where the two of them courted. They looked so in love. Everyone knew that they would marry one day, and we were all so happy when they did. What a joyous way to start a new year!" The Newmans were married in Las Vegas on January 29, 1958.

For a time, the Marmont actually seemed like a West Coast annex for the Actors Studio. The only thing missing was its director, Lee Strasberg. He was one of the last of the group to register at the hotel. In fact, members of his family were old hands around the corridors before he stepped foot inside.

Lee's daughter, Susan, remembers coming to the Marmont with her mother, Paula, for her first motion picture, *The Cobweb*. That was in early 1955. Susan was then sixteen years old and "such a nice, bright girl," according to Corinne. One of the highlights of Susan's visit was sharing taxi rides to MGM with another cast member and Marmont neighbor, Lillian Gish. (Miss Gish is remembered at the hotel not only for her sly side door exits but her frequent comments reminding everyone how happy she was to be working again. *The Cobweb* marked a comeback, of sorts. She had not appeared on the screen for seven years, since *Portrait of Jennie,* in 1948.)

The two Strasbergs, Susan and Paula, were back at the Marmont that summer for Susan's role in the film version of *Picnic*. A frequent visitor to their suite (they always requested 6H, she said) was Susan's *Picnic* co-star, Cliff Robertson.

"Susie was eighteen when I convinced her to come to the Marmont without her mother," says Steffi Sidney, Susan's close friend. "It was her first time out here alone, and I would stay at the hotel with her on weekends. The Marmont was a big party place in those days, especially on weekends, and we assumed that we would get invited to a few. But we never did, and Susie was a young starlet!"

Invitations or not, Susan continued to visit the Marmont often, alone and with her mother. In December of 1964, she also turned up with a handsome young actor, who had sunstreaked hair and a lean surfer's body, named Christopher Jones. There were reports that she dressed in hippie clothes and acted strangely, and that the sounds coming from their suite were not always happy ones. In her candid autobiography, *Bittersweet*, Susan confessed complaining to Christopher, "I'm sick of stuffing towels in the door cracks so the manager won't smell the grass!"

Lee and Paula Strasberg were having problems of their own when they came to the Marmont in 1965. The success of the Actors Studio, and of his now celebrated clients, had brought him considerable fame, even notoriety. At sixty-five, Lee Strasberg was a little man with white hair and glasses. But would-be actresses found him suddenly attractive, undoubtedly blinded by the hope that he could turn them into stars too.

A former desk clerk remembers that "girls would come in off the street and ask for Mr. Strasberg. We would take their numbers and give them to him, and he seemed flattered, but that was all. Maybe not, who knows?

Mrs. Strasberg didn't like the attention her husband was getting. She was very possessive. She watched him like a hawk, but they weren't always together. And when they were, he seemed bored."

Paula's death in 1966 ended all that. Two years later, he married Anna Mizrachi, an attractive young woman, a non-actress, whom he had met during one of his California visits. Lee and Anna were guests at the Marmont in 1968 and 1970.

Then there was the time Paula Strasberg brought her star pupil, Marilyn Monroe, to the Marmont. But that's another story.

# Mr. Ray

Until the arrival of Nicholas Ray, the two-story frame bungalows flanking the Marmont's east side were listed simply by their numbers. From late 1952 to 1958, however, the one called Bungalow 2 took on a more lofty label. In Ray's honor, it became known as "The Director's Bungalow."

Nicholas Ray had been directing feature films for only four years when he came to Chateau Marmont, following his divorce from actress Gloria Graham. But in that short time, his sensitive handling of socially conscious themes and rebellious characters in *They Live by Night* (judged by some critics as the best debut film of an American director) and two Humphrey Bogart vehicles, *Knock on Any Door* and *In a Lonely Place,* had gained him international recognition as an *auteur.* His theater experience in New York, where he had worked with Elia Kazan and John Houseman, had served him well.

Shortly after settling into his quarters at the Marmont, Ray began work on an off-beat Western, the fascinating and strangely symbolic *Johnny Guitar,* starring a rough 'n' tumble Joan Crawford as the proprietress of a gambling house. The film did little to diminish his reputation or his growing cult status.

Then came another Western, *Run for Cover,* with James Cagney, Viveca Lindfors, John Derek, and Ernest Borgnine. Despite a name-heavy cast and a gripping climax, *Run for Cover* received some of the least inspired reviews of Ray's brief career. The overly familiar storyline, concerning the reformation of a duo of bandits, prompted one critic to advise the director to be more cautious in his selection of future projects.

The announcement, in early 1955, that Nick Ray had signed to direct *Rebel Without A Cause* generated little excitement, promising nothing more than a "B" effort among a fall line-up that included such heavyweights as *The Rose Tattoo, To Catch a Thief,* and *Oklahoma!* For one thing, the Warner Bros. release was scheduled to be shot in black-and-white. That fact may have been less meaningful had *Rebel* been slated for production at any of the other major studios, where the notion still persisted that colorless filming could actually enhance mood and dramatic value. But at Warner's, a pioneer in color cinematography, virtually every film with the slightest potential was being shot in the studio's new (as of 1954) and "modestly" termed WarnerColor process. To state that the forthcoming Nicholas Ray production would be colorless was to categorize it along with Warner's other throwaway productions for the year, bottom-of-the-bill features such as *Jump into Hell, Illegal,* and *Target Zero.*

Another mark against *Rebel* was its lack of big-name performers. (*Illegal* could at least boast the highly respected character actor, Edward G. Robinson.) Seventeen-year-old Natalie Wood had been a child actress in over twenty films since her fifth birthday, but she had yet to establish herself as a star. The moody young James Dean had appeared on Broadway, in occasional television commericals and bit in TV dramas, and had made four films. His sole starring role, however, in *East of Eden,* had yet to be seen.

The balance of the cast included talented but unknown youngsters, many making their first appearance on the screen—Sal Mineo, Corey Allen, Dennis Hopper, Nick Adams, Beverly Long, Steffi Sidney (the daughter of Hollywood columnist Sidney Skolsky), and Frank Mazzola—as well as veterans Ann Doran and Jim Backus. Backus, whose credits ranged from stage, radio, and vaudeville to motion pictures, was actually best known for his work behind the cameras as the off-screen voice of the bumbling, myopic cartoon character, Mr. Magoo.

Still, *Rebel* had a powerful and timely storyline that held special appeal for Nick Ray. Anyone even remotely familiar with his work knew of his fascination for rebellious heroes consumed by a quest for love or fast and furious living. The role of teenage Jim Stark, to be played by twenty-four-year-old James Dean, was the ideal Ray character. The uncertainties voiced by others concerning the film's prospects were definitely not shared by Ray. To his thinking, *Rebel* had the ingredients to be a major motion picture.

The early script sessions were held in the living room of The Director's Bungalow at the Marmont, rather than at the studio. It was a bold departure, but Ray wanted the cast members to meet and get to know one another in a comfortable, less intimidating atmosphere, prior to the start of production. Above all, Ray felt the informal gatherings "at home" would help his younger players not only to act but to react to each other and come together as a team.

The casual surroundings made little difference to Natalie Wood, who appeared extremely nervous when she arrived for the first day's session. Starting a new film can be a traumatic experience for the most seasoned performer. But what had her chainsmoking, she said, was the prospect of meeting Hollywood's newest bad boy, James Dean

To make matters worse, Dean did not show up on time. Natalie admitted later, "Like everyone else in town, I had heard stories about him, and I was frankly afraid. The longer we waited, the more frightened I became, because as I thumbed through the script I found he was going to make love to me."

The minutes passed, and still no James Dean. Natalie tried to concentrate on her script, but she was distracted by the slightest sound and often found herself staring at the front door, waiting for it to spring open. When Dean finally did arrive, a half-hour late, he climbed through one of the living room windows.

"He looked a sight," Natalie said. "The rest of us were dressed nicely, especially Sal in his jacket and tie and skinny pegged pants, but Jimmy had on a dirty sports shirt and jeans, with a big safety pin across the front to hold them up."

Natalie told how Dean stood looking about the room before grabbing a script from the coffee table and taking a seat in a corner, off by himself.

"Nick tried to get Jimmy to sit next to me," she said. "He even teased him a little by saying, 'C'mon, Jimmy, you're going to have to make love to this girl.' But Jimmy didn't even look up. He just grunted—and I was so relieved."

There may have been more to Natalie's nervousness than her fear of meeting James Dean.

At the Marmont, Nicholas Ray was regarded as "a kind and friendly man," one who liked people and loved to party. His Sunday afternoon soirees were the talk of the hotel, and his door was open to one and all. He had even been accused of living an open-house existence. "Nick always had the welcome sign out, especially for the kids in the picture," recalled one *Rebel* cast member. "And while he never turned anyone away, he expected us to call first before dropping in on him. At least we were supposed to."

Even before the day of the first reading, Natalie Wood had been infatuated with the lean and lanky Nick Ray. It didn't matter that, at forty-three, he was old enough to be her father. She was wildly attracted to him, and working at Ray's hideaway bungalow made their being together so easy. No one suspected when she was the first to arrive in the morning and the last to leave at night—if she left at all.

If there was to be trouble during the making of *Rebel*, everyone expected it to come from James Dean, whose reputation for being difficult had followed him from New York. But Dean's late entrance through Ray's window, and several sieges of harmless, spirited laughter were his only bids for attention. Without exception, his co-workers found him to be "very cooperative and very professional." How he remained alert, or found time to prepare himself for the free-flowing sessions (script ideas submitted by the director, writer, and cast members were retained or rejected on the spot), no one knew. There were nights when Dean never got to bed, preferring instead to meet with friends for bull sessions at all-night coffee houses and snack shops. One of his favorites was nearby Googie's, where he would join Richard Bright, then a struggling actor himself. "It was never too late for Jimmy," Bright recalls. "We would get together at four in the morning, sprawl out in one of the back booths, and talk for hours." From Googie's, Dean had only to cross Sunset Boulevard for the Marmont and The Director's Bungalow.

The trouble instead came from young Dennis Hopper.

Natalie and Dennis had dated prior to their teaming on *Rebel.* For Natalie, their relationship had ended; for Dennis, it could never end. It didn't take Natalie long to discover Dennis' true feelings or the depths of his emotions.

One weekend, without bothering to call, Dennis arrived at Ray's bungalow. He let himself in, and, not finding anyone on the lower level, he wandered upstairs. As he approached the second floor, he heard voices. The sound led to Ray's bedroom, and he followed it. There he found Natalie and Nick in bed.

Soon after the incident, Steffi Sidney became friendly with Dennis Hopper. "Dennis was such a naive kid at the time," she recalls, "and so in love with Natalie. Seeing Nick and Natalie together was all he could talk about. He kept saying, 'I can't believe it—I mean, she's only seventeen, and look how old he is!' "

"Around Nick," Steffi said, "Natalie dressed older to look more sophisticated." Even at the informal readings, she was seen wearing figure-hugging dresses, jewelry, and very, very high heels.

For Natalie to be interested in older men did not surprise Steffi. She had seen Natalie three years earlier at a USC party, held at a house up the road from the Marmont. "When I saw her, I did a double-take," Steffi admitted. "I had remembered her from the Fox lot as a little kid, and I thought to myself, 'She's younger than I am.' I must have been just eighteen, and she was fourteen or fifteen—but all the guys there were my age or older.

"Everybody was drinking zombies, and Natalie was so loaded she couldn't stand up. I asked one of the guys if he realized she was jail bait—in those days they were very strict about age out here—so he went to find whoever she was with to take her home. By then, Natalie had passed out on a bed near the bar." Steffi was tempted to tell Dennis Hopper about Natalie's earlier escapades, but she didn't have the heart.

Susan Strasberg, fresh from Broadway stardom in *The Diary of Anne Frank,* recalled seeing Natalie lying by the pool in a low-cut bathing suit, eye make-up, painted nails, and smoking cigarettes. "That's what I want to be like when I'm older," Strasberg told herself at the time. She didn't realize they were the same age.

The tension created by Dennis Hopper's discovery began to intensify. According to a *Rebel* cast member, "Nick tried to get Dennis kicked off the movie, but Dennis was under contract to Warner Bros., and he couldn't. So Nick made things very unpleasant for Dennis. To get even, Dennis told Natalie's mother about the affair, which really upset Natalie, because, from then on, her mother was never out of sight. Everyone knew the problems Dennis had created, and he quickly became the goat on the movie."

"Nick had wanted a real camaraderie among the kids in the film," says Steffi Sidney, "but he got just the opposite. Maybe it was that tension that gave *Rebel* its edge."

There were other problems for Nicholas Ray at the Marmont, prior to the start of filming. Writer Irving Shulman, who had worked briefly on the script, withdrew after a series of confrontations with the director. Working with Ray, Shulman charged, was a "nightmarish experience." He was replaced by Stewart Stern.

Young Hollywood photographer Dennis Stock, who was to become one of James Dean's closest friends, first met the actor at one of Nick Ray's Sunday pool parties. "I didn't know who Jimmy was," Stock admitted later, "but I felt he was going to be a really big star, and I wanted to do something with him." Stock soon became a regular at Ray's bungalow.

"He was taking a lot of pictures, which was absolutely against union rules," a friend of Stock's remembers. "Warner's had its own photographer, a still man assigned to the picture, and he would remind Dennis that what he was doing was wrong, but he would let him shoot anyway. He was pretty lenient later on too, when we were on location, but once we got to the studio, he really clamped down on Dennis."

A few days into the filming, in March, 1955, James Dean's *East of Eden* opened to critical acclaim, and he became an overnight sensation. Among Dean's biggest boosters were Hollywood's powerful gossip columnists, Louella Parsons and Hedda Hopper. The two writers traditionally espoused opposite opinions, but in Dean's case they were united with praise. "James Dean is a second Brando," hailed Louella, "and we predict that he is going to be more than a meteor in the Hollywood sky." Hedda agreed, wholeheartedly.

The public's response to Dean's emotional portrayal of the sensitive son in the screen adaptation of John Steinbeck's novel had Warner executives drooling. In *Rebel,* they now had a potential blockbuster on their hands, and they were quick to admit it. Production on the film was shut down immediately, and all existing footage was scrapped. A few days later, filming resumed again, from the beginning—this time in color.

Natalie Wood's close ties with Nicholas Ray continued for several years after the completion of *Rebel Without a Cause.* Gavin Lambert, who later wrote the story and screenplay for Natalie's film, *Inside Daisy Clover,* recalled first meeting Natalie at Ray's bungalow during an extended visit that began in the summer of 1956. "It was the beginning of a long loving friendship," he says, "terminated only by the terrible, absurd accident of her death."

Lambert was brought to California to work as Ray's personal assistant. "I stayed with him at the Marmont for about a year, so it's very bound up with my introduction to Hollywood and my fascination with it." During his time with Ray, they worked on two movies, *Bigger Than Life* and *The True Story of Jesse James,* as well as preparing a draft for a European-made venture, *Bitter Victory.*

Lambert remembered a number of visitors to The Director's Bungalow: "Nick gave a party for the wedding of Don Murray and Hope Lange there. I have a memory of Buddy Adler of Fox blessing the union and the long-term contract he had put them under, and promising them they would never have to make a movie they didn't want to. They had to make several, of course."

There were also Betsy Blair (then married to Gene Kelly), Dennis Stock, Louella Parsons, and the leads in Hollywood's latest off-screen romantic melodrama , Elizabeth Taylor and Eddie Fisher. ("Poor Mr. Fisher was in a trance," a former desk clerk said of their arrival. "It was long before all that nasty courtroom business with Debbie Reynolds, and he looked numb with love. I gave him directions to Mr. Ray's bungalow, but I doubt if he heard me. He kept his eyes glued to Miss Taylor, like some moonstruck puppydog.")

Not all of the visitors to Ray's bungalow were well known. "For a time, Bungalow 2 was vaguely haunted by James Dean," said Gavin Lambert. "When I was living there—after Dean's death, of course—some of his hangers-on used to turn up. There was an oddly tacky crowd, including an ex-actor who became a real estate agent and an artist who specialized in sentimental homoerotic portraits and busts. There was also a girl who called herself Vampyra and claimed occult powers. Nick said, 'But Jimmy finally decided she was a phoney,' and I wondered what took him so long!"

Lambert added: "These people were, for me, the memorable happenings of the Marmont. It's a place I think of with a curious mixture of happiness and sadness—for Nick as well as Natalie died too soon. In any case, it was a unique point of departure for someone coming to work and live in Hollywood—a bit like the Left Bank must have seemed to Americans coming to Paris in the Twenties."

When Nicholas Ray departed the Marmont in 1958, following his marriage to actress Elizabeth Utley, his years in residence were not forgotten. In a CBS television presentation of the early 1960s, John Houseman produced an episode entitled *The Closed Set,* which contained some parallels with Ray's experience directing Joan Crawford in *Johnny Guitar.* For the scenes showing Ray at home, Houseman—a great friend of Nick's and the producer of his first film, *They Live by Night*—had the bright idea of duplicating the interior of Bungalow 2 on a CBS sound stage. It was authentic to the smallest detail. The only liberties taken were with the central characters. Joan Fontaine played the role of the star, Joan Crawford; John Ireland played the role of the director, Nicholas Ray.

# Making A Splash

In a city of sunshine, where swimming pools are as common as palm trees and traffic, Chateau Marmont once stood out as a rarity. For eighteen years, from 1929 to 1947, the Marmont had no pool. Not even a wading pond for little dippers. Few people seemed to mind, least of all the more sedate guests, whose most strenuous outdoor activity was lounging on their private terraces.

The early excuse for not having a pool was lack of land. Until the late 1930s, the only available space had been the grassy courtyard opposite the main entrance, and that was totally impractical. Then Albert E. Smith purchased the adjoining property, and word quickly spread that a pool was in the offing. Ann Little suddenly found herself fending off guests enraged at the prospect. A pool, they cried, would not only disturb Chateau Marmont's precious ambiance of calm and privacy but would attract a decidedly unsavory element. For proof, they pointed to the carnival atmosphere at the Garden of Allah, where a boisterous, boozy crowd of merrymakers frolicked from dawn to dusk as a prelude to the evening's raucous poolside activities. The splashing and squealing could be heard clear across Sunset Boulevard and into the hills.

Actually, the Marmont's unnerved guests had little to fear. Albert Smith had no intention of installing a pool.

Neither did Dr. Brethauer. The man from Germany whose golden pursestrings were tied and padlocked, as many who knew him testified, was the last person anyone expected to splurge on such an extravagance. Brethauer's philosophy had been to cut, not add; denude, not embellish. "He had no choice," Dr. Popper confessed to a lady friend. "Everyone coming to California after the war, especially visitors from the east, demanded a pool."

The ocean was only a short drive away, but many guests from the Atlantic coast seemed wary of the Pacific, with its broad sandy beaches and calm water. As Robert Benchley had noted earlier: "I don't trust that ocean. It's just pretending to be peaceful, waiting for the right time to sweep up and in and over everything."

Many of the newcomers were former servicemen who had been stationed in Southern California, or had tasted the good life during a few days of R&R prior to shipping out to war zones in the Pacific. Some returned with their families for visits, others came to get in on the local post-war boom.

The installation of the Marmont pool during the summer of 1947 was not as traumatic as many old-time guests feared it would be. Even its christening, sometime in the fall, went by unnoticed. Typical of Dr. Brethauer, there were no celebrations, ribbon cuttings, or ads announcing the new facility. It simply was *there* for inquiring guests, as if it had always been.

Perhaps so little fuss was made because the pool was considerably less than Olympic-sized, unlike the Garden of Allah pool, which drew comparisons to the Black Sea. As author/screenwriter Gavin Lambert noted

From his penthouse high above the pool, Howard Hughes viewed scantily clad sunbathers through a spyglass. (*Courtesy of Connie Nelson*)

"There is a pool—rather oddly shaped, like an immense *suppositoire* . . . "

following a visit to the Marmont: "There is a pool—rather oddly shaped, like an immense *suppositoire*—which is some consolation, though it makes one feel dangerously like a Hollywood writer."

Hidden in a grove of trees between the Marmont cottages and the main building, only yards off busy Sunset Boulevard, the pool and its surrounding patio quickly became a private oasis for many of the hotel's guests, the famous and not-so-famous. They came to study lines, exchange the latest movieland gossip, make contacts, or simply to play. Everyone seemed to have time to party.

During the 1950s, when studio expense accounts were more generous and shooting schedules more leisurely, many stars were brought to Hollywood for film roles prior to the start of production. A number of them would wind up staying for months, expense-free, not only throughout the shooting schedule, but for post-production work, such as dubbing and re-takes. It didn't matter if they weren't needed on the set every day, or even every week. The studios wanted their stars on call, and their generosity made it easy for them to linger. According to Donald Spackman, a Marmont regular since 1950, "There was such a leisurely, play atmosphere around the pool in those days. Today it's different because Hollywood's different. It's a nine-to-five, working town now. The stars come out from New York, or wherever, do their roles, and leave."

From the start, lured by the Marmont's roster of celebrities, the pool was a haven for scantily-clad starlets, eager to catch the eye of a visiting producer or director. It's impossible to know how many young hopefuls were discovered at the Marmont, but they aroused the attention of at least one starmaker. From his penthouse window on the sixth floor, Howard Hughes would train a spyglass on the bountiful view below, lurking behind his partially opened French windows. During Hughes' long stay at Chateau Marmont, he never once appeared poolside, but his presence was felt. Anyone who knew where to look had no trouble spotting him.

Marta Toren, the exotic Swedish actress, would often visit the pool when she was in Hollywood. Blossom Seeley became a regular, as did Lucille Ball's favorite sidekick, Vivian Vance. There were Jack Cassidy and Shirley Jones, Geraldine Page, Carol Lynley, Howard Hughes discovery Faith Domergue, Tina Louise, Susan Strasberg, Carroll Baker, Tony Perkins, Omar Sharif, Carol Channing, Dennis Hopper, and, when no one was around, Greta Garbo (floating face down in the water, in case anyone was watching). Helen Kane graciously answered requests for a "boop-boop-a-doop or two. She was in town to coach young Debbie Reynolds for her

Helen Kane role in *Three Little Words*. On Sundays, director Nicholas Ray and his "Sunday fun bunch" would take over.

The view became even richer with the passing years, as swimwear grew skimpier and more revealing. There were see-through creations and poke-through bikinis made of string. The totally daring would go topless or wear nothing at all. A New York advertising executive recalled wandering out to the pool one afternoon to find a topless Diana Rigg sprawled on a lounge. "I was shocked when I recognized her," he admitted, adding, "but, to be honest, it was awhile before I got to her face."

Said another guest: "The European women thought nothing of baring themselves. The American ladies weren't quite as bold, but they weren't afraid to give it a try. They would start on their stomachs, then ease over when they thought no one was looking. The ones who were trying to make an impression were less timid."

Tony Randall, during his long stay at the Marmont, also enjoyed sun-bathing in the nude, but only in the privacy of his bungalow garden. It was during those intimate, relaxing communions with nature that he developed a fascination for hummingbirds.

The poolside display often attracted a gallery of discreet gawkers that included members of the gardening crew. One summer, the plants surrounding the decking were so pampered, pruned, and over-watered, that manager Meemi Ferguson received calls expressing concern over their fate.

Few happenings around the pool escaped Meemi's attention. To make certain things didn't get completely out of hand, she hired a watchdog by the name of Maida Severn to patrol the area. Maida, a beautiful woman who worked occasionally as a character actress, lived directly across the street from the Marmont on Monteel Road. As payment for her services, she was given free pool privileges.

Maida never paid much attention to the skin shows. She was on the lookout for rowdy behavior and excess drinking, which kept her busy. Pool parties were constant. They would start in the mornings, with pitchers of whiskey sours, and last until late afternoon, when survivors would be joined by the lively Five O'Clock group. The regulars, changing almost daily, included Franchot Tone and Zsa Zsa Gabor, T.C. Jones, Jill Jackson, Donald Spackman, Casey Tibbs, Arthur O'Connell, Andy McLaughlin, Audie Murphy, Peter Finch, Graham Ferguson, Christine Jorgensen, and her companion, Patricia Wilson. Jorgensen's flawless complexion and figure were the talk of the Marmont. "She put all the other gals to shame," Jill Jackson confessed, with a sigh of envy.

Meemi froze whenever she saw Christine in the company of her grand-children. Despite repeated reminders to the youngsters, she was fearful that they would spill the beans—or, in this case, let the cats out of the bag. Literally.

Meemi shared her modest accommodations at the Marmont—with two cats, Mitzie and Pinkie. When she had them neutered, her precocious grand-children began calling them Pinkie Christine and Mitzie George. That was fine, until Christine (previously George) Jorgensen registered at the Mar-mont. "Christine is a lovely woman, and she and Meemi became good friends," Meemi's granddaughter, Connie, later reported, "so, of course, we were told *never* to use our nicknames any more. 'They are *Pinkie* and *Mitzie!'* Meemi kept telling us. But we had called them George and Christine for so long—since we were little kids—that Meemi was petrified we would slip. As far as I know, Christine never did find out."

Beatrice Lillie, ever the court jester, made frequent appearances at the pool during her stay for *Thoroughly Modern Millie.* Perched on a chaise under a giant umbrella, with Lord Button snug in her lap, she was rarely without a phalanx of admirers. Bea was never seen bare-headed, out of the pool or in . "Ever since the war years, the blitz," she would explain, haltingly, "I've always gone in the water with a hat on. It must be safe to go without now, but I don't know . . . "

When Hermionne Baddeley wasn't sipping or engaged in conversation, she could be found chin deep in the pool. Her friends dubbed her "the water bug."

Not far away sat Pearl Bailey, book in hand. Frequent interruptions by friends and acquaintances made reading almost impossible, but nothing seemed to rattle the imperturbable Pearlie Mae. Not even the scare she received one steamy afternoon.

Following an exhausting day in town, Pearl returned to the hotel and made her way upstairs to her suite. There, she kicked off shoes before step-ping out onto the balcony for a breath of fresh air. For some reason, she climbed up on the broad cement railing to sit down, letting her feet dangle over the edge. She wasn't there long. Apparently, she became so relaxed that she lost her balance and slid down onto the canvas awning of the balcony below. She struggled for awhile, but, unable to get up or down from the makeshift hammock, she did the normal thing: she went to sleep.

When Pearl's husband, Louis Bellson, arrived at the Marmont he found her shoes and purse, but no Pearl. He phoned downstairs, only to be told by Carmel Volti that Pearl was in the hotel. "Yes, I saw her come in,"

Carmel assured him. Louis grew more frantic with each passing minute. He searched everywhere, placed calls around the hotel trying to track Pearl down, even shouted out her name. He made such a racket that Pearl finally awakened.

When Louis saw his wife swaying on a piece of canvas high above the street, it was all he could do to summon assistance. The full fire department crew, plus a hook and ladder, was needed to get Pearl back on solid footing. She was grateful for the helping hand, but she couldn't understand what the fuss was all about.

Alexander Ives, Burl's son, had an adventure of his own. "When I was around ten," he reported, "we lived in a little suite toward the back of the Marmont, on the northernmost side. One day, after I had been swimming, I came back upstairs and put my wet bathing suit on a towel rack in the bathroom and turned on the heater underneath it. I didn't think the heater would get so hot. The next thing I knew, there was smoke everywhere. Black smoke. The bathing suit must have fallen off the rack onto the heater, starting it smoldering. What a mess!"

That didn't stop young Alex from returning downstairs to continue his "war game" with teenage Brandon DeWilde. The two boys would gather eucalyptus nuts and fling them at each other across the pool. Nearby, seated in a deck chair, Burl could be heard strumming his guitar.

Jonathan Winters got his exercise by running around the pool in giant circles, chasing young Morgan Cavett.

Everyone in Hollywood, it seemed, was waiting for "an important phone call" from an agent or producer. For many years, the Marmont was ill-equipped to handle all the calls to the pool, because only one telephone served the area. Enterprising guests dragged phones out from the surrounding cottages, creating a life-threatening jumble of extension cords and a cacophony of bells.

The ringing of phones could even be heard at the bottom of the pool, where swimmers Wally Cox, Paul Lynde, Michael J. Pollard, and others seemed to gravitate. Whoever was there would surface in a flash, wide-eyed in anticipation. The bobbing went on all day long, but no one hurtled out of the pool—and no one along the sidelines made the first move to answer the calls. Only after a suitable pause did some brave soul give in. Then there was a hush, as everyone waited for his or her name to be called.

"It was controlled panic," one of the regulars confessed, "a kind of disinterested desperation, which was understandable. After all, who in Hollywood would dare appear so anxious, or insecure, as to ask, 'Is it for me?' "

There were few moments of calm around the pool. Even early mornings, when most loyal poolsiders were sleeping off the day before, could be unnerving. One morning, Meemi Ferguson spotted Patrice Wymore strolling around the pool with a baby pig. The little creature had been an Easter gift to her daughter, Arnella, by well-meaning friends who believed it to be much more unique than a baby chick or bunny rabbit. Meemi absolutely adored pets. The hotel was teeming with them. Joan Blondell had just arrived with her two Chinese pugs, Bridie Murphy and Freshness. Sylvia Sidney had her pugs, Madam and Mister. Franchot Tone and Dolores Dorn-Heft had two rare Korean palace dogs: Hermione Gingold had Mr. Pudding; Elizabeth Montgomery and Gig Young had Boo. There was even a *real* French poodle, brought from Paris by its owners, the Leveques. But a piglet? Meemi firmly put her foot down.

Another time, shortly after sunrise, Meemi was awakened by a frantic phone call. "There's a huge hairy thing floating in the pool," a voice shrieked. "It's horrible!"

"My God," Meemi cried, "who could that be?" Her first thought was that a guest, possibly nude, had accidentially fallen in the water. She feared the worst. She had vivid memories of a young child nearly drowning only months earlier. "If it hadn't been for that darling actor, Richard Bright," she told Carmel Volti, "'well . . . '" She couldn't bear to finish the frightening thought.

Meemi hurriedly dressed in her velour jumpsuit and jewels, and made her way to the pool. There she discovered, not a nude guest, but a seal, splashing merrily in the deep end. An emergency call to the Humane Society brought two men with nets who took the lively creature away. How it found its way to the Marmont no one could explain, but Meemi didn't search for answers. Her standard reply, whenever anyone inquired, was a simple, "Anything can happen in Hollywood."

Greta Garbo—homemade stews and
midnight shopping sprees.

Montgomery Clift left word that he
was not to be disturbed by anyone.

Marilyn Monroe shared her weekdays
and nights at the Marmont with Paula
Strasberg, and her weekends with a
secret visitor.

# Chapter 8

## Three Legends

### 'Miss Brown'

She signed the guest register as "Harriet Brown," but there was no mistaking that face, that voice, those eyes. Greta Garbo had come to the Marmont.

She arrived on an overcast day in March, 1955, carrying only a few personal belongings. ("I travel light," she told the desk clerk.) It was Garbo's first visit to the Marmont, despite rumors that she had been a frequent guest for years.

Garbo was initially drawn to the hotel by socialite Virginia Burroughs, who lived with her elderly mother on the fourth floor. Garbo requested an adjoining suite; she wanted to be near her friend, even though "they were so different." A mutual acquaintance at the Marmont remembers: "Virginia had the most gorgeous wardrobe and dressed so elegantly; Greta rarely wore anything but slacks. Virginia styled her hair in a very sleek upsweep; Greta finger-combed hers. Virginia had been married four times and had a son. Greta had shied away from marriage. She would say, 'The world seems too difficult. I would not want to raise a son, or any child, to go to war.' "

If Garbo strayed from her suite during her early days at the Marmont, it was only as far as next door. The two women were nearly inseparable. One day a maid spotted them acting "scandalously" in Burroughs' suite. She rushed downstairs to report, breathlessly, "You'll never guess what I just saw Miss Garbo and Miss Burroughs doing. They're smoking *cigarillos!*" In those days, to see a woman smoking anything but a regular cigarette was considered shocking. The news quickly spread through the hotel.

Everyone knew that Garbo cherished her privacy, but few people realized how much she craved peace and quiet—or how far she would go to avoid being disturbed. It took a spoiled, noisy eight-year-old boy to give her away. One weekend, a family with such a child moved into the suite adjoining her bedroom. Garbo endured the youngster's racket as long as possible; not wanting to complain, she said nothing. Instead she inveigled one of the maids into helping her wrestle her bed into her dining room to get away from the den. There she slept, until the little noisemaker departed. "When the housekeeper saw that bed in her dining room," Carmel Volti remembered, "she was absolutely astonished. It would have been so easy for Miss Garbo to alert the manager, but she didn't want to bother anybody."

Garbo liked to shop at Schwab's Pharmacy, but she refused to go when it was crowded. Said Steffi Sidney, "She was so smart. She knew that Schwab's closed at midnight, so she would time her arrival to get there at five or ten to 12:00. The store would be all but empty, and they would lock the door behind her as she went in. One night, however, an actress was inside when Garbo came in. She was buying something, and when she looked up and saw Garbo, she passed out. It made all the columns.

"Somebody at the Marmont used to tip off my father (Hollywood columnist Sidney Skolsky) whenever Garbo came to town. He knew she liked Schwab's so he would purposely hang around night after night until midnight, never knowing when she would show up."

Once reporters learned of Garbo's whereabouts, they gathered in clusters in the lobby or by the garage entrance, waiting to snare her. For the most part, she eluded them by stealthily using the stairs. Talking with strangers appealed to her as much as having her picture taken. Said one seasoned Garbo-watcher, "She had the radar system of a bat."

Garbo wasn't in flight when Steffi Sidney saw her at the hotel. "I was in the elevator, on my way to see Clifford Odets, when she stepped in. I was looking down at the time, and all I saw were shoes—*big shoes*—but I knew they belonged to *her*. It was the first time I was ever speechless, and I had met stars all my life."

The size of Garbo's feet became a frequent topic of conversation around the hotel. Not everyone agreed that they were as large as they appeared to be. Remarked David Niven: "Garbo's feet were beautifully shaped and long, in correct proportion to her height, but she had an unfortunate habit of encasing them in huge brown loafers that gave the impression that she wore landing craft."

Garbo's 1955 visit wasn't her last. She was back at the Marmont three years later on February 22 and again on March 16 for an extended stay. No longer could she turn to Virginia Burroughs for companionship—both Burroughs and her mother had passed away—but she was not without friends. Through her long friendship with novelist-screenwriter Aldous Huxley she had met Rose de Haulleville, the Marmont's assistant manager. Huxley had once been married to Rose's sister.

One early evening, Garbo invited Rose to her suite for tea. "It seemed like Rose was in with Miss Garbo for an eternity," Carmel Volti remembered, "and everyone was getting so anxious to know what was going on in there— mostly what it was like to be alone with the great Garbo. So the moment I saw Rose come out I rushed up to her and asked, 'What did she say? What did she do?' Rose shrugged and said, 'Oh, Greta just sat there and repeated *How flime ties* (sic)—and that was about it.'"

Though never known to be a scintillating conversationalist, Garbo did have her moments. On occasion, she would stop to chat at the front desk as she wandered in and out, most often recalling with great affection her earliest years in California—a time thirty years in the past—when she lived in Santa Monica. She talked of strolls along the beach, of wandering through the grassy windswept park overlooking the bay, and of visits with her dear friend, Salka Viertel, who lived in a small house in the nearby canyon. Salka was a Polish actress-writer who had been Max Reinhardt's mistress in Vienna before marrying director Berthold Viertel and moving with him to Hollywood in 1929. She had met Garbo at MGM, where she worked in the story department. Over the years, she collaborated on the screenplays of Garbo's greatest films, including *Anna Karenina, Queen Christina,* and *Camille.*

In her autobiography, *The Kindness of Strangers,* Salka Viertel wrote of Garbo's visits: "She came very often early in the morning when the beach was deserted, and we took long walks together.... In the bright light, she was even more beautiful. She wore no make-up, not even powder, only the famous long eyelashes were thoroughly blackened with mascara."

Now Garbo's strolls were limited to the hillside above the Marmont, where she collected spring wildflowers. Said Mrs. Volti, "It was something to see Miss Garbo coming through the lobby carrying a basket of flowers she had just picked. She was so lovely, and she seemed so content." Other staff members commented on how much more relaxed—and daring—Garbo had become lately. If the thought of running into "strangers" made her apprehensive, she never let on. She even took to "milling around" the Marmont gardens, nibbling at times on a sandwich she kept in her pocket. Most often she was seen wearing slacks or shorts, a large sunhat, and, as Salka Viertel had noted, no make-up. To find such "a glamorous star" dressed so casually astounded a number of guests, particularly out-of-towners. They would have been even more surprised to discover, on closer inspection, that she frequently went for her walks with "frownies" taped to the corners of her eyes.

Southern California's long dry spells annoyed Garbo. One day, feeling restive, she commented, "I must have some rain or I'll go crazy." Her solution to the problem was childishly simple. She turned on a lawn sprinkler and, fully clothed, stood in the spray until she was drenched to the skin.

Her days were not always spent in a solitary manner. There were shopping sprees and dinners with friends, such as George Cukor at his secluded, treasure-filled Georgian-style mansion in the nearby hills. One evening, she passed by the front desk wearing a billowing, floor-length black velvet cape. "She was on her way out," Carmel Volti remembers, "and I hesitated stopping her, she looked so lovely, but she hadn't picked up her mail in ages, and I wanted to catch her while I could. So I took the things from her box, held them out for her, and said, 'Miss Garbo, here are your messages and rent receipts.' She looked at me sweetly and, as she continued on her way, replied, 'That's all right. We trust each other.' "

Maurice Chevalier was a neighbor of Garbo's at the Marmont during her extended second visit in 1958. The two stars had known each other since their days at MGM in the early 1930s, but they had barely had time to exchange more than greetings, because of Chevalier's heavy work schedule. They found themselves paired one evening, however, at an intimate dinner party hosted by Cukor at his home. As in the past, whenever they'd had more than a moment to chat, Chevalier tried to follow Garbo's mood, which, he said, tended to change abruptly from "gay, witty brillance to deep sadness or a kind of mysterious despair."

About their conversation at Cukor's, Chevalier later remembered: "We chatted animatedly and easily about many things, and as the evening progressed I began to wonder why I had ever found it difficult to converse with this fascinating woman. Then, out of the blue, as we were discussing the theater, she asked me if I like to swim in the ocean. It seemed like an odd, disconnected question, but I smiled and nodded. 'Good,' she said firmly, 'shall we now go to the beach?' I looked at her rather startled and replied 'Now?' with dismay. It was almost midnight, and the icy Pacific in March held little appeal for me, which I quickly pointed out. This was apparently my mistake, for instantly our warm, friendly conversation was over. The lady still sat beside me, but for the remainder of the party she was so remote and withdrawn and far away that I felt almost alone. I went back to the Marmont that evening, more than ever convinced that the glorious, ethereally lovely, but unpredictable Greta Garbo and I were miles and miles apart." That was the last time Garbo and Chevalier were to see each other in Hollywood.

The "unpredictable" Garbo apparently found Gaylord Hauser, the famed health food advocate, more receptive to her moods, for he visited her on numerous occasions in her suite at Chateau Marmont. Along with Adele Astaire, Clara Bow, and Elsie de Wolfe (Lady Charles Mendl), Garbo had at one time been one of Hauser's celebrated disciples and biggest boosters. They had also been close companions, a relationship the trim and dapper Hauser did little to discourage. Their "planned marriage" in 1940, as reported in newspapers everywhere, had shocked Garbo more than anyone. In fact, when discovered that it was Hauser who had leaked the story to the press, they parted company. But only for a time. The friendship not only resumed, but they became partners in a real-estate venture on Beverly Hills' fashionable Rodeo Drive.

Hauser's "secrets of good health" remained with Garbo over the years, even though she generally ignored his favored maxim: "It has to look good, taste good, and do good." At the Marmont, a vegetable salad or watery soup often sufficed for her dinner, even a cluster of raw garlic. One morning, a maid was surprised to discover Garbo ambitiously preparing "something" in the kitchen alcove of her suite. "Would you like breakfast sent up from downstairs, a roll and coffee?" the maid inquired. "No," Garbo answered busily, "I'm fixing myself a little vegetable stew."

Although Garbo's visits to the Marmont were relatively few, she has become more closely identified with the hotel than any other star. In fact, the Garbo legend at the Marmont has, if anything, grown stronger with the passing years.

Gaylord Hauser stayed at the Marmont briefly in the 1930s, shortly after the publication of one of his early nutrition manuals, which had earned him a considerable following within the movie colony. As Mrs. Volti remembered: "It seemed as if everyone was eating celery stalks and raw carrots, wheat germ, blackstrap molasses, and 'Hauser Broth.' One night Mr. Hauser didn't get home for dinner, and his cook, whom he had brought along, called down to see if anyone would be interested in eating the meal he had prepared for Mr. Hauser. One of the girls said yes, without thinking. Well, she was expecting the raw carrots and all, but it turned out to be a steak, baked potato, and a salad. Was she relieved!"

# Miss Monroe

After spending a little over a year in New York, during which time she divorced Joe DiMaggio, filmed *The Seven Year Itch,* and had a falling out with Twentieth Century-Fox, Marilyn Monroe returned to Hollywood in March, 1956. Her homecoming was noteworthy on several accounts: not only had she made peace with Fox and obtained a lucrative new contract, she had landed the much sought-after starring role in the film version of William Inge's play, *Bus Stop*

A huge, clamoring turnout of press greeted Marilyn and her entourage at the airport in Los Angeles. She was accompanied by Milton H. Green (New York's most talked about fashion photographer and Monroe's partner in their newly formed MM Productions); Green's wife, Amy; and Paula Strasberg, with whom she had worked while studying at Lee Strasberg's Actors Studio. With Monroe no longer able to attend classes in New York, *Bus Stop* director Josh Logan had been persuaded into accepting Paula as Monroe's dramatic coach. The arrangement pleased Marilyn; she was now as dependent on Paula Strasberg as she had been earlier on Natasha Lytess, her coach for years at Fox.

It was Paula Strasberg who brought Marilyn Monroe and her new friends to the Marmont. They came not because fellow *Bus Stop* cast members Arthur O'Connell and Casey Tibbs would be there throughout the filming, but because Strasberg was familiar with the hotel. According to a family friend, "She felt the quiet surroundings best suited Marilyn's need for privacy." Such a setting would also enable Strasberg to better control her star pupil. Strasberg's fierce attachment to Monroe had her known, in some circles, as "a witch" and "a sorceress." (She was also known as "the black mushroom," because her small, squat frame was usually garbed in formless black chemises).

At first, Paula Strasberg found herself fighting a losing battle. Around the Marmont, Marilyn seemed to be constantly upset, on edge. "It was her fear of Natasha Lytess," an unidentified cast member said. "She couldn't help but feel responsible for having caused Natasha to lose her job at the studio, and she was deathly afraid that Natasha was out to get her for that. She had nightmares about running into Natasha. She couldn't make a move without thinking she would run into her."

Precautions were taken to protect the studio's—and America's—reigning blonde goddess. An item in the trade papers noted that Lytess had been barred from the Fox lot after Marilyn refused to leave her dressing room between takes. At the Marmont, strict instructions were left at the switchboard that "Miss Monroe was not in," should her former coach call. Calls were received. They came in the early morning and late at night. The messages were left unanswered.

Even if Monroe had wanted to talk with Lytess, it is doubtful Lytess could have gotten through. Night after night, Paula placed calls through the switchboard to her husband in New York, and they would talk for hours. The calls were not personal in nature, as would be revealed later. She phoned Lee for advice on how to prepare Marilyn for an upcoming scene that was scheduled to be shot, and to confer with him about the problems she was having with her star pupil.

Anyone who caught a glimpse of Marilyn at the Marmont during the early filming could see that there were problems. "It wasn't only the Lytess thing," one of her co-workers said. "She had gotten a lot of publicity because of her ties with the Actors Studio, and she was under pressure to prove that she could really act." The role of Cherie, *Bus Stop*'s tawdry southern cabaret singer, wasn't an easy one for Monroe. She returned exhausted to the hotel each night, wearing toreador pants, a plain house coat, and with her deadly chalk-white film make-up, created by Milton Greene, still intact. Seeing her drag in one evening, Meemi Ferguson's grandson, Lee, quipped, "Is she trying to prove she can be ugly?" Her apparent disregard for her appearance raised a few eyebrows. Everyone knew her reputation for spending hours perfecting her "look" before she dared be seen in public. Now it seemed as if she didn't care—or she was too tired to care.

Actually, not that many people saw Marilyn. Her time at the Marmont was spent exclusively with Paula Strasberg and the Greenes; everyone else, including Arthur O'Connell and Casey Tibbs, was carefully avoided. If anyone would have come in contact with her, it would have been Tibbs, the champion rodeo star, who spent his off hours "living it up" around the hotel. He arrived with his pal Andy McLaglen, Victor's son, one change of clothes, and "a trunkload of stories to tell." Whenever he wasn't on the set he was around the pool, surrounded by anyone willing to "listen to me bullshit the cowboy."

The somber intensity that characterized Marilyn's behavior during the week vanished on weekends, with the arrival of her secret visitor. She was seeing playwright Arthur Miller, whom she had met during her stay in the east, and no one was to know . "His weekend visits to the Marmont were *very* hush-hush," a former desk clerk recalled. "He was supposed to be in residence in Reno, obtaining his divorce. Instead, he was sneaking away to be with Miss Monroe."

On Fridays, filled with the anticipation of Miller's arrival, Marilyn's personality turned from somber to playful. "She so looked forward to her weekends with Mr. Miller that she could hardly contain herself," Corinne Patten wrote in her journal. "She became the Marilyn we all knew and loved."

Another entry in Corinne's journal, recorded one Friday evening, reads: "Marilyn Monroe sauntered through the lobby tonight—or should I say *bounced*—wearing a most revealing low-cut blouse, a tight, *tight* skirt, and spike heels. Her face was glowing as she hummed a little tune and gaily swung her arms." Other witnesses identified the tune as *That Old Black Magic,* the song she sang in *Bus Stop.* "It was as if she couldn't get it out of her head," they remarked.

There was another Marilyn admirer at the Marmont, who made no secret of his infatuation. He stood in the lobby not only on weekends but day after day, patiently waiting for an opportunity to speak with her. It was playwright Clifford Odets. "Poor Clifford," a mutual friend recalled. "He was absolutely dying to meet Marilyn, and he made no bones about it. He was probably the only person who didn't know about Marilyn's involvement with Arthur. It might not have made any difference if he did. Once Clifford became enamored with someone, he was impossible. Clifford's problem was that nobody really ever took him seriously. He had a crush on everybody at one time or another."

The *Bus Stop* troupe remained at the Marmont through the completion of filming in late spring. Then Marilyn Monroe and her friends, led by Paula Strasberg, returned to New York. Not much later, Marilyn and Arthur Miller were married.

# Mr. Clift

He looked like a fugitive as he waited outside the Marmont that March night in 1957, pacing nervously until the lobby cleared. His head was bowed at an awkward angle . He wore sunglasses, even though the sun had set hours earlier. His coat collar stood on end, shielding his face, even though the night air had yet to bring a chill.

It had been years since Montgomery Clift had been inside the hotel. In those days too, during the rain-delayed filming of *Red River,* he had taken special precautions to avoid being seen, although he had yet to appear on the screen. His face was famous now—but it was not the face that belonged to "the most beautiful man in films," the one that moviegoers had come to know so well.

He was lucky to be alive. Less than ten months earlier, he had wrapped his car around a telephone pole, following a party at the Coldwater Canyon home of Elizabeth Taylor and Michael Wilding. The automobile had been totaled. Its driver hadn't fared much better. His nose and sinus cavity had been shattered, his jaw crushed, his cheeks severely slashed, his upper lip ripped in half. His face, as a friend described it, "was literally torn away."

In the agonizing interval since the near-fatal crash, he had spent weeks in traction—unable to speak or eat solid foods because of his wired jaw—and had undergone extensive dental surgery and therapy. Yet somehow, against all odds, he had managed to complete his role in the multi-million-dollar epic, *Raintree County,* that he and Taylor had been filming at the time of the accident.

Montgomery Clift had returned to his home in New York following the stressful assignment at MGM. Now, for some unexplained reason, he was back in Hollywood, signing in at the Marmont. He offered no real explanation. A brief reference to *Raintree* was taken to mean that he had been summoned for additional work on the film. Perhaps he wanted to say more, but found talking difficult. He spoke in a soft, slow, almost unintelligible manner that slurred his words. He would start sentences, then leave them unfinished. But he was able to make it known that he was not to be disturbed during his stay, not by anyone, not even his close friend Kevin McCarthy, whom he knew to be a Marmont "regular." Above all, his mother was not to know his whereabouts. "If she . . . calls," he said haltingly, "tell her . . . I'm not . . . here."

There was some speculation that the reason behind Clift's return to Hollywood was his growing concern about his appearance in *Raintree*, specifically in those scenes that had been filmed after the accident, and that he was anxious to view the footage privately before the film's release. According to one source who saw the actor at the hotel, he looked "odd."

The left side of his face appeared paralyzed, lifeless. His nose was deformed, his mouth oddly shaped. His eyebrows, the source said, were bushier and blacker than she had recalled, and his eyes had a wild look in them.

Clift had requested "a room" on the sixth floor, but none was available. Instead he was given 3F, a two-bedroom suite on the northeast corner on three. From the moment he stepped inside, a "Do Not Disturb" sign was seen dangling from the knob of his door. He later left word with the switchboard that maids were not to enter 3F while he was there.

The suite remained off-limits for nearly a week. When Clift finally departed for a short, unexplained absence, the third-floor maid was allowed access. But she wasn't prepared for the sight that awaited her—once she had found a workable lamp switch. "He had taken out the bulbs in every fixture except one, and that had a very dim light in it. The windows were closed tight, and the shades and draperies were drawn. The place was as black as a cave!" She also discovered that all the large framed mirrors were gone, removed from their wall hooks and hidden in a corner with their backs facing outward. Those permanently attached were shrouded with towels and sheets.

Blankets, stained sheets, and dirty clothes were lying in heaps everywhere, but she found one bedroom in particular a complete shambles. "The mattress was falling off the bed, pillows were twisted and crumpled, a chair and lamp had been tipped over. You could hardly walk for the empty liquor bottles on the floor." There were also pills, she said, scattered like confetti.

One afternoon, the switchboard received an angry complaint from a woman who identified herself only as "a neighbor." She told of "a crazy man" shouting obscenities from a third-floor terrace at the northeast corner of the Marmont. From the sound of her voice, it was impossible to tell which she found more offensive: the man's language or the sight of him naked.

On another occasion, the swtichboard lit up with calls from guests who had been awakened by a late-hour disturbance on the sixth floor. A houseboy was immediately summoned to the scene, where he found a stuporous, barefooted Clift, wrapped only in a loose-fitting bathrobe, slumped in the corridor outside the door to the penthouse, his head lowered and his face buried in his hands.

"He was pounding on the door, hollering for somebody named Libby," one of the guests in an adjoining suite told the houseboy . "He kept calling for her to let him in —making an awful racket—but nobody answered. Then he started crying. I guess he finally realized there's no Libby here. As far as I know, the penthouse isn't even rented."

With the help of the houseboy, Clift was led back to his darkened quarters and put to bed. The troubled actor offered no resistance.

The following day, an item in *The Hollywood Reporter* revealed that Montgomery Clift was recuperating at Chateau Marmont, following his near-fatal car crash. It also stated that Clift was the guest of his wealthy "protectress," Libby Holman, in her $1,000 a month penthouse, where he was receiving "all the tender loving care possible."

Clift may have been the recipient of Libby's special attention at her Connecticut estate, Treetops, which they often shared whenever he was on the east coast, but they were not together at the Marmont in 1957. For the most part, he was alone throughout his stay, closeted behind the doors of his third-floor suite.

Perhaps it was the memory of another time that had drawn Montgomery Clift to the penthouse. Perhaps, in his tortured mind, he was again secretly slipping away from the location filming of *Red River,* as he had eleven years earlier, to be with Libby Holman.

Certainly, he had known happier days at the Marmont.

Liberace dangles sixty feet above Sunset Boulevard to symbolically light replica of his trademark candelabrum held by the new Sahara showgirl during publicity stunt in early 1966. (*Courtesy of E.T. Legg & Co.*)

The Sahara showgirl stands perched above billboard at the curve of Sunset Boulevard and Marmont Lane, 1957. (*Courtesy of E.T. Legg & Co.*)

# Chapter 9

## Do Not Disturb

## A Dark Day

Flatbed trucks carrying massive steel girders were the first to arrive. Then came the construction crews, brawny men in hard hats, tee-shirts, jeans, and boots. They parked along Sunset, directly beneath the Marmont, before making their way to an unused strip of land between the hotel and Preston Sturges' restaurant, The Players.

No one at the Marmont gave a second thought to the sudden activity that early morning in May of 1957. Even the sound of drills boring into the rock-hard earth failed to create a stir. After all, workmen were always doing *something* along the boulevard.

By noon, however, there was cause for alarm. Beams of steel, set in holes deep enough to draw water, were towering skyward. Atop the beams, the frame for yet another structure was on the rise.

From the construction site came the unhappy news that a super-sized billboard, known in the advertising trade as a "spectacular," was being erected so the Sahara Hotel in Las Vegas could promote its showroom and lounge attractions. The marquee display was to be one of a kind and absolutely unique. It wasn't made clear just how "unique" the billboard would be, but it didn't take long to find out. Within the week, a giant crane was lifting into place not only a massive replica of a silver dollar but the crowning glory—a giant forty-foot-tall likeness of a Las Vegas showgirl, scantily clad in Western garb and posing provocatively on one leg. And she revolved!

Never had guests at the Marmont raised such a fuss. Dr. Popper and Dr. Brethauer were beseiged with complaints and urged to take action against the outdoor advertising company and its client, citing the display as "sleazy and garish," "an eyesore," and "an outrage." Longtime guests with suites overlooking the Strip were particularly outraged. "Our magnificent view has been destroyed," they moaned. Others claimed that the structure's appearance marked "a dark day" in the history of the hotel.

The owner and his associate were strangely unmoved by it all. For some reason, they refused to let the billboard (or their disgruntled guests) upset them. Rumor had it that they had secretly agreed to relinquish a portion of the Marmont's sprawling vista in exchange for "a tidy sum."

If the doctors believed that objections to the Sahara spectacular would fade with time, they were wrong. The billboard was impossible to ignore. It was always in full view, day after day, night after glaring night. Spotlights lit up the showgirl like a torch, as she moved in dizzying, non-stop circles atop her pool-sized, silver-dollar pedestal.

A group of diehard guests circulated a petition around the Marmont, gathering signatures in an attempt to force removal of "the thing." Calls were made to city officials. When no one listened, Marmont teenager Brandon DeWilde, who was at the hotel while filming *Blue Denim* with Carol Lynley, took to the terrace of his parents suite with an air rifle. He soon became quite the marksman, able to hit the showgirl's revolving strategic parts almost at will.

The Sahara billboard became such an eye-catcher—and instant landmark—that it spawned a tongue-in-cheek takeoff. Directly across Sunset, outside the offices of Jay Ward Productions, a miniature (by showgirl standards) pirouettting Bullwinkle J. Moose—with outstretched hand that balanced his feathered friend, Rocky—was installed as a publicity stunt for Ward's cartoon series on television. Fox's Marilyn Monroe clone, Jayne Mansfield, handled the unveiling.

To the dismay of the people at the Marmont, the leggy Las Vegas showgirl remained in sight atop the Sahara billboard for nearly a decade. (During that time, her brief cowgirl outfit was replaced by more stylish red, white, and blue patriotic scanties.) In 1966, she was dismantled and hauled away. Four years later, however, Twentieth Century-Fox brought her to the screen for the highly publicized film version of Gore Vidal's *Myra Breckenridge*. Thanks to the magic of Hollywood, she was once again seen twirling on her famed billboard perch. Gratefully, she never made it back to the Strip.

Portions of *Myra Breckenridge* were shot on location at the Marmont, where Vidal had written his best-selling novel. For those scenes, the studio moved in lights, cameras, production crews, and stars, including curvaceous Raquel Welch for her unlikely role as the mannish young woman who had undergone a sex change. Hauling the heavy equipment to the upper floor "set" was too much for the elevators. They promptly broke down, forcing guests to use the stairs until repairs could be made. One Marmont oldtimer, who was familiar with Vidal's novel, blamed the problem on "the curse of that goddamn go-around showgirl!"

Today the Sunset Strip is littered with spectacular billboards from one end to the other; they are as common as the stars along Hollywood's Walk of Fame. But none can compare to the one and only original—the ultimate traffic-stopper. Unfortunately, its commercial impact was lost within the walls of Chateau Marmont.

# Mr. & Mrs. Merrill

Life was not particularly sweet for Bette Davis, when she and her fourth husband, actor Gary Merrill, checked into the Marmont from their home, Witch Way, in Cape Elizabeth, Maine, in early February, 1957. Finances had become somewhat a problem. She was supporting her mother, Ruthie, in high style down the coast in Laguna. Her sister, Barbara ("Bobby"), required psychiatric treatment and occasional confinement in costly nursing homes. Her—and Merrill's—incurably retarded adopted daughter, Margot, needed constant attention and specialized care, which she was receiving at the Lochland School, an institution on Lake Geneva in upstate New York. She was determined to give her two robust and healthy children, daughter Barbara ("B.D.," by her husband number three, handsome landscape artist, William Grant Sherry), and adopted son, Michael (with Merrill), the finest educations possible. Davis did not begrudge spending such enormous sums of money; she was only too happy to share her income with members of her family, whom she deeply loved. But she was earning far less now than she had in the past.

Since 1950, Bette Davis had made only eight movies, the exceptional *All About Eve,* plus several of rather dubious quality that failed to attract much interest, even among her most dedicated followers. That compared to nearly twenty prestigious films during the 1940s and more than forty during the previous decade. Roles had become fewer and farther apart.

Fortunately, her plight wasn't yet desperate enough to force her to take drastic measures. That would come soon enough. Her much ballyhooed ad in Hollywood's show-business bible, *Daily Variety* was still several years away: "Situation Wanted: Mother of three—10, 11 & 15—divorced, American. Thirty years experience as an actress in motion pictures. Mobile still and more affable than rumor would have it. Wants steady employment in Hollywood . . . "

Now, there were at least offers to appear on television. Not too long before, Bette Davis would never have considered working for "the competition," a view shared by most of her fellow big-name film stars. Switching from the big sceen to the rival small screen was not only considered *declasse* but unthinkable.

But circumstances have a way of altering a person's thinking. In an interview given to Cecil Smith of the *Los Angeles Times* during one of her early Marmont visits, Davis admitted, "I had to get into the medium eventually. I had to find out what this new thing was. And now that I'm in it, I love it. Simply love it!"

About the only thing she didn't love was appearing live. She was all set up to star on television's foremost dramatic program, the very live *Playhouse 90*, when she suddenly panicked and withdrew. Such a move was not typical of Bette Davis. After nearly thirty years in the spotlight, both in Hollywood and on Broadway, she had deservedly earned a reputation as "a fearless old pro ."

Between February, 1957, and January, 1960, Bette Davis checked into the Marmont no less than seven times, not always with Gary Merrill, whose own career was somewhat stalled following years of activity. It's a wonder either one of them returned at all. Most of the visits were memorable, though not for positive reasons.

Carmel Volti recalled those occasions quite well: "We were expecting Mr. and Mrs. Merrill but we didn't know how long they were planning to stay. So Meemi Ferguson made a point of asking me to find out when they arrived. Most people didn't resent it, so I simply asked her when she registered. Well, if looks could kill, I would have been gone on the spot. Those big eyes of hers got even bigger as she glowered and roared, 'I don't know! And why do you have the nerve to ask?!' "

One of Davis' former co-stars was staying at the Marmont at the time and overheard the outburst. He later tried to soothe hurt feelings by saying, "Bette is under a great deal of stress, or she wouldn't have spoken so abruptly. That isn't her way." Still later he admitted, "Oh, yes, I've known her to get rather testy and pull rank at the studios, but only to make a point, particularly when she's in the right. Generally she's very cooperative—a wonderful lady."

Her stress wasn't all money and career related. Another problem was her relationship with Merrill, which was often severely strained. Shared mutual interests weren't enough to overcome clashing temperaments, and from the sound of bleating voices emanating from their suites, they cared little how many people knew their shabby state of affairs. They bickered and fought, yelled and cursed at one another. Once, when they were living on the first floor, their exchanges could be heard all the way to the lobby, prompting Corinne Patten to remark: "They won't be together much longer."

Then there was the time she was staying in one of the bungalows with her cat. She had returned to the Marmont after signing to appear in the pilot of a proposed television series, *Paula,* late one evening. As Mrs. Volti recalled, "She was watching television, concentrating on one of her old movies. She must have dozed off and absentmindedly dropped a lighted cigarette onto the upholstered chair where she was sitting. If Lou Jacobi hadn't happened by when he did, it might really have been horrible." An omen perhaps. The pilot didn't sell.

A guest appearance on the popular western series *Wagon Train* brought her to the Marmont for the last time on January 7, 1960. Once again she came alone; by now she and Merrill had separated. (Oddly, she registered as "Mrs. Gary Merrill," whereas she had previously signed in as "Bette Davis.") This time an electrical short in one of the closets triggered an alarm. It was one scare too many, even for the admittedly accident-prone Miss Davis. Said Carmel Volti, "She just gave up and said she would never be back. And she has kept her word."

# Mr. & Mrs. Brando

New Year's Eve, 1958. Traffic snarled the Sunset Strip, as boisterous partygoers made their way toward the glittering nightclubs to join the gala festivities. On a hillside overlooking the Strip, Anna Kashfi, lovely Indian actress, and wife of Marlon Brando, quietly checked into Chateau Marmont with their seven-month-old son, Christian Devi. A taxi had delivered them from their home atop Mulholland Drive, where, not much earlier, a heated argument had taken place.

Since their marriage in October of the previous year, the papers had been full of stories about the Brandos and their stormy off-and-on relationship, reports of violent brawls and subsequent reconciliations. As Anna complained about her husband's increasingly distant and uncommunicative nature, Hollywood gossiped about his newfound interest in the beautiful Eurasian actress, France Nuyen. Marlon countered that his wife was having "a serious affair" with her *Night of the Quarter Moon* co-star, young John Barrymore, Jr. It seemed the Brandos had more dirty linen than a laundromat. The columnists had a field day.

The months of headlines had fueled Marlon Brando's reputation as the rebellious, non-conforming prototype of the 1950s "Beat Generation," an image not too far removed from the wild and brutish characters he portrayed so successfully on the screen. All too often, he was being depicted as a real-life Stanley Kowalski, a modern day Zapata. Cruel, heartless, uncaring. The suffering Anna, fed up with his antics, labeled him "a solipsist." She would later claim that he had been so shaken by one of her "escapes" from their Mulholland Drive home that he had mounted one of her used sanitary napkins and nailed it to his bedroom wall.

By the time Marlon checked into the Marmont in December, 1959, Anna was long gone. Their marriage was over (they had been divorced since April), but the brawling Brandos had remained in the spotlight. There had been non-stop court battles over visitation rights to their son, as well as endless allegations of beatings, uncontrolled rampages, and general harassment. While that was going on, he had been faced with unforeseen problems (and interminable delays) during the production of his latest film, *One-Eyed Jacks,* on which he functioned not only as star but producer and director. It was a challenging assignment that tested his temperament and sparked a few well-reported outbursts. One paper had told its readers that he was "spreading himself too thin with too many responsibilities." Another had him "on the brink of nervous collapse." The Marmont staff was steeled for the worst.

"We really didn't know what to expect from Mr. Brando," Corinne Patten used to tell her friends. "We had heard all the stories about his temper tantrums and his violent moods. To tell the truth, when he first came to the hotel, no one wanted to have anything to do with him. He had a look that said 'Stay away.' " He made it easy to do just that.

It is doubtful many people knew Brando was at the Marmont. He received few phone calls (which were screened at his request), and he responded to even fewer. Nor did he stray far from his second-floor suite. For a time, according to Corinne, he was "practically invisible. There were days when no one saw him at all. He just seemed content to remain behind closed doors." He probably wouldn't have been "content" had he known that his quarters, 2G, were directly adjacent to 2F, which had been occupied earlier by Mrs. Brando and little Christian. The potentially touchy arrangement had been purely accidental.

Carmel Volti remembers Brando as being "quiet and withdrawn," a loner who kept very much to himself. So it came as something of a shock when she received a call from him late one evening. She was working the switchboard at the time; Brando wanted her to come to his suite during her break. He didn't explain why, but she agreed anyway, mainly because he sounded "so troubled."

When Carmel arrived at 2G, sometime later, she found the actor not only troubled but "very agitated. He seemed desperate for a sympathetic ear. He needed to talk with someone. Anyone."

Carmel stayed with Brando throughout her scheduled break, and longer, listening to him elaborate on his problems. "He was very perturbed over his ex-wife," she remembers. "He seemed most concerned that she might try to exploit their relationship by writing a book. He didn't want that. He intimated that he was prepared to offer her money *not* to write it." His fears proved to be accurate, though somewhat premature. Twenty years would pass before the publication of Anna Kashfi's stinging *Breakfast with Brando*.

In time, Marlon Brando gained the friendship and admiration of other staff members. Manager Meemi Ferguson became most fond of him. "Marlon was going through an extremely difficult period when he came to the Marmont," she recounted later. "But he was never the raucous bad boy we had heard so much about. To the contrary, he was always subdued, always so kind and thoughtful. Quite the gentleman."

He was also generous. When he departed the hotel for Tahiti to film scenes for *Mutiny on the Bounty,* he presented the staff—everyone he came to know—with handwritten notes of thanks, as well as gifts of money and expensive jewelry. Said Meemi, "He went out of his way to be nice. He may have had us shaking when he arrived, but he had us in the palms of his hands when he left."

# Mr. & Mrs. Muni

Paul Muni, the distinguished stage and screen actor, checked into the Marmont on March 19, 1958, following a highly praised *tour de force* performance on television's premiere drama series, *Playhouse 90.* It wasn't that the sixty-two-year-old Muni's role in the live production had been that demanding as much as the manner in which he had pulled it off. As one critic put it, "He unbagged more tricks in his ninety minutes than I have ever seen over a comparable period on TV." Because Muni was no longer able to memorize his pages of dialogue and he was unable to read the Teleprompter because of failing vision, director George Roy Hill ingeniously suggested outfitting Muni's character with a hearing aid, through which he could feed Muni his lines. The idea worked brilliantly. Muni's slight pauses to listen to Hill before reciting his speeches, filled in with such "tricks" as impromptu smacks of his lips, a tug at his vest, a scratch of his head or hands, were thought to be masterful touches of drama.

Now the veteran actor was in Hollywood to begin rehearsals on a new venture. He had signed to play an aging song and dance man in the musical version of Vicki Baum's venerable *Grand Hotel,* retitled *At the Grand,* to be presented by the Los Angeles Civic Light Opera Association. Muni had taken the role, played in the classic 1932 film drama by Lionel Barrymore, at the urging of his wife, Bella, who longed to see him strutting around a stage again in white tie and tails. She had fallen in love with him during his early days with the Yiddish Art Theater, nearly forty years before. That's how she remembered her "Munya" best. That's how she had to see him once more.

At first, Muni seemed pleased that he had given in to his wife's wishes. He departed the Marmont each morning—followed closely by Bella, who rarely let him out of her sight—with a smile on his face and a doff of his hat for anyone he happened to see. Says a former garage boy, "Mr. Muni was a kindly gentlemen of the old school, very well mannered and very proper. As anxious as he was to get to work, he would go out of his way to say hello and wish everyone well."

Afternoons found the Munis eagerly rushing back to their spacious fifth-floor suite, the small penthouse, where the actor conscientiously prepared for the following day's rehearsal. As was his custom, he worked with multiple tape recorders, reciting his lines and playing them back, over and over again, usually at full volume, late into the night. One of his neighbors sarcastically remarked that he easily qualified as Muni's stand-in. "I know all the lines backward and forward," he said, half smiling. "I should, I've heard them enough."

It took less than a week of rehearsing with the cast for Muni's enthusiasm to fade. He had no quarrel with his role, he said; he loved the challenge it afforded him, and the welcome change of pace. But the show itself, as it began to unfold, was proving distasteful. Much of the dialogue, spoken by others in the cast, offended his puritannical heart, and the revealing costumes worn by the dancers shocked him.

Most disheartening was his belief that the show's director, Albert Marre, and his wife, Joan Diener, were plotting against him. Muni was certain that Marre was purposely flaunting Diener's wildly bloated bosom (witnesses reported that she made the reigning cleavage queen, Jayne Mansfield, look like a toddler) to make his life miserable. There was no way for Muni to avoid Miss Diener. She was his co-star, cast in the role Greta Garbo had played in the film version.

Muni protested loudly. He ordered script rewrites. He demanded costume changes. He succeeded only in antagonizing not only the creative staff but also his fellow cast members.

The tension that pervaded the rehearsal hall quickly spread to the Marmont. No longer was Paul Muni the mild-mannered, gentle man—or even the gentleman—he at first appeared to be. He walked gruffly through the corridors, as if he were headed for death row. His morning departures were cheerless, his expression frozen with gloom. He rarely had time for anyone. When he did, he made no attempt to hide his unhappiness. The desk clerk was only a nodding acquaintance, but she knew more about *At the Grand*—a distorted view, surely, of the backbiting, in-fighting and chaos—than many people connected with the show.

Muni's evenings were no better than his days. Night after sleepless night, he roamed the rooms of his suite, shouting into tape recorders while sidestepping the French doors that opened onto his wrap-around terrace. The view had become especially distasteful lately. The sparkling lights of the city below were breathtaking, but Muni could not see past the floodlighted Sahara billboard, with its scantily clad showgirl. Round and round she twirled, flaunting every inch of her curvaceous anatomy. "It's the whore Hollywood!" he bellowed. "The whore show business!" His cries could be heard all the way down on Marmont Lane.

Following one particularly stressful evening, Muni summoned *At the Grand's* creative team to his suite. Not much later, Albert Marre, Robert Wright, George Forrest, and Luther Davis marched through the Marmont lobby and made their way upstairs to meet with their increasingly temperamental star. They were not seen again for over three hours. They departed with "dumbstruck looks on their faces."

A friend close to Mrs. Muni at the hotel later confided to Corinne Patten that "the emergency session went nowhere. Paul wanted the men to hear his suggestion on how to improve the show—ramblings he had recorded during the night—but his tapes offered little, other than long drawn-out pauses. Only once did Paul say something really constructive—but it was hardly earth-shattering. In fact, one of the men told Paul he had been given similar advice while attending a university drama school. With that, Paul's face turned sour and he rushed from the room. Everyone but Bella believed Paul had suddenly become ill. Bella knew better. She simply excused her husband by saying, 'It upsets him to be reminded that you went to college and he didn't.' "

Ads touting the July 7 "World Premiere" of *At the Grand*—and its illustrous star, Paul Muni—generated heavy interest despite negative reports of "troubles behind the scenes." Fed with backstage gossip from insiders, columnists seemed delighted in telling their readers that all was not right with the production. Until opening night, however, no one could have guessed the extent of the difficulties. There were unexpected problems with the huge sets, and the theater's enormous revolving stages, used for the many changes in scenery, didn't always work smoothly. There was also a bomb threat.

When the reviews were in, Muni was singled out for his usual bravado performance. But there were few cheers for *At the Grand*. Critics labeled it "tedious" and "less than grand." Still, business was brisk, thanks to the Civic Light Opera Association's impressive list of subscribers and heavy advance ticket sales.

The show ended its run in August, and the Munis departed the Marmont for San Francisco, where *At the Grand* was scheduled to play through early September. "Mr. Muni was very upset when he left," Meemi Ferguson said. "He looked so tired and disillusioned. He had given his all, but that wasn't enough. The poor man wasn't accustomed to being in anything but a critical success."

Everyone at the Marmont followed the fortunes of *At the Grand* during its San Francisco run. They read of frantic efforts to revamp the production, rewrites, and changes. As in Los Angeles, theatergoers ignored the notices and flocked to see Paul Muni in a musical. The response was heartening, bolstering hopes of taking the show to Broadway. But Muni had had enough. He wanted out, and he got his way. Without its star, *At the Grand* went nowhere.

Fortunately, Paul Muni was not left to dwell on what he termed "an ugly experience." While still in San Francisco, he signed to appear as the aging slum doctor in the film version of *The Last Angry Man*. It would be his last screen appearance, and one of his strongest, earning him a fifth Academy Award nomination.

Vivien Leigh's suite at the Marmont
held a secret she thought no one would
discover.

Warren Beatty—locked out.

# Chapter 10

## The Party's Over

## Mr. Beatty

Dozens of struggling young actors have migrated to Chateau Marmont over the years, but the least known—and believed least to succeed—was a handsome, bespectacled, twenty-two-year-old named Warren Beatty. (One of his challengers for that dubious honor was an unknown Dustin Hoffman, who stayed at the Marmont in 1967, after just having finished filming *The Graduate*. Instant stardom was ahead, but until the picture opened, he lived in obscurity, waiting for offers and collecting his weekly pittance from the unemployment office to pay his rent.)

Warren Beatty checked into the Marmont on June 22, 1959, hoping to start a career in films. He had made the usual tests, but his experience had been limited to stock and minor appearances on television. Prior to that, he had been a bricklayer's assistant, construction worker, and sandbagger on New York's Lincoln Tunnel project, after dropping out of college (Northwestern) following his freshman year. His greatest claim to fame was that he was in the running for the lead in William Inge's play, *A Loss of Roses*.

The people who knew Warren Beatty at the Marmont say he displayed a confidence far beyond his years. Corinne Patten used to tell her friends about "the nice young man in 1F." She admired his ambition and chastised anyone who even suggested that he might be a trifle arrogant. "There's nothing wrong with being sure of yourself," she would say. "He simply knows what he wants and where he's going."

Unfortunately, he wasn't going much of anywhere. That's not to say he idled away his time. Corinne was constantly intrigued by the number of female visitors who passed through the door of his bachelor quarters. She could understand the attraction. Whenever she spoke of Warren, she frequently fluttered over words like "boyish charm" and "adorable." She avoided any reference to his virility; she was much too proper for that.

Meemi Ferguson tended to take a more critical view of his activities, particularly with Dr. Popper hovering about. She liked Warren, and she went overboard to help him by not pressing to collect his overdue bills. She knew he was in dire financial straits, unable to keep current on his eight dollar-a-day tab (the hotel's lowest rate at the time). Never mind the extra charges for the continuous phone calls. "That Warren," she would say with a tsk! tsk! in her voice. "He's an absolute phoneaholic!" He was, too. He could barely function without a telephone in his hand. It was his security blanket.

The penurious Dr. Popper did not take kindly to bending rules when it came to delinquent accounts. He made exceptions, of course, but never, never for nameless, unemployed actors. Had he known about Warren's precarious situation—and growing debt to the hotel—he would have clamped down immediately. But Meemi so filled him with optimistic fabrications about Warren that she almost had herself believing her chatter. When she wasn't making up stories about calls from producers and interviews Warren had lined up, she was fantasizing about his future. Her favorite line, which she repeated at frequent intervals for Dr. Popper's benefit, was, "He's so much talent in one person. He's going to make it big one of these days."

But Warren wasn't making it, except in his overactive social life. He was raising everthing but the money to pay his past-due bills.

One evening, Warren returned to the Marmont to discover that he couldn't get into his room. It seemed something was wrong with the door lock—or the key. He tried again and again, but he couldn't get either one to work; the door simply wouldn't open.

He double-checked the lock and found that someone had tampered with it. He stood for a moment, puzzled. Then, his anger mounting, he made his way to the front desk. "What's the meaning of this?" he demanded to know from Mrs. Volti.

Carmel knew full well, but she wouldn't say. Instead she tried to pacify him by putting in a call for Meemi Ferguson.

By the time Meemi arrived, Warren was seething. Her news didn't make him feel any better. "Dr. Popper was going through the books today," she told him, almost apologetically, "and he came across your account." She shrugged and added, "He had me install a lockout key in your door. I'm sorry, but that's policy."

"What am I supposed to do?" Warren asked, defeated.

"Pay your account," Meemi said. "I can't let you in until you do."

Warren stared at Meemi through narrowed eyes. "Just you wait!" he bellowed. "One of these days I'm going to buy this goddam joint and have you fired!"

Meemi disappeared for a moment; when she returned, she had a plan. If Warren could offer some collateral—anything—to show his good faith, she would see that he gained access to his room.

He had nothing of value. But he did have one cherished possession, a big old-fashioned radio, which he agreed to hand over. Meemi accepted it gladly. "It was huge," remembers Meemi's granddaughter, Connie, "about three feet long and a foot high, made of light blond wood and covered with knobs—really ugly, but Meemi loved it so much that Warren never got it back. It stayed in our family for years, until it got too heavy to lug around."

Warren Beatty never carried out his threat to buy the Marmont, although that wouldn't have been an impossibility following his string of film successes that began in 1961. Nor did he harbor any resentment over the lockout incident. Over the years, he continued to return to the hotel, living with Joan Collins for a time in one of the upper-floor suites, as well as visiting the succeeding ladies in his life—Julie Christie and Diane Keaton, who registered on his recommendation.

# The Oliviers

When Sir Laurence Olivier arrived in Hollywood to begin his role as Marcus Crassus in Universal's epic, *Spartacus,* it was widely rumored that he had moved in with art director Roger Furse and his wife, Inez. There was no reason to question the reports. Olivier and Furse had been longtime friends and associates. Furse had worked as set designer on Olivier's Shakespearean productions at the Old Vic Theater and as art director on several of Olivier's films, including the Academy Award-winning *Hamlet.* If Olivier did stay with the Furses, it wasn't for long. On April 8, 1959, he checked into a $425 a month suite—5F—at the Chateau Marmont. There he would remain until the early days of June.

Tracking the peripatetic Olivier has created some confusion over the years. This item turned up in a by-lined *New York Times* article: "When he was a young man and making his first trip to Hollywood in the late 1930s, Laurence Olivier found a note waiting for him at the Chateau Marmont on Sunset Boulevard, where he was staying. It was from C. Aubrey Smith, then the ranking British actor on the scene. It read: 'There will be set practice tomorrow afternoon at 4 p.m.. I trust I shall see you there!' " The hotel's records do not show Laurence Olivier as ever having been a registered guest during the 1930s.

Stories on Olivier's living arrangements were of marginal interest, however, compared to other published revelations concerning his personal life. Not many months earlier, the public had read with disbelief that he had asked his wife, Vivien Leigh, for a divorce. There was even talk that he would marry another actress, young Joan Plowright. Millions of moviegoers wondered how he could abandon the frail and often sickly, lovely woman who would remain forever Scarlett O'Hara in their hearts. The Oliviers—Laurence and Vivien—were legend, an historic pair. It seemed unthinkable that one of the world's great romances was over.

While others speculated about Olivier's future with Joan Plowright, he remained silent, even with his wife. He later confessed that, during one of their final sentimental moments together—the occasion was Leigh's forty-fifth birthday in November—"I was able to talk calmly to her, lying that there was no question of anyone else in my life. I just knew that our relationship must come to an end. I said we should take advantage of the separation that was forced on us by my approaching departure to Hollywood for *Spartacus* to learn to accept the situation."

Olivier had arrived in the film capital earlier than expected, to confer with blacklisted screenwriter Dalton Trumbo (writing under the pseudonym, Sam Jackson), in the hope of expanding his rather limited role in the film. Joan Plowright did not accompany him; she was appearing with Robert Morley in a play, *Hook, Line and Sinker,* in London.

At the Marmont, Olivier was said to be "very kind and friendly," despite having to "constantly avoid the press." Had he been busier, his stay might have been more enjoyable, but long delays during the filming of the multi-million-dollar spectacle made it seem interminable. "Nearly eight weeks passed," he reflected in his memoirs, "before I found myself dressed, made up with applied classical-shaped nose, coiffured, and ready to portray the part . . . , which God knows, I'd had time enough to learn. It was a good thing that Joan and I had made up our minds to a long parting . . . There was nothing for me but to wait to be called and enjoy the rich company of my Hollywood friendships." There were also letters to read from London, which arrived daily, and occasional overseas calls to ease the painful separation.

Laurence Olivier departed the Marmont for England on June 4, 1959. Thirteen months later, almost to the day, Vivien Leigh signed in. She had arrived from New York with her cat Poo Jones, for a four-week stay, while appearing in a play, *Duel of Angels,* at the Hollywood Playhouse.

The last time Vivien Leigh had visited Hollywood was in 1953. She was then in the midst of filming *Elephant Walk,* with scenes still to be shot on the Paramount lot, after weeks on location in and out of the stifling jungles of Ceylon, an island off the tip of India. Her delicate condition had made it difficult for her to cope with the demanding role and strenuous schedule. She became hysterical without warning. She had turned to alcohol to calm her frazzled nerves. Ultimately, she was forced to withdraw from the film and had to be flown out of Hollywood under sedation (some say in a straightjacket). Elizabeth Taylor, nearly twenty years her junior, was hired to replace her.

Vivien Leigh was troubled on her latest visit to Hollywood as well. The failure of her marriage, made publicly official during the New York run of her play, gnawed at her. She was still tied to Olivier—the divorce had not yet been granted—but in name only. She was under the constant supervision of a doctor and reportedly receiving shock treatments.

Working in *Duel of Angels* had been a tonic of sorts for Vivien. She had grown close to her costar, Jack Merivale, an actor she had known since 1940, when they appeared together, along with Olivier, in the touring *Romeo and Juliet.* Merivale was the lean and handsome stepson of dignified British actress and beauty, Gladys Cooper. At the Marmont, Vivien Leigh and Jack Merivale occupied adjoining fifth-floor suites.

Word around the hotel that summer of 1960 was that Leigh and her stage husband were more than workmates."They seemed very close," an intimate and fellow guest from England recalls, "quite inseparable." Indeed, they were rarely apart. They shared meals together, often at the nearby house of director George Cukor. They strolled arm in arm through the hotel's gardens, and spent long moments gazing at the "luscious view" from her terrace. They even planned to travel to San Francisco, where *Duel of Angels* would continue its run, apart from the other cast members, in Vivien's sleek new Thunderbird. The car, she admitted, was a gift to herself on being offered the title role in the forthcoming film of Tennessee Williams' *The Roman Spring of Mrs. Stone.* The thought of portraying another

Williams' heroine on screen thrilled her. In 1951, his Blanche du Bois creation for *A Streetcar Named Desire* had earned her a second Academy Award.

According to onlookers, Vivien Leigh did everything possible to make it appear that she and Merivale were "mad about each other." She even told a visiting columnist that she was "completely over Larry and hopelessly in love with Jack." Insiders at the Marmont knew better, particularly Corinne Patten, who all but dedicated her waking hours to becoming friendly with Leigh, long one of her favorites. Their moments alone together—without Merivale's lingering presence—were rare, but the two women chatted on at least two occasions in the main-floor drawing room.

"Our conversations invariably turned to Mr. Olivier," Corinne reported. "She was utterly preoccupied with him, and not in a nasty way. Her every other word was 'my Larry.' Always 'my Larry.' The only resentment she harbored was against those who criticized him for abandoning her. It upset her if anyone spoke about him in a negative way. And no wonder—she still loved him. All that talk about her and Mr. Merivale was just that. No matter what she wanted everyone to believe, her heart belonged to Mr. Olivier." Corinne didn't think it the least bit odd that Leigh still referred to herself as Lady Olivier—or that her hotel registration card bore the signature, Vivien Leigh Olivier.

Few people relied on Corinne as a source for reliable information. She was known to exaggerate at times, even fabricate, when it came to the retelling of her "intimate" conversations with the stars. But this time there was little reason not to believe her. One of the maids inadvertently helped to substantiate her story, after making an innocent discovery. The maid told of a magnificent painting on display in Vivien Leigh's living room. She felt certain it didn't belong to the Chateau, as she had never seen it before during her rounds. It turned out to be an original Renoir that Leigh had brought with her from England. Said the actress later, "I thought I might need something to brighten my hotel rooms in America, a touch of home."

Corinne *had* to see the painting. She got her chance one quiet afternoon, while Leigh and Merivale were visiting friends.

The fifth-floor maid accompanied Corinne inside Leigh's suite, 5D; they went directly to the living room to view the painting, passing a docile Poo Jones along the way. What really caught her eye were the other personal objects on display—beautifully framed photos of Laurence Olivier that crowded virtually every flat surface in sight. She found them on bookshelves, table tops, cabinets, the fireplace mantel—handsome images in profile and full face, in casual dress and ornate costumes.

Fascinated, and somewhat overcome by Olivier's "presence," as she described it, Corinne began wandering from room to room, only to discover similar displays at every turn. It wasn't until she reached the bedroom, however, that she was moved to tears. Instead of masses of photos, the room contained just one, a loving dual portrait of the golden couple—Vivien and Laurence—taken during happier days. It was set in a sparkling silver frame placed on the bedstand adjacent to Leigh's pillow. Commented Corinne, dolefully: "The picture was the first thing she saw each morning—and the last thing she saw each night."

# Mr. & Mrs. Flynn

Errol Flynn, his wife, Patrice Wymore, and four-year-old daughter, Arnella, were living at the Garden of Allah in 1957, when the roguish actor, best known for his amorous off-screen escapades and barroom brawls, was offered a major role in Darryl F. Zanuck's production of Hemingway's *The Sun Also Rises*. The film was to be shot on location in Mexico. Taking the part meant months of separation for Flynn and his family, but his wife begged him to accept. It wasn't that she wanted him to go; he simply had no choice. Errol Flynn hadn't been in a successful picture in years. He was deeply in debt. And she could no longer tolerate watching him wasting his days, destroying his health with alcohol. His problem, he admitted, was in reconciling "my gross habits with my net income."

Flynn's troubles began in the late 1940s, as his career began to fade. Always a heavy drinker and smoker, he began to experiment with drugs as well. In 1949, his marriage to Nora Edington ended, and the following year he married actress Wymore. Without work and financially strapped, an embittered Flynn departed for Europe, where he hoped to play off his former fame. The few films he made overseas were failures. To make matters worse, he invested his recently earned capital in an ill-fated historical epic, *William Tell*, which was never completed. Then the United States Government brought charges against him, claiming over $800,000 in unpaid back taxes. He began to disappear for long stretches, taking refuge aboard his yacht, the *Zaca*, as he cruised aimlessly around the Mediterranean in a futile attempt to escape his troubles.

Flynn's offer from Zanuck came shortly after his return to Hollywood, following his self-imposed exile. The role of the drunken wastrel, Mike

Campbell, in the Hemingway classic was tailor made for the forty-nine-year-old star, whose once dashing looks had been described as "disarmingly handsome." Now his face was puffy and lined, his eyes deadened with sadness.

*The Sun Also Rises* brought Flynn his first rave notices in years and led to another bit of perfect casting, a portrayal of his hard-drinking friend from past days, John Barrymore, in the film *Too Much Too Soon*. It was Flynn's old boss, Jack Warner who had first thought of Flynn for the role. Later Warner commented: "He came back to the lot, but I could not bear to watch him struggle through take after take. He was playing the part of a drunken actor, and he didn't need any method system to get him in the mood. He *was* drunk. *Too Much Too Soon*. The words should have been carved on a tombstone at the time, for he was one of the living dead."

During the filming at Warner Bros., Flynn was introduced to blonde Beverly Aadland, a pretty, bright, fifteen-year-old, who was working at the studio as a bit player in the new Natalie Wood picture, *Marjorie Morningstar*. As Flynn's career—and interest in Aadland—escalated, his marriage fell apart. Patrice Wymore had remained with her husband through his most agonizing years. She summed up their life together by saying, "I wish I could hate him, but I can't. He could charm the birds out of the trees, but he was an adventurer with people . . ., he loved to tease. Looking back, I don't think he should ever have gotten married. He was too mercurial . . . I felt out of it completely."

No formal announcement of a separation was forthcoming. Wymore simply packed her bags and, with little Arnella in hand, departed the Garden of Allah. On May 17, 1958, they moved across the street to the Chateau Marmont.

It was impossible for Flynn to settle down. He drank his way from city to city, even country to country, in search of work—always with his young companion, Miss Aadland, at his side. Following much publicized treks to France and Africa (for the *Roots of Heaven*) and the Caribbean (for his disastrous semi-documentary, *Cuban Rebel Girls*), the couple returned to Hollywood, where Flynn was scheduled for several television appearances. He told a local interviewer who questioned his unorthodox behavior, "I never thought the public would be interested in my so-called antics [so] . . . I've lived hard, spent hard, and behaved as I damn well chose. You'd think I'd be ready for the wheelchair after the last twenty years of hell-raising, but I never felt better." The truth was, his doctor had given him less than a year to live.

When Flynn and young Aadland arrived in Los Angeles, she was wearing an engagement ring. He was determined to marry the teenager, but that was impossible, with Wymore blocking his way. She had yet to file for divorce, despite on-going reminders of Hollywood's latest—and steamiest—May/December romance.

One evening in early October, 1959, a raging Errol Flynn stormed into the Marmont, demanding to see Patrice Wymore. He had been drinking. His bloated body trembled as he spit out garbled commands. "He was in a terrible state," Carmel Volti remembers. "I've never seen such a reprobate in all my life!"

Carmel put in a call to Wymore in Bungalow C, more to alert her to the arrival of her drunken husband than to announce him. No one answered. "She's not in," Carmel told the staggering Flynn. He stared angrily at Carmel for an instant, then turned on unsteady legs and made his way toward the stairway leading to the garage.

He hadn't been gone ten minutes when word reached the front desk that "a bellowing lunatic" was trying to break into Bungalow C. He had tried to force his way through the front door, the caller reported, and was now attempting to get inside through a bathroom window.

Two houseboys were sent to Wymore's bungalow. They found no one there.

A few minutes later, Flynn reappeared in the lobby. He was drenched in persipiration, his complexion was gray. "He could barely walk," Carmel says, "but that didn't stop him from holloring at everyone he saw. Oh, what a commotion he made! It was so sad to see him that way. To think that he was once a dashing matinee idol."

On October 14, less than a week after his futile visit to the Marmont, Errol Flynn was jolted by a sharp pain, so sharp that he lapsed into unconsciousness. He was dead within hours.

## Goodbye To The Garden

On the morning of April 12, 1959, the Los Angeles papers broke the news that the Garden of Allah, the once-glorious haven for many Hollywood notables, was to be sold by owners, Morris Markowitz and Mrs. Beatrice Rosenus. The story wasn't particularly surprising. Markowitz and Rosenus had been undecided for some time whether to invest in a much-needed renovation or divest themselves of the fading Sunset Boulevard property.

The decision was made for them when Markowitz's financial backer died suddenly. What followed came as a surprise, particularly to everyone close to the storied Garden. A *Los Angeles Times* announcement in June read: "The Garden of Allah, once an oasis, awaits Kismet. The day of its grandeur was awesome, but it will be razed in September to make way for Lytton [Savings & Loan]."

In its heyday, the Garden of Allah was a Hollywood landmark. As one West Coast writer noted, "It would have stood out for any one of many things—high prices, illustrious patrons, agreeable design, wild parties, and zany shenanigans. But taking all its attributes together, it was truly unique." Following World War II, however, the Garden began to fall on hard times. Its picturesque villas and bungalows, while rarely unoccupied, attracted fewer long-term guests than one-nighters. Its dimly-lit terraced bar, once a hangout for filmdom's elite, had become a haven for hookers and neighborhood elbow-benders. Harold Ross, one-time editor of *The New Yorker*, labeled the Garden "a pesthole of pettifogging vaudeville actors and fallen women."

The Garden of Allah may have been doomed, but it wasn't dead—not yet anyway. In 1927, the Garden had opened with a rip-roaring Hollywood party; Markowitz wanted it to end the same way. He invited three-hundred and fifty guests, requesting that they attend dressed as glamorous stars of the Twenties who had attended the christening; such luminaries as Rudolph Valentino, Clara Bow, Charlie Chaplin, Mae West, Lon Chaney, and shimmy queen, Gilda Gray.

Markowitz's guests arrived, plus about six-hundred outsiders who "crashed" the festivities, including dozens of barely dressed starlets hoping to catch the attention of studio bigwigs. Even Lee Francis, Hollywood's reigning madam, made a rare public appearance. She too came looking for business, flanked by several of her loveliest girls. She knew the territory. In the old days, many of her clients, Hollywood's top stars, would frequent her establishments on their way to the Garden for cocktails.

By midnight, the enormous Garden pool was bobbing with empty liquor bottles, soggy hors d'oeurves, and assorted pieces of clothing. Luckily, *Life* magazine had sent a photographer to capture some of the action for its popular feature, *"Life Goes To A Party."* It was the costume ball to end all.

The next day, a public auction was held to sell the surviving furnishings and fixtures. Errol Flynn's bed received the greatest attention.

All but one of the Garden's residents had departed willingly. Patricia Medina, the beautiful English actress, was the lone holdout. Even with the threat of an oncoming wrecker's ball, Medina couldn't bear leaving her cozy cottage, which she had occupied since 1951.

In desperation, she contacted Morris Markowitz and told him that she wanted to buy her bungalow. She had thought of relocating it at the beach, if possible. She didn't have a specific spot in mind, but that was beside the point. At zero hour, she was grabbing at straws.

Markowitz offered no hope. "It's too late," he told her, "the wreckers are coming tomorrow."

She called the company handling the demolition, hoping to work something out. She talked to the man in charge, who promised to send out a representative first thing in the morning. A young man did arrive, but too late, as Markowitz had warned. "As we talked," Medina recalled, "every bungalow, all of them empty of furniture, including mine, was being bulldozed to the ground. I realized there was nothing I could do, so I collected my clothes, put them over my arm, and walked across Sunset Boulevard to Chateau Marmont."

Chateau Marmont, early 1960s.

# PART IV

# CHANGING TIMES

# CHANGING TIMES

In the early spring of 1960, Corinne Patten stood quietly at the outer edge of the Marmont's front lawn, overlooking Sunset Boulevard. Seeing "that hideous thing"—the Sahara billboard—made her fume. And now, across the way, she faced a gaping hole in the ground where, only months earlier, the charming Garden of Allah had brightened her view. Corinne did not like what was happening along the Strip. Indeed, she thought even less of the changes taking place throughout her beloved Hollywood.

Once again, Hollywood was in transition. A deadly atmosphere permeated the town. The breakup of the studio system was in full swing. The majority of stars were no longer under contract, and fewer of the old guard—the legendary moguls—remained. Independent productions were becoming firmly established. "Hollywood glamor," once the industry's trademark, was giving way to a new on-screen permissiveness. More and more films were being shot on location, away from once-busy sound stages, leaving increasing numbers of local actors and technicians out of work.

If it weren't for television, observors noted, Hollywood might fade away. Thank God for television. And the music industry. And tourists.

It seemed inconceivable that the news could get more alarming. Yet the worst was still to come. Hollywood, like the rest of the nation, would soon be rocked by one devastating happening after another: the Cuban missile crisis; equal rights demonstrations; the assassinations of President John F. Kennedy, Martin Luther King, Jr., and Senator Robert Kennedy; the escalating war in Vietnam; and anti-war riots.

Corinne Patten did not often stray to the outer reaches of the Marmont property. She preferred staying within the hotel, shutting herself away from the fast-changing outside world. At the Marmont, almost everyone felt, time stood still.

But even within the fortress-like walls of the hotel, unexpected changes were taking place. In 1961, Scotty Thompson died suddenly. The garage boys all turned out for his funeral, serving as pallbearers, honoring the man who had been so influential in their lives. It was a small funeral, held not far from Scotty's home. Screenwriter Anne Morrison Chapin was there, squired by her chauffeur. Carmel Volti came with Gene Gordon. Red, the mechanic, showed up alone, looking strangely presentable. As someone remarked, "He scrubbed down real good."

"Scott Thompson had a strong moral texture that somehow rubbed off on all of us, "Morgan Cavett said later. Added Tom Wheat: "If it hadn't been for Scotty, there would have been four very strong juvenile delinquents running around Hollywood. But he sure kept us in line."

Following Scotty's death, the garage boys began drifting away from the Marmont to pursue other interests. Cavett went on to make a name for himself in the recording industry, as discoverer and record producer for the Captain and Tennille, among others; Tom Wheat became associated with one of Southern California's top real estate firms; Ken Schwarz followed in his father's footsteps as a studio technician. The last anyone heard from Pete Dickel was years ago, when he joined the Air Force.

The news of Scotty's death shattered Meemi Ferguson. Not many months later, she too became a casualty, of sorts.

During the summer of 1962, after years of dreaming of a European vacation, Meemi called her travel agent and packed her bags. When Jolie Gabor, recently married to handsome Hungarian Edmund De Szigethy, heard about Meemi's plans, she told another staff member that Meemi's money would be better spent on a face lift. The comment soon got back to Meemi, but she ignored it. (The two women were actually quite close. Meemi had once told a mutual friend: "Her girls may never amount to anything, but I really like their mother.") Meemi should have paid attention to Jolie Gabor's remark, because she returned from Europe to find herself out of a job.

"While Meemi was away," a former co-worker reported, "the relief switchboard operator plotted against her. The woman wanted Meemi's job, so she filled Dr. Popper's head with a pack of lies. Meemi had been such a wonderful manager—a real workhorse and a doll. There wasn't anything she wouldn't do for the hotel and the guests. She even did all her own typing. But Dr. Popper never appreciated her. He thought she was too frivolous. So when he heard the trumped up story from the relief operator, he believed her. It was her word against the rest of the staff, but all he would say was 'I don't want to hear about it!' He had the excuse he needed to fire her."

The "pack of lies" concerned a piano that was given to Meemi as a gift. Over the years, she had been lavished with any number of expensive presents from guests and admirers—such valuables as a white 1956 Buick, a mink coat, a Baroque pearl necklace from Jolie Gabor, and a glittering crystal bracelet from Marlon Brando (which she wore to "spark up" her jump suit)—who preferred tipping with something personal rather than money. The relief operator claimed that Meemi had taken the piano from socialite Virginia Burroughs' suite when Burroughs died, and that the piano belonged not to Burroughs but to the hotel. The truth was, the piano *did* belong to Burroughs. She had willed it to Donald Spackman, a "gentleman farmer" from Pennsylvania, who, in turn, had given it to Meemi. Spackman thought the world of Meemi Ferguson. "She *was* the Marmont", he once commented.

No one ever accused Dr. Popper of being a compassionate man, but for some reason he offered Meemi free lodging for one year to compensate for her loss of position. Perhaps he felt he had acted in haste, after other staff members rallied to Meemi's defense. She accepted and, along with her two cats, Mitzie and Pinkie, moved into the only available space, a large restroom off the main-floor breakfast nook. Meemi wasted little time in transforming the lavatory into a stunning little suite, complete with a piano, two television sets, and two couches. "Twice a year," recalled her granddaughter, Connie, "Meemi bought bolts of yardage in little checks and flowers, all different designs and patterns, and had one of the maids, Lila Mae, whip up curtains, slipcovers, pillowcases, everything. One season the room would be all in yellow, the next all in blue, or green, or whatever. Meemi was so proud of her place that she was always having her friends in, especially the two English girls, Ann Todd and Glynis Johns."

For nearly a decade, Meemi Ferguson, Carmel Volti, and Corinne Patten had been a team. Charles Boyer, Franchot Tone, and Duke Ellington spoke adoringly about the three ladies of the Marmont. Carroll Baker, touched by their warmth, regarded them as "adopted aunts." Marlon Brando and Greta Garbo fell under their spell, as did almost everyone who knew them. Now the trio had been reduced to a duo. Meemi may have been cut from the staff, but Corinne and Carmel carried on.

Carmel's unaffected natural charm and easygoing way made her a favorite with the Marmont's celebrity clientele. In turn, she was captivated by show business and the people who made movies. Working the night shift, doubling at times as desk clerk, she met them all. "It was wonderful seeing and knowing all the great stars," she said, reeling off a few select names: Harlow, Monroe, Hayworth, Bea Lillie, and Dorothy Parker. They, and others, would often stop to chat with her late in the evening when they were least involved, and most lonely. They confided in her to such a point that Paul Newman began referring to her as "boss." Tony Perkins ("that little rascal") jokingly nicknamed her "Madam Spy." Sitting crosslegged on the front desk counter, he repeatedly tried to pump her for information with a sly smile and an inquiring, "What's new?"

Few guests could resist Carmel's gracious charm—or her occasional display of free spirit. She could be outrageously candid. When Shirley Booth (at the Marmont throughout her long-running television series, *Hazel*) paraded before her, modeling a new coiffure—only to confess that she was wearing a wig—Carmel chastised her. "Never tell anyone *that*!" she scolded.

"Let people think it's your own hair."

Corinne Paten would have been more tactful with Miss Booth. She might even have told her a tale or two. No story was too wild for Corinne. Hardly a day passed that she didn't record at least one happening in her crowded Marmont journal. Her celebrity photo album was growing considerably thicker too, and it didn't take much encouragement to get her to open its covers. Among her treasures were personally inscribed shots of Greta Garbo, Yul Brynner, Maximillian Schell, Roddy McDowell, and Carol Lynley.

During the early 1960s, the Marmont also welcomed a number of famous parents and their children.

Walter Matthau was a doting father. Time after time he would bring his young son, Charlie, to the lobby, plop him on the front desk, and entertain him with jokes. All bystanders were welcome to listen, but the performance was for little Charlie. Said Carmel Volti: "Mr. Matthau worshipped that boy."

There was a slight problem with Claire Bloom and Rod Steiger's little girl. One day the desk received a complaint that she was romping around the second floor, "making enough noise for a horse." Bloom was "very apologetic" and put a stop to the racket in a hurry.

Rip Torn, Geraldine Page, and their twins lived in Bungalow B for a time. Almost everyone who caught a glimpse inside the Torn living quarters came out shaking their heads and muttering to themselves, words like: "A cyclone must have just passed through!" If the little ones were a handful, the Torns didn't seem to mind. From all reports, they were devoted parents.

Carol Lynley first came to the Marmont when she was fourteen years old. She later returned with her own little girl, Jill. As one of the desk clerks remembered: "Jill was a sweet child, who came down to the lobby almost every day after school to practice on the piano." The youngster was either new to the instrument or underexposed to the wealth of available sheet music. The only tune she was heard to play was "Hello, Dolly"—and she played it over and over and over.

Two of the Marmont's smallest guests, Carol Channing's son Channing, and Patrice Wymore Flynn's daughter Arnella, had other interests: one another. "Channing and Arnella were young lovers," Wally Seawell reported, adding that they were about two years old at the time.

Also on hand were director Stuart Rosenberg and his young son, Benji; Diahann Carroll with her daughter, Suzanne Kay; Debra Paget's niece,

Meg; and Joan Crawford's daughter, Christina.

Anne Baxter arrived at the Marmont from Australia to await the birth of her daughter, Melissa. Lee Remick also came to the hotel expecting. Lee Grant and her husband, playwright Arnold Manoff, *left* the Marmont with expectations. On a photo to Corinne Patten, Grant inscribed: "I lived, worked, and conceived a daughter in this barogue shelter." The offspring was Dinah Manoff.

Donald Sutherland also sired at the Marmont. "I had three kids born there," Sutherland confessed, "but then I lived at the hotel for years, starting in Bungalow A, then shifting to Bungalow B, before moving from suite to suite." At one time, Sutherland even offered to buy the penthouse.

Sutherland was too late with his offer, however. Had he made it several years earlier, he might not have been turned down.

A double tragedy led Dr. Brethauer to sell the Marmont. In late 1962, following a lingering illness, Dr. Popper died. Within months, Dr. Brethauer's wife, who had somehow survived on lettuce leaves and bread crumbs for much too long, died of malnutrition. Stunned by the loss of the two people dearest to him, Dr. Brethauer remarked darkly, "I no longer have any interest in the hotel."

Within a period of only two-and-a-half years, starting in March of 1963, the Marmont was acquired by three different owners: William Weiss, Guilford Glazer, and Longridge, Ltd. (a corporation).

Of the new owners, Guilford Glazer took the most active interest in the hotel. Rumor had it that he was a wealthy ammunitions manufacturer, and that he bought the hotel as a birthday present for his wife. Actually, Glazer was a real-estate developer. He did have a wife, Francois (who later married Albert S. Ruddy and co-produced *The Godfather*), and together they set about sprucing up the Marmont, which was badly in need of repair and "freshening" after years of neglect under the parsimonious Dr. Brethauer. They hired a decorator, whose most lasting contribution is still on view in the main-floor drawing room—and the view always brings shudders. It seems that the decorator considered the priceless, one-of-a-kind Persian rug gracing the floor too large for the room, so he had several yards lopped off at each end. It wasn't a total loss. The "clippings" made fine hall runners.

The renovation was still underway when Glazer called a halt to the costly expenditures. "We added some touches and upgraded to some extent," he says, "but it became a pain in the neck. I poured a lot of money into the place before I sold it [in late 1965]. For me, it became an expensive project and a losing proposition."

Unfortunately, that would be the prevailing opinion for several years to come—and yet the stars continued to come to their beloved Marmont, even during these years of transition.

Boris Karloff—a sweet, gentle man.

# Chapter 11

## Strange Sights, Odd Happenings

## Mr. Karloff

Sherry Hackett, the wife of comedian Buddy Hackett, told this story of the time in 1955 when she and her husband were staying at the Marmont, shortly after their marriage. "Buddy and I were in the garage, on our way somewhere," she recalled, "when I remembered that I had forgotten something in our suite, so I left Buddy at the car and went back upstairs. I was on my way to rejoin him, waiting for the elevator, when the doors slid open. Who was standing alone inside—staring at me—but Boris Karloff! There I was, a young bride, and all I could think of was that ghoul I had seen in the movies. I got so scared I started shaking. He didn't calm me down any when he said, in that soft, sinister voice of his, 'Won't you come in?' I did, but I couldn't stop trembling, and I shook all the way downstairs, until I saw Buddy again. Then I ran to him and cried, 'I don't want to stay in this place anymore. They've got monsters living here!' He did a very compassionate thing. He laughed!"

Despite the lasting impression created by many of his film roles, Boris Karloff was not the monster Sherry Hackett feared him to be. At the Marmont, he was considered meek, kind, and unassuming, at all times the perfect gentleman. Meemi Ferguson called him "the nicest man in Hollywood."

The silver-haired Karloff was sixty-seven years old when he and his wife, Evie, first came to the Marmont in early 1955, believing that they would remain no more than three weeks. His career, which had already spanned over four decades, was picking up again, following a slow-down after World War II. Karloff credited the resurgence of horror movies to "that newly hatched monster, television." He had no idea, however, how much in demand he would be. Except for brief trips to England and Italy for film assignments, and time out in New York for the Broadway run of *The Lark*, in which he appeared opposite Julie Harris, the Karloffs would make the Marmont their home for the next seven years.

"Mr. Karloff was not an easy man to know," Meemi admitted. "He was a sweet, gentle man, but so shy. He kept very much to himself, preferring to let his wife handle everything—even his money. Mrs. Karloff was definitely the boss."

Meemi was Boris Karloff's closest friend at the Marmont. He appreciated her elegant style and Boston manner, which brought out his seldom-seen playful nature—to the point of embarrassment. One evening, as he entered the lobby on his return from the studio, he smiled playfully at Meemi (she called his expression "flirtatiously wicked"), then proceeded to his suite. A short time later, Meemi received a phone call from Karloff. "Go to the elevator," he told her. "I'm sending something down for you."

Meemi waited for the elevator to arrive. When the doors opened, she found he had placed a cocktail on the elevator floor. It was a very dry martini, garnished with a stuffed olive on a colorful toothpick. Meemi took the drink and put it aside, then called Karloff to thank him for his thoughtfulness. That was a mistake. Every night after that, as long as he was in town, she was presented with an elevator-sent martini. "I didn't have the heart to tell him that drinking on the job was taboo," Meemi said, adding with a wink, "of course if he had asked me to join him in his suite, I might have bent the rules. But he never did."

With Boris' penchant for privacy, the Karloffs rarely accepted invitations, preferring to spend quiet evenings in their suite. But one night in 1957, Evie talked her husband into leaving the hotel on the premise that they were to join old friends at a secluded restaurant for dinner. They would end up instead in a television studio, where the unsuspecting Karloff faced a live audience, as the surprise subject of Ralph Edwards' prime-time hit, *This Is Your Life*. Karloff sat strangely subdued throughout both the sentimental proceedings and the gathering that followed, surrounded by family, friends, and colleagues who had come to honor him. He was still in a reflective mood on his return to the Marmont. Stopping briefly at the front desk, he reported, "We had a most wonderful evening, with such nice people."

During his years at the Marmont, Karloff pushed himself unmercifully.

He starred in four motion pictures (including one in which he actually played Dr. Frankenstein and *not* the monster); hosted an NBC anthology series of suspense dramas, *Thriller*; guest starred with such television favorites as Red Skelton and Donald O'Conner; and narrated a popular Mother Goose story record for children. Many of Karloff's friends at the hotel, including Meemi Ferguson, felt he was pushing himself too hard. Their concern was his health. He had developed emphysema, which made breathing difficult for him at times, and walking was often stressful; his legs were arthritic, and he suffered from an old back injury. But suggestions of slowing down or retirement caused him to bristle. "I never will," he answered emphatically. "I'm not alive when I'm not working. I want only to die in harness."

Was it Boris Karloff's powerful screen image or the wild imaginings of guests that set off a chain of strange happenings at the Marmont?

In a sixth-floor suite once occupied by Dr. Popper, two guests reported seeing visions of a girl floating about the rooms and caressing the furniture. Other visitors to the same suite told of similar sightings. The girl, whom they were able to describe in detail (she had long black hair and wore a pink dress, they said), was a dead ringer for one of Dr. Popper's long-departed girlfriends.

Two prominent entertainers from New York, a popular husband and wife team, called the front desk in a frenzy late one night. They had been awakened from a deep sleep by "an eerie sound," only to discover a woman, dressed in white, hovering above their bed.

A noted musician, who admittedly had fled from his wife after a stormy domestic battle, complained that he couldn't sleep at night because "someone or something" kept waking him up.

Two male guests swore the suite they shared was "haunted by spirits." They told of repeated knocks at their door, yet, when they answered, no one was ever there. And the faucet in their bath kept running mysteriously. They would turn it off, and moments later it would be on again—"not dripping but gushing water."

Several employees began to talk of a "mad room" in the turret (haunted, no doubt, by memories of such films as *Jane Eyre* and *Psycho*). The night auditor, John Howell, bit the bullet one night and investigated. He discovered a room with sealed windows, filled with elevator equipment. There were no surprises, except for the stacks of "dirty magazines", left by an unknown visitor.

Lynn Redgrave told of the time she prepared a school lunch for her daughter, Kelly. "I got a sandwich ready for her the night before, and put it in a bag by our front door. The next morning, the bag was empty." Redgrave said that, while the bag appeared undisturbed, she did discover a small hole in it. "We suspected a really virulent mouse," she said, trying to be rational.

Lee Remick actually caught a glimpse of her goblin. It was during her third visit to the Marmont. ("Being from New York," she said, "I liked being among New Yorkers. One had the feeling of retaining one's easternness by staying there.")

Remick was pregnant at the time, and married to William Colleran, executive producer of *The Judy Garland Show* for CBS Television. She remembered: "It happened while we were living in the main building on the fifth or sixth floor. We had just finished dinner, and we had moved from our dining room into the living room, when we saw an enormous dark shadowy thing pass by. I ran into the bedroom and called downstairs, while Bill tried to trap it in the hall and get it into a closet. We had a long, long hall, full of doors. I talked to two lovely little ladies who told me that absolutely nothing could be done at the moment. If I would call back in the morning, they promised to send some help."

"In the morning," Remick said, "a lovely little man named Scotty, who worked in the garage, appeared with a broom. He was wonderful, so filled with glee. Well, it took Scotty about fifteen minutes until he finally got the creature out of the closet—and that was cause for such excitement. He was squealing and having a good time. Then off he went, happy for having saved me and knowing all was well.

"Later, one of the little ladies from downstairs called back to explain that a possum must have crawled up into a palm tree and made its way into our suite. She was so charming that I was reminded of Tennessee Williams and his poetic visions."

The mysterious "something" that swept through Sophia Loren and Carlo Ponti's penthouse bedroom was more easily explained. One of the garage boys, Morgan Cavett, had a huge crush on the glamorous Signora Ponti. Catching an occasional glimpse of her was exciting, but hardly enough for young Cavett. He wanted a personal rememberance, and he waited patiently for an opportunity to get one. It came one morning after the Pontis departed the Marmont for the day. With assistant manager Rose de Haulleville's teenage son, Siggy Wessburg, as moral support, Cavett made his way up to the penthouse. The door was locked, but that didn't stop the youngsters. They climbed in through the terrace. "We got inside before the maid," Cavett confessed later, "so the bed hadn't been changed yet. That gave us a chance to feel the sheets where Sophia had slept!"

Desi Arnaz was another unsuspecting guest whose actions intrigued the garage boys, and created a stir.

Arnaz was at the Marmont for months following his divorce from Lucille Ball in 1960. He soon earned a reputation as "quite a swinger," based on the wild parties he tossed and the large number of "gorgeous but wayward ladies" who appeared at all hours to visit him.

One of the girls, a very shapely blonde, frequently pulled into the garage, then sat in Scotty's small underground office while awaiting Desi's call to join him upstairs. She never sat alone. The garage boys practically smothered her with attention. "We knew why she was coming to the hotel, and that made her even more exciting to us," Morgan Cavett recalled. "She must have been about twenty, only a couple of years older than we were, but we thought of her as *that mysterious older woman*. We all had a crush on her." Arnaz didn't know that she had a crush on a baseball player, one of the Dodgers new to town. Nor did he suspect that the boys spent many entertaining hours sneaking peaks at him and his beauties. Only now does Cavett confess that "we would climb down fire escapes and over balconies to watch the performances." If Scotty and his teenage boys were especially attentive to Desi Arnaz, it wasn't only because of Arnaz's swinging ways. They considered him "a genuinely nice guy"—and one of the hotel's Big Tippers.

James MacArthur didn't qualify as a teenager (he was twenty), but the maids claimed he acted like one, when he ran down the halls naked chasing his girlfriends. As one eyewitness later explained, "Jamie was built so close to the ground he probably felt being unclothed gave him an edge." MacArthur's mother, Helen Hayes, was shocked to see her son when she checked into the Marmont. He was dressed at the time, but his head was shaved, Mohawk-style, for a role in Disney's *The Light in the Forest*.

During the summer of 1960, columnist Jill Jackson had a surprise when she ran into a revered colleague. According to Jackson: "I had just finished a long, hot day in town, covering the Democratic Convention for NBC's *Monitor*. It was a tiring job, and I couldn't wait to get back to the hotel to relax. I made it, only to discover that the Marmont elevator was out of order, which meant having to climb the stairs. As I was approaching the third-floor landing, who did I find sitting there but Ed Murrow! He was at the hotel while covering the convention for CBS. Well, he smiled and asked me to join him while he rested before making it up the rest of

For Lee Remick, an after-dinner visitor.

Springtime in the Hollywood hills with "Gypsy" and Hermione
Baddeley. (*Courtesy of James Haake*)

the way. I did, and we had the nicest chat. A wonderful man!"

Jackson had another surprise during her stay. As she remembered: "I must have been daydreaming one day, when I got off the elevator and went to what I thought was my suite, 4G. I put the key in the lock, opened the door, and walked inside. The room looked different, but it didn't register that I was in the wrong suite until I saw someone sitting stark raving naked in a big wing chair. It was Walter Slezak. I froze for a second, then said, rather feebly, as I backed toward the door, 'I think I'm in the wrong place.' Walter didn't make a move. He simply stared at me and muttered, 'I think you're right.' The next day, we met downstairs and had our pictures taken; this time Walter had his clothes on. The strange thing was, which I didn't learn until later, every key that the desk handed out was the same. I found that hard to believe, until I went from door to door, and sure enough, my key opened every one. One key fit all!"

With the departure of the Karloffs from the castle on the hill in 1962, reports of strange and bizarre happenings slowly began to subside.

And the locks to all the doors were changed.

# Mr. Harris

Ann Little used to marvel that guests never caused her a moment's trouble during the Marmont's early days. "If they had," she reflected many years later, with a touch of authority still in her voice, "out they'd have gone."

It's probably a good thing Richard Harris wasn't around during the filming of *Mutiny on the Bounty* in 1935, instead of during the 1962 version; Ann Little would never have put up with him. As it turned out, he didn't last long anyway.

Harris first checked into the Marmont for a short stay in August of 1960, returning briefly several times over the next twelve months. With each visit, he would amaze the staff with his ability to put in a full day's work, then play till dawn. The consensus was that "he had an uncanny zest for living—and an unbelievable capacity for spirits." (Others described his tippling in harsher terms.) There may have been more raucous individuals at the Marmont, even during Little's time, but no one caused such widespread havoc as the actor from Limerick, Ireland. His boisterous shenanigans finally got him in trouble in the fall of 1961.

As the story goes, Harris stopped at a Hollywood pub one evening after work, before returning to the Marmont. He was still in the bar at closing time, 2:00 a.m., when he was asked to leave. Finding himself on the street, not ready to call it quits for the night, he went looking for some excitement. He found it at the Marmont. Actually, he didn't find it, he created it. Instead of returning to his suite for a few hours sleep, he stumbled along the corridors, banging on doors and bellowing, "They've dropped the bloody bomb!"

Within minutes, the hotel was deserted, as startled, groggy guests ran screaming for the street. One terrified young actress fled in such panic that she reportedly found herself halfway down the stairs before realizing that she was in the buff.

When calm was at last restored to the hotel, and the prank revealed, Harris was told for the second time that evening to "take his celebrated presence elsewhere." As far as anyone knows, he's the only person to get tossed out of the Marmont.

## Miss Mazeppa

Faith Dane was one of the surprise stars of Broadway's *Gypsy*, stopping the show nightly as the trumpet-tooting, pelvis-pounding stripper, Mazeppa. In late 1961, she was brought to Hollywood to recreate her role in the movie version of the hit musical. She took up residence at the Marmont and quickly established herself as one of the hotel's most bizarre characters.

How an uninhibited, lusty performer like Faith Dane could be lured to the quiet of Chateau Marmont, with its fairly reserved clientele, remains a mystery. Faith was neither quiet nor reserved. Her background was sideshows and carnivals, where life was a twenty-four-hour celebration, loose and lively. She craved excitement, and attention; she was always "on," even when she wasn't before the footlights or cameras.

Long before the filming started on *Gypsy*, Faith began appearing on her balcony in hot pants and a strapless stretch top, fully revealing her statuesque, full-blown wonder-woman proportions, to rehearse her part in the big number, *You Gotta Have A Gimick*. She was especially proud of that song. "Who do you think inspired it?" she would say. "I'm the one who gave Jule Styne [the composer] the idea to do it—and put it in the show."

There were others who weren't quite so pleased with her *Gimmick* routine, particularly her next door neighbors at the Marmont, Boris and Evie Karloff. "Faith would stand on her balcony and blow her trumpet to the winds," an inside source reveals. "The Karloffs got very upset with her, and complained frequently. But that didn't faze Faith. Nothing bothered her.

Always on the lookout for good times, Faith soon became a regular on the Marmont's party circuit. She never missed an open house hosted by Donald Spackman, nor an opportunity to entertain with her *Gypsy* number and other highly suggestive songs and bawdy jokes from her repertoire.

Connie Nelson attended many of Spackman's get-togethers with her grandmother, Meemi Ferguson, Connie remembered. "There were some young people who would drop in, kids in their teens and early twenties. We had read *Catcher in the Rye*, and we knew all of 'those words' but we didn't dare say them—not in front of my grandmother. Faith didn't care. She liked being wild and raunchy. Everybody was stunned—and pretty embarrassed—at those parties."

Following one of Spackman's affairs, Meemi cornered the gentlemanly Spackman to say, "Don, I'm really offended at your knowing someone like *that!*"

Meemi didn't stay offended long. A few days later, on a Sunday, she was driving to Church, when she stopped for a red light at Sunset and Fairfax. Standing at the corner in front of the drugstore was Faith Dane. Meemi was about to drive on, when Faith spotted her and ran to the car. "I'm late for Church," Faith said. "Can you give me a ride?" Meemi couldn't say no.

Says Connie Nelson, "When Meemi found out that Faith was a very devout churchgoer, Faith became a 'very lovely girl.' She honestly believed that the other Faith—the obnoxious one—was simply a put on; a character she had assumed for her movie job. Of course, the real Faith Dane *was* Mazeppa. The only time she calmed down was for church."

From that Sunday on, Faith could do no wrong in Meemi's eyes. Meemi even made excuses when the Karloffs, and others, called to complain about the sour trumpet solos (interspersed with some rousing bumps and grinds) sounding from Faith's terrace. After all, Meemi would explain, Miss Dane was dutifully at work perfecting her craft. Meemi never failed to add that the near-naked subject of the complaint was also "a very lovely girl."

Had James Haake known Faith Dane during her stay at Chateau Marmont, the walls might still be quivering. Known professionally as "Gypsy", he's not only a working actor (Mel Brook's *To Be Or Not To Be* and television mini-series, *Hollywood Wive's*) but the reigning King of female impersonators and the sharp-witted, outrageous and unpredictable star/M.C. at Los Angeles' popular night spot, La Cage Aux Folles. "My mother was one of the first female doctors to graduate from Columbia Medical School. My father was a mechanic. Now you know why I'm a drag queen."

Gypsy is no ordinary drag queen, however. For one thing, he never wears wigs, ("The parts people look at have nothing to do with hairdos.") For another, he was married for eight years, has a grown daughter and two grandsons, and holds a Master's degree from NYU. "In high school," he noted, "I wanted all the football players on the team to appreciate the fact that I was about to marry the prettiest girl around, after they had made fun of my not having any muscles. That's exactly what I did. She was the captain of the cheerleaders. Now she's a size 14 and has six grandchildren of her own—and I'm still wearing a size 10. How many husbands can say that after all these years!"

A tall and willowy former broadway "gypsy," he began his career as a chorus boy in Cole Porter's *Kiss Me, Kate*. Haake was initially drawn to the Marmont through his friendships with Nellita Choate Thomsen (one of his mother's close classmates at Stanford); Larry Bordeaux, Thomsen's companion and confidant; and actress Hermione Baddeley (for whom Bordeaux later worked). Through his frequent visits, he soon became a regular around the hotel, and a fixture at various functions. Once, while wearing an Oscar de la Renta creation, he was confronted by Betsy Bloomingdale, also gowned by the noted couturier. "She wasn't too thrilled about *that*," said Gypsy. "The first thing she asked me was, 'How did you get *your* dress?' I looked her straight in the face and said, 'The very same way you got yours—with a discount!' That was the end of our conversation."

Whether he turns up in Levis and boots or in spangles (he admits to having over six-hundred designer gowns), life is never dull with Gypsy on the scene.

# Bedding Down

Until recently, the majority of smaller suites at the Marmont featured Murphy beds, tastefully concealed behind closed doors. For the children, the "hideaways" were an exciting part of Marmont living, a secret locked in a closet. For many adults, they were a terror.

Columnist Jill Jackson remembers returning to the hotel late one evening, admittedly "feeling no pain" and ready to collapse in bed. Her hideaway was concealed in the dining area of her suite; getting to it was no easy feat, even when she was in full command of her senses.

"I had to reach in to pull it out," she recalled, "and that's what I was doing when a rod snapped. I felt myself falling backward and saw the damn thing coming after me. When we landed, I was on the floor, with my hand pinned in such a way that I could not get loose, and the bed on top of me. As God is my judge, I was trapped. Unhurt, but *trapped*. I couldn't free my hand, I couldn't stand up, I couldn't get to the phone. And yelling was senseless. The door and windows were all closed.

"I was starting to panic, when I noticed an ashtray on a nearby table. I reached for it with my free hand and heaved it out the window. The next thing I heard—after the shattering of glass—were some people down on the street. I was encouraged, until one of them said, 'Some drunk must be throwing things!' Then it was quiet again. They had left without paying any attention to me."

Jackson said that she could picture her predicament lasting for hours— at least until the arrival of the maid, sometime during the coming day. Driven by that terrifying thought, she tried to concentrate on other possible ways to free herself. The telephone was completely out of reach, but maybe . . .

"The cord was lying on the floor several feet away," she reported, "but after much stretching and struggling, I was able to hook it with my foot and pull the phone over." Exhausted, she alerted the switchboard to her plight.

By the time help arrived and broke down the door—"they couldn't find a pass key"—the sun was rising. "After all that, I knew I would never be able to sleep," Jackson said. "Besides, it was getting too late. So I folded up the bed and went to work."

At the Marmont, future superstar Barbra Streisand turned heads even though few people recognized her.

# Chapter 12

## Signing In And Out

### Mr. & Mrs. Hill

In 1948, Burt Lancaster joined with his agent, Harold Hecht, to form the independent production company, Hecht-Lancaster. Eight years later, the company became Hecht-Hill-Lancaster, with the addition of producer James Hill, resulting in such praised pictures as *Sweet Smell of Success, The Devil's Disciple,* and *The Unforgiven.*

James Hill was a bright, distinguished-looking man and one of Hollywood's most eligible bachelors. In 1957, however, during the production of *Pal Joey,* he met the movie's former "Love Goddess," Rita Hayworth. He not only convinced her to play an aging fashion model (her first non-glamorous role) in his company's screen version of Terence Rattigan's hit play *Separate Tables,* but he talked her into marrying him. The next year Hill became Hayworth's fifth husband, following in the footsteps of such headline-makers as one-time "boy wonder" Orson Welles; Prince Aly Kahn, playboy son of the spirited leader of millions of Moslems; and debt-ridden crooner Dick Haymes.

The Hayworth-Hill marriage did not run smoothly. In the three years they were together, there were all too frequent fights and separations. Hayworth wanted to settle down and lead a "normal" family life, spending quiet evenings at home; she bought a nine-room house in Beverly Hills, just north of Sunset Boulevard. Hill wanted her to continue her career.

During those unsettled times, Hill turned to the junior penthouse at Chateau Marmont, which his company had converted into an office of sorts.

Says Hill: "It was a place for me to stay, a place to go. Then Rita and I would patch things up and get back together again."

Hill was in the fifth-floor penthouse more often than not. Warm, friendly, and down-to-earth, he soon established himself as one of the Marmont's favorite hosts. His door was always open, no matter the hour, and his bar became a popular gathering place.

One day, Burt Lancaster arrived with a gift. As Hill remembered: "Lancaster brought me a hibachi to cook steaks, and we put it to use out on the terrace. Billows of smoke began drifting up past the windows of the penthouse above us—thick, choking clouds of smoke. Desi Arnaz was living over me, and when he saw all the smoke he came out screaming. The girl who was staying with him tried to calm him down. I heard her say, 'Well, at least they're eating!'"

A former desk clerk at the hotel recalled seeing another visitor, Hayworth's daughter, Rebecca Welles. "When Rebecca came to see Mr. Hill," the staff member said, "she would wait patiently down by the piano. She looked very pregnant."

Between separations, Hayworth continued to appear in films, giving in to Hill's wishes, despite her opposition. In 1959, she co-starred with Gary Cooper in *They Came To Cordura* and, the following year, in Clifford Odets' *The Story on Page One*. By the time *Story* was released, the problems in the Hill household had reached the press, fed by rumors of "drinking bouts and fights over nothing." With Hill back at the Marmont, the marriage appeared doomed.

By the early spring of 1961, however, Rita and her husband were again living together and planning new ventures. They even formed their own production company and set off for Spain to film a comedy about art swindlers called *The Happy Thieves*. If there were problems overseas, they didn't surface, but Hayworth's co-star, Rex Harrison, would later comment that she was "desperately uncertain of herself, although she had worked for so many years."

*The Happy Thieves* received dismal notices, forcing the Hills to abandon another film they had planned when they returned to Hollywood. On June 30, 1961, the press announced in a formal statement issued by Hayworth's publicist: "Rita Hayworth and producer James Hill have separated, and a divorce is imminent." In September, she filed for divorce.

Rita began seeing actor Gary Merrill, whose stormy marriage to Bette Davis had ended the previous year. Merrill could hardly have been a calming influence on Hayworth; he was involved in a bitter battle with his former wife over the custody of their children.

On December 12, 1961, Rita Hayworth paid a surprise visit to the Marmont. She arrived with luggage and requested a suite near Hill on the fifth floor.

Carmel Volti remembered Hayworth's arrival; she was working the front desk at the time and checked the actress in, "She looked so beautiful, absolutely lovely, but she was not the same Rita Hayworth I had seen on the screen. Her hair was a mousey dark brown, not its flaming red or strawberry blonde. She was much smaller in person, and she seemed terribly frightened and bewildered. Such a shy, quiet little thing. She even had some difficulty speaking."

Not for long. According to reports, Hayworth became quite eloquent once she reached her suite, 5F. Before she could unpack, she was on the telephone to a nearby liquor store, and within minutes, a delivery was on its way to her door. Then she was on the phone again, this time placing a call to the small penthouse. Her speech was no longer hesitant. Her tone was sharp, demanding; the words came rapid-fire. A source close to the actress at the Marmont claimed: "Once Rita had a few drinks, her personality changed completely. Drinking gave her confidence, and she needed all she could muster. She was determined to get Jim [Hill] back, to give the marriage another chance. When Rita wanted something, nothing could stand in her way." A determined Hayworth kept the line to Hill's penthouse *busy.*

It wasn't long before her ploy paid off. After only two weeks, Rita Hayworth and James Hill departed the Marmont to try once again to salvage their broken marriage. The reconciliation was brief. Before long they separated again, this time for good.

## Miss Pitts & Mrs. Lanning

ZaSu Pitts, the delightful, scatterbrained comedienne of movies and television, was at the Marmont in late 1962, while filming back-to-back films (*The Thrill of It All* and *It's A Mad Mad Mad Mad World*), when she discovered that Roberta Sherwood, her singing idol, was not only in Hollywood to cut a record album but staying at the hotel. ZaSu *had* to meet Roberta Sherwood, and so she prevailed upon Jill Jackson to arrange an introduction.

Jackson had met ZaSu Pitts earlier, through her good friend, screenwriter

Frances Marion. She had known Sherwood even longer. "Roberta was guesting on my television show in New Orleans all the time during the 50s," Jackson says. "That was shortly after Walter Winchell had discovered her singing in a bar in Florida, and she was really hot."

Setting up a meeting between the two performers wasn't difficult; Sherwood had long been an admirer of the zany ZaSu Pitts as well.

As Jackson remembered: "I invited them to my room one afternoon for tea and cookies. ZaSu was so excited she arrived a half hour early, dressed to the hilt and all girly and giggly. Then Roberta walked in. She looked as plain as could be, but that was her way. She wore the same get-ups onstage.

"Well, it was an instant admiration society. They hugged and swooned and complimented each other. They talked about their beginnings in show business, their homes, their children (Roberta, who was married to Don Lanning in real life, was at the hotel with one of her boys), their diets, and everything under the sun. Then Roberta sang her big hit, *Cry Me A River,* and her favorite song, *Take Me Along.* ZaSu couldn't have been more thrilled if she had won the Irish Sweepstakes—she looked about to faint. Her eyes rolled round and round. She clutched her hands—she had a way of wringing them—and she fluttered, 'Oh, me, oh, my! Oh, my goodness!' On and on it went. I've never seen such a love fest in my life!"

"It didn't take those two ladies long to decide that they were one terrific team and should be working together. ZaSu suggested a television series. She had recently been with Gale Storm for three seasons on *Oh! Susanna.* And that's the way the party ended—with lots of hugging and kissing and promising to get together soon. It was wonderful!"

"Of course, they never did a show together. I doubt if ZaSu and Roberta ever saw each other again. ZaSu had cancer and died shortly afterward. But she never once let on that she was so ill. She had been a trouper for nearly fifty years, but that afternoon at the Marmont she gave the greatest performance of her life."

# Miss Streisand

In the best tradition of the theater, Barbara Streisand was a virtual unknown when she made her Broadway debut at New York's Shubert Theater in *I Can Get It For You Wholesale.* But when the opening night curtain fell, she was, if not the glamorous star, a *somebody.*

That was on March 22, 1962. Six months later, twenty-year-old Streisand was in Hollywood to tape a Dinah Shore television show. She checked into Chateau Marmont, where Shore's executive producer, Henry Jaffe, had called home for many months. ("I lived next door to Burl Ives in Bungalow A," Jaffe commented. "When Burl moved out, Sidney Poitier moved in with Diahann Carroll. Then Pearl Bailey moved in. There was a constant flow of celebrities.")

Streisand's accommodations at the Marmont weren't nearly as impressive as Henry Jaffe's. She was given 1F, a morning bright but virtually viewless (except for the driveway leading to the garage) single, previously occupied by John Emery, Buddy Hackett, Warren Beatty, Elizabeth Montgomery, and a French refugee and teacher of languages, Mr. Thomas, who shared the quarters with his two collies. The room was adjacent to the main-floor lavatory and was entered through a door set in a recess created by the off-lobby staircase. Although spacious, and visually appealing inside (a soaring high ceiling added to the illusion), it seemed to be an architectural after-thought. Streisand didn't complain, but then, no one thought she would. After all, wasn't she the kooky kid from Brooklyn who bought her clothes in thrift shops?

The young singer's unusal way of speaking and dressing certainly made her easy to spot, not that it mattered. She could pass through the lobby as often as she pleased, generating stares and turning heads, but few people recognized her or knew who she was. Her Broadway fame, and her name, had yet to become bell ringers on the West Coast.

Despite her success as the frumpy put-upon Yetta Tessye Marmelstein in *I Can Get It For You Wholesale,* Streisand intimated that she welcomed a few days away from the role and its nightly routine. (While in Hollywood, she was replaced by her understudy, TV's yet-to-be-Mary Hartman and future Marmont guest, Louise Lasser.) Though she didn't say it, there were indications that she wouldn't be unhappy to see the show close. She was starting to receive offers to play nightclubs around the country, and there was talk that a record company was interested in signing her for a solo album—her first. Streisand was grateful that she was being accepted as a singer.

For a time, she doubted that would ever be possible. Most of the New York critics hailed her performance, but there were brambles among the tossed bouquets. Such comments that she was "too different" and "a possible flash in the pan" were less disturbing than those attacking her personal appearance. She was labelled "drab and unattractive," even "homely," and likened to such creatures as an anteater and a Borzoi. The latter comparison was in no way meant to imply elegance. The reviewer went on to advise that Streisand should have her prominent nose bobbed if she had any aspirations for a movie career.

The barbs hurt, but Streisand was determined to sing, and *Wholesale* had put her in the spotlight. She had been given the chance to display her vocal talents, as well as her funny side; she was grateful that her *work* had received such high praise. But as the weeks passed, she began to fear that Miss Marmelstein might pigeonhole her as "a natural comedienne" (an ethnic one at that!), and displaying her comedic abilities was not her goal. More than once she said stubbornly: "I do not want to become another Fanny Brice!" The offers she would receive for personal appearances and guest shots on television were gratifying. Still, she had a lot to prove.

Newcomers to Hollywood often find the going rough, and Streisand was no different, although it wasn't the town—or closed doors—that had her on edge. She desperately missed the one person in her life who gave her strength, the young man she worshipped and adored. And needed.

Streisand had fallen in love with Elliott Gould during the early run of *I Can Get It For You Wholesale.* He had the lead in the show. He was tall, good-natured, and, being nearly four years older, more experienced. He sang, he danced, he had appeared on television. He had attracted attention in *Say, Darling* and *Irma La Douce* on Broadway. He had a reputation as a *lady-killer;* he brimmed with self-confidence. His role in *Wholesale* was to make him a star. It didn't. As his career stalled, hers began to escalate. He needed her as much as she needed him.

Their first separation came with Streisand's visit to Hollywood, and it was a painful one. Corinne Patten later commented: "It was easy to see that she was hurting while she was at the hotel, but she tried to put up a brave front, and we [the staff] tried to be as attentive as possible—though I doubt that we were much consolation. She looked terribly lost, even teary at times. Poor thing seemed to be marking time, simply counting the days. Her heart was miles away."

As Streisand's stay came to an end, her mood began to brighten. She talked eagerly about returning to New York and even quipped about the future. "No one dared imagine what a big, big star she would become," Corinne remembered, "but at that point in her young life, she seemed more committed to Elliott Gould than to Miss Marmelstein or her career."

# Mrs. Howard

Dorothy Lamour, the movies' one-time glamorous "sarong girl," had been living in Maryland for ten years with her husband, William R. Howard III, and their two sons, Ridge and Tommy, when she was brought back to Hollywood to appear on a Bob Hope television special for NBC. She checked into Chateau Marmont on April 10, 1962.

The Hope show was essentially a promotion for the latest (and last) of the "Road" films, *The Road to Hong Kong*. Since *The Road to Singapore* in 1940, Lamour had teamed with Bob Hope and Bing Crosby in no less than six "Road" pictures, playing the sultry, breezy foil to her two co-stars. The newest in the highly popular series marked a change, however.

For years, there had been talk of reteaming the popular trio. But when plans for *The Road to Hong Kong* were at last released, the only definite cast members named were Hope and Crosby. Lamour, it seemed, had been bypassed. "I read that because I'd been in retirement for four or five years," she commented later, "Gina Lollobrigida and Sophia Loren were the top choices to take up where I had left off. It was apparent that Bing, Bob, producer Mel Frank, and director Norman Panama had decided that I had been off-screen too long to be a major asset to the film."

If Lamour had been overlooked, it wasn't for long. Eventually she received a script with an offer to appear in the film, to be shot in London. What she read had her fuming. Her role consisted of one song ("not one of the greatest that Sammy Cahn ever wrote") and a few lines of dialogue, little more than a bit part "for old time's sake." The co-starring role, once hers, had been assigned to sexy Joan Collins.

The normally cooperative Lamour let it be known that she would not appear in the film as written, under any circumstances. There was even talk of a feud brewing between Lamour and her young replacement. She told a reporter: "There is no feud. I have never had a feud with anyone, but *if* I ever considered having a feud, it would be with one of the *stars* of the film."

It wasn't until *The Road to Hong Kong* was about to go into production that Lamour had reconsidered, mainly out of loyalty to her fans and former co-stars. She had heard that Bob Hope was fighting for her to be in the film. That pleased her. (His reported reference to her as "the old gal in the sarong" didn't.) She arrived in London with her puny part intact and a hefty raise for added incentive.

Lamour claimed to have had such a good time working again "with those two guys" that she readily accepted Bob Hope's invitation to help publicize the movie. It was during her stay at the Marmont, after completing the Hope Show, that she learned Bing Crosby was planning a similar promotion on his upcoming television special. She phoned Crosby to tell him that she would gladly remain in Hollywood a few extra days, if he wanted her to make an appearance. The idea failed to interest him; he told her that it was too late to write her into the script.

"Miss Lamour didn't say a word to anyone at the hotel," Corinne Patten confided to a friend, "but it was obvious that she was devastated. It wasn't until later that we learned about the snub."

Later, when the show was aired, Lamour was shocked to find herself one of the pivotal characters. Large blowups of her were used as backdrops, and her name was mentioned frequently throughout the show.

Lamour's fans weren't quite as fickle. Donald Spackman remembered seeing her during her early 1962 visit to the Marmont. "We rode up in the elevator together, and I couldn't stop staring at her. She looked so gorgeous. Without a doubt, she was the most beautiful woman I had ever seen."

However slighted Lamour may have felt by her small part (and treatment) in *The Road to Hong Kong,* she believed she had a chance to right matters by accepting an offer to appear in Paramount's *Donovan's Reef,* a John Ford comedy, with John Wayne and Lee Marvin. Ford had promised that there was "a wonderful part" in the film for her. But when she arrived back at the Marmont in August, she learned that her role was not much bigger or better than the one she had recently completed. She complained, and Ford promised to give her added scenes, but he never delivered. One day, following a confrontation on the set, Ford came to her dressing room to apologize. Within minutes, they were both laughing and crying. "That man could charm apples right out of the tree," she confessed later. "Angry and indignant as I was, he won me over."

She returned again to the Marmont on November 6, 1963, while she worked on *Pajama Party,* a teenage beach party picture with an unlikely science fiction twist. The movie starred Tommy Kirk and Annette Funicello. Among the supporting players were Elsa Lanchester, Buster Keaton, and Dorothy Lamour. If the still lovely Lamour's previous two screen appearances hadn't convinced her that her starring days in films were over, this one almost certainly did.

# Chapter 13

## Playing The Lobby

## Miss Garland

For eight years, starting in 1956, the multi-talented Billy Barnes and his friends rocked Los Angeles with a series of intimate satirical revues. Since Meemi Ferguson's granddaughter, Connie Nelson, worked for a time in the Barnes box-office (and "stowed away" in vacant Marmont suites whenever possible with her brother, Lee), the hotel lobby became the site of several gala, celebrity-filled opening-night celebrations.

In April of 1964, composer Barnes and his sketch writer-director, Bob Rogers, held a backers audition for their latest production, *Billy Barnes' Hollywood*, starring regulars Ken Berry and Joyce Jameson. The success of their previous ventures heralded another triumph, filling the Las Palmas Theater off Hollywood Boulevard with potential investors. Who could turn down an invitation to be a part of the money-making madness, or to have an advance look at one of Hollywood's most eagerly awaited theatrical events? The would-be "angels" were prepared for a wild time. They knew that, when Barnes and Rogers tackled a subject, nothing was sacred; all of Tinseltown, from the stars and studios to the hot tourist attractions, were certain to be subjects for songs and sketches.

Joyce Jameson had the big show-stopper, to be performed toward the end of the first act. Entitled "Judy," it was a stinging spoof not only of Miss Garland's marriages but her hot-and-cold career, her unmistakable vibrato and mannerisms, her fluctuating weight, even her bouts with pills and booze. Barnes overlooked nothing in composing the caustic musical critique. He admits: "It was written because I was upset with Judy at the time."

As Jameson waited offstage to perform her number, the song's namesake arrived unexpectedly at the theater, escorted by fashion designer Ray Agyhan. The late arrivals were taking their seats, as word reached the cast that Judy Garland was in the audience. Jameson grew tense, then began to panic, but she pulled herself together long enough to get through the song in flawless fashion. A moment of awkward silence followed, as heads turned toward Garland, waiting for her reaction. She made it easy for the crowd: she rose to her feet cheering, prompting a standing ovation.

Following the run-through, Garland made her way onstage to congratulate the cast. That done, she pulled Billy Barnes aside. He remembers the face-to-face confrontation. "She seemed upset at first, then she got coy. There was a slight chuckle in her voice when she said, 'No audience is going to accept anyone saying those naughty things about me! With that, she pulled five-hundred dollars from her purse, told me that she was an investor, and, as an investor, she didn't want the number in the show. She walked away, sat down at the piano and glared at me, while she sang "Make Someone Happy." It was the first time I had heard it sung as a threat. The next day, I got a call from her. She told me, 'You do that number, and I'll sue your ass!' "

Two nights later, a tipsy Judy Garland wandered into Chateau Marmont, supposedly to meet a friend. Over the years, she had been in and out frequently; she was always a favorite guest at hotel parties. This time, however, she never made it upstairs, not even to the front desk. She barely made it across the drawing room to the piano, which, at that time, was located at the far west end. She appeared to be in a playful mood as she sat momentarily on the bench, hit a note, then stood, all the while making exaggerated gestures with her hands. Her face contorted, she began croaking out a song. But it wasn't one of her traditional numbers that she chose to perform for the sparse gathering of disbelieving onlookers. She was doing her own version of Billy Barnes' "Judy." Actually, it was Judy Garland doing a blistering take-off on Joyce Jameson impersonating Judy Garland.

Months later, Barnes had the last laugh. Prior to the show's opening, he had replaced the "Judy" number with an equally biting "Elizabeth," based on Miss Taylor's marital escapades, her bouts with booze, her fluctuating weight, etc. The trade paper *Variety* called "Elizabeth," as performed by Joyce Jameson (spectacularly gowned by up-and-coming designer, Bob Mackie), "the highlight of the show." But as *Billy Barnes' Hollywood* neared the end of its run, Barnes devilishly "slipped in the Garland song." As far as he knows, she never found out. If she did, nothing came of it.

Judy Garland's 1964 performance at the Marmont piano was her final hotel appearance. Less than four years later, however, memories of Garland were revived with the arrival of Liza Minnelli and her long-sideburned husband, Australian singer-songwriter Peter Allen. Both were young, wide-eyed, and bristling with energy. Said former night auditor John Howell: "At the time, we knew very little about Miss Minnelli and even less about Mr. Allen, except that they were both trying to make it as entertainers. But it was impressive to know that she was Judy Garland's daughter."

## The Sounds Of Music

Judy Garland wasn't the only entertainer to "play" the Marmont drawing room. Drawn by the ever-present baby grand, many of the greatest names in show business have filled the huge room with music over the years.

Ann Little loved to recall Jose Iturbi's visits during the 1930s. "In those days, he wasn't the well-known figure he later became, from his appearances in MGM musicals. He was mainly a piano soloist, and an occasional guest conductor with various orchestras. He once told me that he came to the Marmont to relax. But he seldom did. I would catch him at all hours of the night, playing in the lobby. There were times when he would stay at the piano till dawn, fingering the keys so softly he would never disturb anyone. Then he would order breakfast. He always wanted his eggs cooked in olive oil."

Victor Borge, the clown prince of piano, has displayed his serious side at the Marmont keyboard. Erroll Garner and George Shearing, when they weren't playing before crowds along the Strip, played for their own enjoyment off the hotel lobby. Duke Ellington worked on his film score for *Paris Blues* on the old piano. Rickie Lee Jones, like Iturbi preferred to do her practicing (and wailing the blues) at "strange hours." Maximillian Schell, said to be "a brilliant pianist when he isn't charming the ladies," continually surprised everyone with his polished performances. As Meemi Ferguson, who was no slouch at the ivories herself, used to say, "Few guests can resist running their fingers across the keyboard. As long as it's there, everyone wants to touch it."

It only seemed that way. The piano *did* attract attention, but there were generally far too many musical celebrities on hand for one instrument to

Judy Garland tossed a few barbs during her unscheduled performance in the main-floor drawing room.

Many of the world's top talents have played the Marmont's baby grand.

Beatle John Lennon.

Diahann Carroll and Sidney Poitier's on-going rendezvous at the Marmont resulted in two shattered marriages.

Rod Stewart. (*Photo by Jim Frank*)

Alice Cooper. (*Photo by Jim Frank*)

accommodate. They came to the Marmont for film and television commitments, for recording dates, and while playing the night spots and appearing in stage productions. And they came in droves.

There were singers—and recording stars—Ray Eberle, Dick Haymes, Andy Williams and Claudine Longet, Norman Luboff, Ray Charles, Nina Simone, Roger Miller, Quincy Jones, Sarah Vaughn, J.P. Morgan, Fabian Forte, Sylvia Syms, Shani Wallis, John and Michelle Phillips, Peggy Lee, and John Lennon.

There were songwriters and composers Hugh Martin and Ralph Blane (working on a Betty Grable score for Twentieth Century-Fox), Alan Lerner and Frederick Loewe (writing "Thank Heaven for Little Girls" and "I'm Glad I'm Not Young Anymore" for *Gigi* in the penthouse), Burton Lane, John Kander, Paul Williams, Jerry Goldsmith, Stephen Sondheim, Mary Rodgers, Bob Merrill, Michael Cacoyannis, and Hector Villa-Lobos. Meredith Wilson created his score for *The Music Man* at the Marmont.

There were stars of the musical stage: Florence Henderson, Carol Lawrence, Elaine Stritch, Chita Rivera, Doretta Morrow, Juanita Hall, Richard Eastham, Robert Guillaume, Tammy Grimes, Carol Channing, Ronny Graham, Valerie Bettis, Robert Coote, Elizabeth Allen, Lotte Lenya, Liliane Montevecchi, Jack Cassidy, Nancy Walker, and Robert Goulet.

At the Marmont for concert or club dates, aside from George Shearing and Erroll Garner, were Eartha Kitt, Della Reese, Dave Brubeck, Josephine Premise, Miles Davis, Billy Strayhorn, Hugh Masekela and Odetta, Dizzy Gillespie, Gerry Mulligan, Leon Bibb, Buddy Pepper, Chris Conner, and Tito Puente. Also on hand were Miriam Makeba, Carmen McRae, Grace Bumbry, Louis Bellson, Line Renaud, Luther Henderson, Peter Matz, and Fran Warren (that "Sunday Kind of Love" gal).

On hand for film work were Shirley Jones, Pearl Bailey, Burl Ives, Julie Andrews, Petula Clark, Harve Presnell, Pat Suzuki, Nancy Kwan, Mary McCarty, Lillian Roth, and Maurice Chevalier.

It was never a secret when Paul Whiteman stayed at the Marmont. Each evening, as he pulled into the garage, he would announce his arrival by tooting his car horn, a custom contraption that blared the first few notes of his trademark theme from Gershwin's *Rhapsody in Blue*.

Josephine Baker was the most sought-after and highest paid entertainer in Europe during the late 1920s and 1930s. The American-born dancer-singer had been hailed as "the international black queen of Paris music halls" and "society's darling." But she was no longer rich or in demand when she came to the Marmont in the spring of 1960, with her touring one-woman show. Nor was she the driven performer of her earlier years. Her interests had turned to the five children, all legally adopted war orphans, whom she was raising at her home in France. "I want more little ones, a whole housefull," she told Meemi Ferguson. "I must prove that people of all creeds and colors can live together in harmony."

Baker got her wish; the tour was so successful that she was able to adopt seven more youngsters. The added responsibility was more than she could handle, however, and she was forced to embark on another fund-raising tour to pay off her many creditors. By the time she arrived back at the Marmont for her Los Angeles engagement, she had lost her home *and* her family. Nearing seventy she was balding, and her beauty had faded. She confessed to Corinne Patten, "I am so afraid that my fans in America have forgotten me." She needn't have worried. Her return was a triumph. Night after night, audiences rose to their feet to salute the former star of the Folies Bergere. For the many cheering fans who watched Josephine Baker prancing about the stage in towering headdresses and wigs, feathers and glitter, time had stood still.

The same year, 1960, *Los Angeles Times* columnist Art Seidenbaum interviewed Duke Ellington at the Marmont. He later wrote that "Ellington spread out in a large suite and lay down on a long couch as we talked. He had his grapefruit in the kitchen, his phonograph in the living room, and his associate, Billy Strayhorn, answering the phone."

Liberace's arrival at the Marmont always generated excitement. But it was not the flashy showman everyone wanted to see as much as it was his incredible car, which he parked on Marmont Lane in front of the hotel. "Whenever Liberace came to visit," Carmel Volti remembers, "we would drop everything and run outside to join the crowd that was gathering around the longest limousine I had ever seen. It was enormous, all black except for the back end, which was painted black and white like a piano keyboard."

Renowned jazz flutist Paul Horn met his wife Trentje Bom, at the Marmont. "Miss Bom Bom," as she was called, was a lovely, artistic Dutch girl and a former fashion model, who spent her years at the hotel as a knitwear designer for Catalina Swimwear. She also had hopes of creating costumes for Beatrice Lillie. It was said that Miss Lillie was so fond of Trentje that she longed to pair her up with her business manager, John Phillip Hock, so she could be "auntie" to their children. (Trentje liked to joke that her first-born would be named "Adam Bom".) Trentje wasn't interested in Hock, not with Paul Horn on the scene. How she made her point clear to Bea Lillie without offending her, and jeopardizing a possible business deal, isn't known, but she probably handled the situation in her usual fearless fashion. Trentje had a devilish streak, and a mind of her own.

A former Marmont desk clerk tells this story about her: "One morning, Sam Weisbord [head of the William Morris Agency] met Miss Bom in the lobby and said, 'I wish you wouldn't flush your toilet so early in the morning.' So what did she do? The very next morning she flushed eight times non-stop! Then she went to Mr. Weisbord and asked him if he would arrange a screen test for her."

Diahann Carroll was in Hollywood working in *Porgy and Bess* at the Goldwyn Studio when she met her co-star, Sidney Poitier. At the time, neither one knew they were sharing the same roof at the Marmont; Carroll had a suite on the first floor, Poitier a suite on the third. Although they were both married, Poitier talked her into having dinner with him. As he told it in his autobiography, *This Life,* "During the following weeks, I saw as much of her as she allowed. We went out to dinner again, to the movies, a couple of visits to night clubs on Sunset Strip, and best of all, there were evenings when we would study together in her apartment . . . " There were also moonlit walks up the hill behind the Marmont. "Halfway through the picture, we fell in love," Poitier confessed. The affair continued long after the completion of *Porgy and Bess,* often at the Marmont, when the two stars were in Hollywood.

Carroll and Poitier ultimately obtained divorces from their respective spouses, and for awhile, it appeared they would marry. But their times together, while sweet, did not always run smoothly. There were fears and anxieties, fights and loud shouting matches. "I should have gotten a clue when she threw that brush at me at the Chateau Marmont Hotel," Poitier says. "I should have known that this child was going to have the last word whenever she could."

After six years and two shattered marriages, the relationship ended. Diahann Carroll and Sidney Poitier continued to visit the Marmont, but their stays no longer coincided as they had in the past.

When Molly Picon arrived at Chateau Marmont on September 4, 1962, she seemed so thrilled that she nearly lurched into one of her patented cartwheels in the hotel lobby. Long an established star of the Yiddish theater and Broadway, Picon had taken a leave from her smash hit, *Milk and Honey,* to appear in the movie version of Neil Simon's *Come Blow Your Horn.* (The film's producer, Norman Lear, and director, Bud Yorkin, had filled her third-floor suite with flowers, necessitating a tranquilizer to quell her excitement.)

Hardly a day passed that Picon and her husband of forty-three years, Jacob ("Yonkel") Kalish, didn't act like typical tourists. They wandered about the Marmont in search of celebrities then in residence, important visitors such as Shelley Winters, Samuel Spewack, George Grizzard, Kim Stanley, Cathleen Nesbitt, Kevin McCarthy, and Diana Hyland. They dined at the best known celebrity hangouts, including Chasen's and Romanoff's. They "did" Disneyland. And they were quick to accept an invitation from the film's star, Frank Sinatra, to fly in his private plane for a few days in Las Vegas, where they were treated to all the shows and introduced to his current flame, Juliet Prowse. Picon was so filled with stories on her return to the Chateau that she gushed: "I could get used to so much red carpet treatment. Such pampering! *Is this a life?*"

The musical stars and musicians who frequented the Marmont were part of an era—a golden age in music—that would soon fade. Before the end of the 1960s, the hotel, like the rest of America, would be dancing to a different beat.

## Rockin' Along

The Sunset Strip, Hollywood's glittering playground for nearly three decades, was in a state of decline. The great attractions that had made the Strip famous were gone. Ciro's stood boarded up. The Trocadero, Mocambo, and Crescendo had been demolished. Shiny chauffeured limousines, carrying fur-clad glamor girls and tuxedoed leading men, no longer motored leisurely along the Strip. They had been replaced by teenagers in black leather and Levis, cruising in hot rods and on motorcycles.

Forlorn Strip operators sought answers to the boulevard's deterioration. They blamed entertainment taxes and Las Vegas, which was luring top talent to its hugh hotel showrooms at sky-high salaries. "We simply can't compete," they cried. The old-time nightclub had become all but obsolete.

In their desperation, the Strip operators began experimenting with an idea borrowed from Europe, the *discotheque*. The basic premise was simple. It required little more than a dance floor, a jukebox or combo, and available food and drink at affordable prices. But nothing in Hollywood remains simple for long. In a once dignified building, formerly occupied by a branch of Bank of America, the new showplace of the Sunset Strip was born. Painted a gaudy green, the Whiskey a Go Go opened its doors in the mid-1960s. Inside were light displays, a platformed bandstand, blaring amplifiers, and scantily-clad, wiggling human "birds" in glass-enclosed cages. Outside were Kleig lights, Hippodrome-like poster displays, and lines of clamoring customers stretching into the hills. The Whiskey quickly became the most successful nightspot in America. Everyone from the Shah of Iran and a Russian track team to movie stars and teeny boppers wanted in to see the action.

Following the success of the Whiskey, any old shell of a building was soon wired for sound, as trendy discos opened up and down the Strip. The old elegance hadn't returned—far from it—but business was booming.

With its close proximity to the Strip's hot new clubs, the Marmont became a natural haven for rock musicians and singers. Many of the young performers weren't fussy about their accommodations or privacy. As one of the hotel's new breed of guests commented: "Where else can a group traveling nine deep, with instruments and sound equipment, get a better deal?"

Ann Little and Meemi Ferguson would have recommended other accommodations. In recent years, however, Chateau Marmont, like the Strip itself, had lost much of its luster. The hotel continued to attract its faithful, plus an impressive roster of new arrivals, but there was no denying that the Marmont, once the Grand Dame of the Strip, was in a decline. "Things were changing so quickly in the late 1960s, and not always for the best," a former employee admitted. "The hotel was beginning to open its doors to all comers—even those who couldn't afford the rates, which weren't all that steep. The people at the desk used to joke that they didn't care if a guest had money or not. They only checked their pulse rates."

The Marmont was taking on a decidedly different atmosphere as rock groups began to descend upon the hotel. Among the groups who stayed at the Marmont during this period were Ambergris, the Moody Blues, Dan Hicks and his Hot Licks, Yellow Bird, The Velvet Underground, Blood Rock, and Blue Breakers. They were followed by the Steve Miller Band, Sea Train, The Band, Meatloaf, the Jerry Corbett Group, Lewis and Clark, J.Geils Band, the Jeff Beck Group, Quicksilver, Jefferson Airplane, MotherEarth, Crosby Stills Nash & Young, The Charlie Daniels Band—and six Brazilian teenagers from a new and nameless South American combo.

There were budding stars and superstars as well: Richie Havens, Leo Sayer, Rod Stewart, Joe Cocker, Gram Parsons, Ricki Lee Jones, Boz Scaggs, Grace Slick, Jimi Hendrix, John Sebastian, Cat Stevens, Mary Travers, James Taylor and Carly Simon, Terry Reid, Robbie Robertson, Rick James, Marvin Gaye, Laura Nyro, Linda Ronstadt, and Mick Jagger.

Many of the younger Marmont employees were thrilled to have the rock stars at the hotel. "It nearly blew my mind when Janis Joplin walked in," a former desk clerk remembers. "I had seen her at the Monterey Festival in 1967, and she fractured everybody, including me. I had had a preconceived notion of what she would be like in person, but she was totally different. She was staying in 1F, and every once in awhile she would stop by the desk to talk. What surprised me was how pleasant and polite she was. That and her voice. It was very feminine, almost dainty. Then she would walk onstage and sound like a truck driver."

Phoebe Snow was another staff favorite, even though no one could understand why she lived in the hotel, while her friends lived in a parked van on Monteel Road.

Titian-haired Irish rocker, Van Morrison, found himself alone over the holidays during one of his Marmont stays. At a loss for something to do, he camped at the piano in the lobby, where he offered a private concert for some of the staff.

Graham Nash checked in for one night and stayed five months. He brought with him his own piano, on which he churned out one new song after another.

Of all the groups to visit the Marmont over the years, The Clash received the highest marks. "They present a pretty tough image," a staff member told an interviewer, "but they are all nice, pleasant guys."

Not all of the reports on rock groups have been as positive. From the manager of another rock 'n' roll-infested Sunset Strip hotel came news that members of Led Zeppelin had held motorcycle races down one of the hotel's main corridors. That wasn't all. Some of Alice Cooper's "roadies" had been caught playing football nude on the mezzanine. "Most of them don't worry about damages," the harried manager moaned. "If I could draw 18,000 fans at ten dollars a ticket I wouldn't worry either."

The Marmont never encountered anything quite so rowdy, even after Led Zeppelin and the Alice Cooper group switched bases, but there were problems. Unpleasant, and potentially dangerous, problems.

An incident involving Jim Morrison, lead singer with The Doors, made the papers, following a bizarre encounter with a female companion, in which blood-soaked sheets were discovered in his suite. Later, for an encore, he fell out of a second floor window, injuring his legs and back. That one went unreported.

Many of the suites were left in shambles. "Richie Havens was practically banned from the hotel," reported John Howell. "And we had to be very rough with Bob Dylan because of his visitors."

Long-haired, super record producer Phil Spector arrived at the Marmont late one night, wearing wraparound dark glasses, a flowing black cloak, Cuban-heel boots, and carrying a large cage containing two cats. Carmel Volti, who signed Spector in, admitted that he looked "very bizarre." She also added: "He had the cage with the two cats, and people with pets are always stable. So we let him in."

"It was a crazy time," admitted Donald Spackman. "Word was getting out that the Marmont harbored drug addicts and hippie groups, as well as rock stars. That wasn't entirely true, but there were a lot of scruffy people roaming around."

One afternoon, a writer from London entered the Marmont to find a dozen or so long-haired bodies squirming harmlessly about the Persian rug in the adjacent drawing room. "It looks like the cast from *Hair*," he said facetiously. It *was* the cast from *Hair,* rehearsing under the watchful eyes of director Tom O'Horgan and composers Gerome Ragni and James Rado.

During the late 1960s (and even into the 1970s), the hotel was highly vulnerable. Never had it ever been so abused and battered. Or so helpless. The owners—whoever they happened to be at the time—were never present. The Marmont was being run by an interim manager, a young Scandinavian more interested in becoming a film star than a hotel executive. He could not chance offending anyone in show business who, if not in a position to further his acting ambition, could "connect him to the right people." Besides, he wasn't around all that much either. He often feigned headaches, leaving the hotel in the hands of underlings, while he supervised the installation of a swimming pool at his home. For his construction crew, he spirited strongarm workers from the Marmont's payroll.

The action around the Marmont pool, where members of British rock groups like Pink Floyd frolicked unattended, was more fascinating. Stripped down for a bit of quick color, their pale skin stood out like snowflakes on a summer day.

From outside came calls complaining about the racket being made by the young rock musicians, especially those living in the bungalows, who all-too-frequently returned to the hotel following a night's performance and played till dawn. "It's not only the noise," the neighbors screamed, "they park their cars and vans everywhere, so we can't get ours out!"

There were calls from inside the Marmont too. Late one evening, an advertising executive from the east angrily phoned the switchboard to report a disturbance in the next suite. The disgruntled guest blamed a blasting radio. The operator didn't argue, even though she knew a radio wasn't the cause; night after night she had received similar complaints from various parts of the hotel. But she tried to placate the gentleman by assuring him that "we'll take care of it."

She placed a call to the offending suite, and after countless rings, someone finally picked up the receiver. The background noise that greeted her nearly dislodged her headset. "I'm sorry, but we've had a complaint . . .," she began.

The line went dead. She tried again, with the same result.

On the third try, she didn't even have a chance to speak. A barely intelligible voice cut her off with a screeching *"Rock 'n' roll forever!"*

The switchboard operator just sighed.

Beatrice Lillie brought new meaning to the phrase "balmy days" during her visits to the Marmont.

Hermione Baddeley—wild parties and intimate gatherings.

# Chapter 14

## The British Invasion

### The Crown's Jewels

For nearly sixty years, travelers from Europe have found their way to the Marmont. There have been wealthy industrialists, financiers, artists, and designers, even royalty, but no group has outnumbered the British stage and screen stars. At times, they have arrived in such waves that the hotel's corridors have sounded more like Piccadilly than the heart of Hollywood.

The movement began during the Depression, picked up speed after World War II, then all but exploded during the 1960s. Guests included Terry-Thomas, Stanley Holloway, Patricia Medina, Trevor Howard, Claire Bloom, Lionel Jeffries, Wendy Hiller, Diana Rigg, Nigel Green, and Estelle Winwood.

They were followed by Hugh Griffith, Julie Andrews, Anthony Steele, Beryl Reid, Georgia Brown, Martita Hunt, Ann Todd, and Glynis Johns.

And still later: Sean Connery, Lynn Redgrave, Pamela Franklin, the Fox brothers (James and Edward), Peter Finch, Shani Wallis, Peter Coe, Tom Courtenay, Petula Clark, Susannah York, Tony Richardson, John and Hayley Mills, Donald Pleasance, Charlotte Rampling, and David Warner.

Wilfred Hyde-White, the puckish, white-haired actor, stayed at the Marmont while filming *Let's Make Love.* Everyone believed that the mischievous twinkle in his eye came from working with Marilyn Monroe—until they saw his stunning, very young wife.

Cedric Hardwicke, the veteran actor, was apparently all thumbs. Each day the switchboard received an urgent call from his wife asking to send someone to their suite to zip up her dress.

Roddy McDowell impressed the staff as being "a very witty, very busy, and very charming young man," who moved from one picture to another. When he wasn't at the studio, he was seldom seen without a camera in his hands. Corinne Patten used to brag to her friends that he was the hotel's "star photographer." He may have been—when he wasn't eating. One of the garage crew noted, "Roddy liked the food from Greenblatt's delicatessen. Three or four times a week, he would send out for sandwiches, then we would get the call to pick them up and deliver them to him." (Greenblatt's was the place where they used to display bad checks from famous customers in the store window. They stayed up, for all to see, until the debts were paid.)

British actor Richard Haydn remembered visiting the refined Isobel Jeans during her stay at the Marmont. She was there while making *Gigi,* in which she played Leslie Caron's mother. "We were reminiscing, when she stopped in the middle of the conversation and said, rather fearfully, 'I've heard so many reports about earthquakes in California. Why do I feel as if I'm living on the third floor of a piece of merinque?'"

It was also at the Marmont that Haydn overheard the indomitable octogenarian, Estelle Winwood, tell an aspiring young actress, "Go home and stop acting silly!"

David Hemmings would have appreciated an occasional cold shoulder. His problem was receiving too much attention from American actress Gayle Hunnicutt. Hemmings did everything possible to elude the persistent Hunnicutt, short of switching hotels. He even had some of the guests covering for him. One day, as one of his "accomplices" recalls, Hemmings was in the lobby when he caught sight of a fast-approaching Hunnicutt. He dashed for the nearest hideaway, which happened to be the lobby phone booth; with its heavy Gothic door and small window, it provided excellent protection. Before he disappeared, however, he somehow managed to persuade an innocent woman bystander to post guard at the door, as if she was waiting to use the phone. When Hunnicutt came into the lobby, there was no sign of Hemmings. She glanced quizzically at the lady blocking the telephone booth, then at the closed door. "Oh, somebody's in there," the bystander smiled. "I'm just waiting to use the phone." The subterfuge worked, but only temporarily. Hunnicutt eventually caught her man and married him.

Several years before John Williams, the Academy Award-winning composer-conductor, made a name for himself, the Chateau had a John Williams dilemma. It seems the hotel frequently had two John Williamses registered at the same time. One was "an old, old man from Dallas who had made a fortune in Monte Carlo." The other was the distinguished British character actor. To help solve the confusion, the desk assigned a middle initial to one of the gentlemen.

John Williams, the actor, and his wife, Helen, also made their home in La Jolla, California, but they stayed at the Marmont whenever Mr. Williams was working, which was often. Since neither of the Williamses drove, John took taxis to the studio. Helen seldom left the hotel, but she was not reclusive. Each afternoon, around five o'clock, she appeared elegantly dressed in the lobby to await the arrival of her husband's taxi. She always brought along a martini, which she delicately sipped, to keep her company and help pass the time.

There was also a slight problem with the two Hermiones—Gingold and Baddeley. Though no one knew why (or would dare admit it), it seemed that the two ladies weren't the best of friends. They were rarely, if ever, seen together. In fact, their closest mutual friends were careful to avoid being seen by one Hermione while in the company of the other. There was even an unwritten rule at the Marmont: "Never put Gingold and Baddeley in the same room."

Despite the behind-the-scenes chatter, neither Hermione would stay anyplace but the Marmont while in Hollywood. Perhaps they were drawn by the hotel's old-world atmosphere. Perhaps it was the ever-present English crowd that attracted them. Looking back, Hermione Baddeley remembered "a lady at the desk—her name escapes me, but I think she was Scottish—who was most kind to British people." (Probably Meemi, of the Ferguson clan.) More than anything, however, she talked about "the good times and good fun. It was a *very* special place."

Around the Marmont, Miss Baddeley had a reputation for being rather unique herself.

## Miss Baddeley

It's hard to believe that someone who was so much a part of the Marmont for so many years, once ran from the hotel in tears, vowing never to return. Hermione Baddeley did just that. But the Marmont wasn't the only place she wanted to put behind her. She had had it with Hollywood *and* America.

The emotional departure took place following her third visit to Chateau

Marmont. Her two previous experiences held much fonder memories.

Hermione Baddeley was one of the chosen few when she first arrived at the Marmont on March 26, 1960, to attend the Academy Awards ceremony, having been nominated as Best Supporting Actress for her role in the British production, *Room at the Top.* She didn't win (she lost to Shelley Winters in *The Diary of Anne Frank),* but her stay had enough high spots to have made the long journey worthwhile. She was being courted by Bill Sitwell (a cousin of noted English poet, Dame Edith Sitwell) and partied with magnums of champagne. "Hermione loved the bubbly," a mutual friend recalled, "and Bill kept her well stocked with the stuff—he must have had a pipeline to the Liquor Locker. Many an afternoon, they would have guests in for champagne and what Bill called 'canaps.' It took me a while to figure that one out. 'Canaps, *canaps!* he would say. It was his way of pronouncing *canapes.*"

Hermione was also friendly with the Marmont's unofficial housemother, female impersonator T.C. Jones. T.C. lived next door to Hermione on the third floor, and when she wasn't the object of champagne toasts, she frequently made her way to T.C.'s suite. There they shared an odd mutual interest: dyeing shoes. T.C. had entire rooms filled with shoes that had either just been dyed or were slated for a color switch. There were pumps, wedgies, platforms, ankle straps, slings, even ballerinas, in every hue— and all enormous.

In those days, Hermione was far better known in England than in America, despite her long career on stage and in films as an actress-comedienne. There were the occasional mix-ups with Miss Gingold, who had made such an impression in *Gigi,* and with Hermione Baddeley's sister, veteran actress Angela Baddeley. The role that would make her a household name in America, that of the guzzling, demented, old cockney, Mrs. Naugatuck, on the hit television series, *Maude,* was still years away.

Jill Jackson remembered her first encounter with Baddeley at the Marmont: "Hermione loved to hang around the pool and sun. We were both there one day, when I looked over and thought, 'My God, that lady looks familiar.' I wasn't really sure, so I went over and said, 'Excuse me, but aren't you . . . Hermione Baddeley?' She turned and replied, in a terribly thick-as-pudding accent, 'Yes, and who are *you?*' When I told her I was a columnist, she warmed up and we talked. But I couldn't get over how timid she was, even after we became friends. Very, *very* timid. If we went anywhere together, she would always get behind me. I always had to lead the way."

A few years later, in February of 1964, Hermione returned to the Marmont while working in two films, *The Unsinkable Molly Brown* and *Mary Poppins*. She was back again on June 18, 1966.

She had been summoned to Hollywood by Walt Disney himself for the title role in his next big picture, *Mrs. 'arris Goes to Paris*. "It had taken Mr. Disney nearly a year to get the rights to do the film," she recalled. First Jean Arthur had them—she wanted the story as a vehicle for herself—then Ray Stark. Disney was having a successful discussion with Stark when he sent for me. I remember him coming to me and saying, 'Isn't this wonderful? I've got my little comic charlady. I'm going to do for you what I did for Miss Andrews [in *Mary Poppins*]!' For some reason, he was crazy about old English actresses like Julie Andrews and Gladys Cooper and me."

Preparations began for the filming, but there were delays and *more* delays. "It was very odd sitting and waiting for this film to begin," Baddeley said. But she didn't seem to mind too much . She was on an expense-paid vacation, happily ensconced in the Marmont's Bungalow B ("my very favorite place"). She had her dog with her—"I *always* have a dog with me"—and a friend, Joan (Lady Ashton Smith), to keep her company. There were relaxing hours by the pool and visits with her Marmont neighbors, Peter Finch and his twenty-two-year-old wife-to-be, Jackie. And there were parties. Always parties.

"While I was waiting at the Marmont," said Hermione, "I gave a little party for Paul Gallico, the author of *Mrs. 'arris*. I do believe that dear Gladys [Cooper] was there, Rex Harrison and Rachael Roberts, Peter Finch—he could get marvelously drunk—his Jackie, and so many others. It was great fun."

By Thanksgiving, the picture still hadn't gone into production. To make matters worse, Walt Disney had taken seriously ill. His doctors discovered a tumor on his lung. The patient survived the surgery, but he was stricken with acute circulatory collapse and died in mid-December. "Suddenly there was no *Mrs. 'arris,* no money, and it was all rather ghastly," Hermione recalled. "I ran home in tears. I never wanted to come back."

But she did. She returned to the Marmont the following year for another Disney film, *The Happiest Millionaire* (*Mrs 'arris Goes to Paris* was never made), and again year after year.

While living at the Marmont, Hermione became one of Hollywood's great party-givers and a much in-demand guest. She hosted "a wild birthday party" for Gladys Cooper, who arrived wearing a floor-length mink coat over a stunning silk leopard evening gown. Paul Lynde was also there.

Not to be upstaged, he walked in wearing long turquoise earrings and Estelle Winwood's hat, then pranced around in Cooper's coat until she pointed a finger at him and yipped, "Take off my coat!" To show there were no hard feelings, he picked up her birthday cake and bit off one entire side.

On another occasion, Hermione hosted an intimate gathering for Rex Harrison in the Marmont lobby and main-floor drawing room. According to Hermione's good friend Marshall Stewart, "Everyone was there. Flora Robson, Terry-Thomas, Donald Pleasance, Sybil Burton and Jordon Christopher, Margaret Leighton, Glynis Johns, Lila Kedrova, Roloff Benny, Elsa Lancaster, Greta Keller, Dame Edith Evans, Edward Mulhare, Christopher Isherwood, Tennessee Williams—*everyone*! Hermione had the largest platter imaginable stacked to the ceiling with lobster tails, and the champagne flowed like water. Lady Ashton Smith was just in from London, and she wore a creation with huge cabbage roses—and a flock of birds—popping out of her bosom. That was the evening Dame Edith cornered Peter Finch with a bit of advice. She told him: 'You know, you used to get wonderful laughs, but you're not getting any lately, are you? Comedy is like firing powder puffs out of a cannon—and you're firing cannon balls!"

There were brunches in her bungalow, lunches at Poopies (a snack shop next to Schwab's), and swims at 4:00 in the morning. During one of Baddeley's late-night soirees, at which Lady Ashley Smith was present, comic Larry Storch turned to a friend and said, "I want you to meet a *real* Lady." They found her passed out on the floor, "like a gargoyle," between two of Hermione's rooms.

One New Year's Eve, Hermione received a call from Marshall Stewart to inquire about her plans for the evening. "Oh, I'm going to some boring party," she replied.

"Let's meet at the Marmont and do midnight," Marshall suggested. Hermione was all for that. They wound up house-hopping, driving from one wild party to another in Hermiones' limo. Way past midnight, as they were departing their seventh celebration, believing the night's festivities were at last winding down, a neighbor's door suddenly opened. "Come on over!" yelled somebody with waving arms. Because of the noises coming from within, it sounded like a party was still in full swing. One was. Inside were clusters of chattering people, tables filled with fancy delectables, and a piano, which Marshall, an accomplished pianist, found irresistible. As Marshall remembered: "I was playing away, and Hermione was running back and forth bringing me platters of food, gobbling along the way. We had made ourselves completely at home—taken over, actually—when we were confronted by a rather imperious lady, who happened to be Helena Kallianiotes, the Greek woman from *Five Easy Pieces*. 'Do you know whose house this is?' she inquired. Hermione drew herself up and gazed boldly about. 'Not really,' she replied in her best British accent. Miss Kallianiotes couldn't wait to inform us. 'You're in Jack Nicholson's house,' she said, with a touch of hrumpf, then departed. I returned to the piano, and Hermione resumed eating. A few minutes later, Mr. Nicholson appeared, as if someone had just tattled on us. He couldn't have been more charming, but we didn't push our luck. As soon as Hermione finished her plate, we headed back to the Marmont."

On another occasion, Hermione was on her way to the airport from the Marmont with Lady Ashton Smith (Lady Joan) and her rare French bulldog, Lottie, when they smelled a foul odor. Looking about, they discovered that old Lottie had lost control. Hermione nudged Lady Joan, who quickly pulled out a tissue. "But Joan," Hermione said darkly, "it's *more* than *that*." Lady Joan tucked the tissue away, as Hermione unraveled a luxurious silk scarf and dropped it over the pile. When they reached their destination, Hermione handed the chauffeur fifty dollars and said, with typical British reserve, "There's been a little something in the back seat."

Hermione Baddeley was in and out of the Marmont through 1974, the year she became a regular on *Maude*. Of that experience, she cracked: "They kept giving me less and less to do, because Maude herself didn't care for the competition, and by the fourth season, I was only being allowed to put my head around the door with a tea tray. I didn't want to get into the 'Yes, mum, no mum' thing, so when they reduced me to one line a week, I stopped showing up."

When Hermione departed the Marmont, she bought a house not far from the hotel in the Hollywood Hills. She told a reporter from the *London Times:* "I now live mainly in California, where there's still a lot of work in television for old English eccentrics, especially if you can do a cockney accent. If the money gets short, I go on the chat shows and do all my old Coward numbers. That seems to keep them happy, and it pays for the dog food."

# Rub-A-Dub-Dub

In all its years, the Marmont has never had a cocktail lounge, a restaurant, a doorman, or uniformed bellboys, some of the usual amenities considered *de riguer* at first-class hotels. But it did have Joe Leigh.

For nearly two decades, Joe Leigh plied many of the most famous bodies in Hollywood. It was said that his talented hands could ease away flab and relax even the most stubborn, tense muscles. Leigh was the Marmont's masseur *par excellence*—and one of the world's great gentlemen. "Lucky for Joe that he was," a former associate commented. "He could easily have gotten in real trouble."

When Leigh, an Englishman with a heavy Mile End Road accent, first came to the Marmont in 1960, it was not legally permissable for a man to massage a woman. Joe shunned the law and got away with it. "No one complained about Joe," said Carmel Volti, "because he was strictly business. He did his job, and that was it. He never even discussed his clients. But we knew who they were, because he received all his calls and messages through the switchboard. The stars were always calling to set up appointments." The fact that "gentleman Joe" refused to discuss his illustrious clientele nettled Corinne Patten. She dogged him for years, hoping to pick up tidbits for her Marmont scrapbook.

Joe had his own little black book that listed names, dates, hours, and places. Most of his patrons were guests at the hotel. He preferred seeing them in their suites, but he willingly traveled to the studios for sessions, if they were working.

Peggy Lee was one of Joe Leigh's regulars. So were Ann Sheridan, Richard Boone, Vivien Leigh, Donald Sutherland, and Stella Stevens. Diahann Carroll called on Joe almost every day. Burl Ives, when he weighed in at 350 pounds, insisted on complete massages with a wintergreen astringent. On those days, Joe was forever washing his hands. "That's very heady stuff," was his only comment.

He also worked on Ann Sothern. Ann, who loved to eat, was not one of Joe's most disciplined customers. If she didn't have a banana in her hand, she had a chocolate bar. She claimed the candy gave her energy, but the only exercise she got was climbing one flight of stairs, from the lobby to her second-floor suite. She wouldn't have done that if she hadn't been so terrified of elevators.

Joe didn't approve of Ann Sothern's sedentary lifestyle or eating habits. He was one of the earliest believers in "the body is a temple" credo. He placed special emphasis on its care and feeding, especially his own. He exercised. He watched his diet. He encouraged his wife, his daughters, his friends to follow his lead without being preachy.

If anyone was a walking advertisement for healthful living, it was Joe Leigh. He was solid and lean; his muscles were well defined. He had the look of a featherweight champion.

One day, that look began to fade. For the first time in his life, Joe admitted that he didn't feel "right." He saw a doctor; he took tests. The results were not encouraging. Joe had cancer.

"As sick as Joe was, he came to work every day," Carmel recalled. "We would see him growing thinner and thinner, but he refused to give up—or slow down. Joe *had* to keep working. And he did just that, almost to the day he died."

# Lady Peel

She wore the most enormous mink coat ever seen at Chateau Marmont, a great mass of fur that billowed as she crossed the lobby from the elevator to the front desk. In the crook of her arm, all but lost in mink, she carried a wildly fuzzy black Pekingese with huge round eyes.

Reaching the counter, she paused momentarily to straighten the small pillbox that crowned her sleek, boyish bob. Then, picking up a pen, she cut the air with a flourish, and began printing in bold letters: L-A-D-Y P-E-E-L. For good measure, or the unworldly, she added in rather miniscule handwriting, *Beatrice Lillie.*

At the front desk, two women stood watching the grand entrance. One of them, her curiosity piqued, leaned forward and asked, 'Are you *really* a Lady?"

Beatrice Lillie straightened noticeably and answered, in a voice that could be heard clear to the Pacific shore, "You're goddamned right!" It was a line she would use over and over during her stay at the Marmont, one she had borrowed from one of her early revues. She would, at times, explain its origin. Then again, depending on her mood, she would leave the startled questioners with their mouths open.

Bea Lillie first checked into Chateau Marmont on May 23, 1966, accompanied by her longtime companion and manager, John Phillip Huck, and her beloved Pekingese, Lord Button of Henley-on-Thames. She had returned to Hollywood to do a film, her first in eleven years, but she had no idea how long she would be staying. "Weeks, months . . ., who knows?" she told the desk clerk. "I tend to get stuck in places."

Bea's movie, *Thoroughly Modern Millie,* was to be a musical comedy, starring Julie Andrews, Mary Tyler Moore, and another Marmont guest, Carol Channing. Over a dozen songs were scheduled, but none for Bea, despite her years in British and American musical revues.

Huck, a large, heavy-set Englishman, made no attempt to hide his displeasure with Bea's appearance in the film. The fact that her role was non-singing was not the issue. He simply didn't want her working. "Someone got to her when I wasn't around," he confided angrily to a friend. "It's a difficult part, much too strenuous. If it were up to me, she wouldn't be doing it."

Huck's interest in Beatrice Lillie was more than professional; he was totally devoted to her, and he rarely let her out of his sight. A former singer himself, Huck had served as a lieutenant in the Marine Corps before starting as her personal representative in the late 1940s.

His concern was for her health. At seventy-three, Bea had suffered a series of "little strokes or something." Her odd behavior was nothing new. It had been so much a part of her wonderfully outrageous personality for so long that no one was quite certain if she had been born balmy or if she had taken on the quirkiness of the characters she had played. Recently, however, she had become strangely vague at times—or so it seemed. As a friend at the Marmont commented, "With Bea, how can one really tell?"

Bea took to wandering the corridors of Chateau Marmont shortly after her arrival. One day she came across an open door, and, seeing a woman gently rocking a child, she quietly stepped inside to join them. When she got close enough, she blurted, "I see you've got a baby there."

As if responding on cue, the "baby" sprang from the woman's lap. "Hello, I'm Alison Arngrim," she said brightly, "and this is my mommy, Norma. Want to see my new rocking chair?" The tiny four-year-old youngster took Bea by the hand and sat her down, then climbed aboard.

Bea was charmed by the precocious Alison (who as a teenager would play "the prairie bitch," Nellie Olson, on TV's *Little House on the Prairie*), and returned often to the Arngrim suite not only to rock her newfound little friend but to entertain with comical dances and cockney sketches. For her performances, the living room furniture had to be rearranged against the walls. She needed leg space, she said. There were also macabre songs. As a gift, Alison had received a "baby first step" doll. Bea could not resist working it into a ditty. "Little baby first step," she sang darkly, "will it be her last step . . .?"

When little Alison celebrated her fifth birthday at the Marmont with a party in her parents' suite, Bea Lillie was there, along with John Philip

Huck, to entertain Alison and her playmates with a ditty in English and French. "Mouse, mouse, come out of your house," she sang. "You shall sit on a tuft of hay, I will frighten the cats away . . . Mouse, mouse, when you've gone to bed, I shall give you a large loaf of bread . . ." The youngsters were enthralled.

Lillie's gift to Alison was an East Indian head. As Alison's mother remembered: "It was a beautiful thing, with big eyes—but no body. Bea came up to me later and said, rather pitifully, 'I just don't know what to give little children.' " It took John Phillip Huck awhile to warm up to the occasion. He stayed in the background throughout the games and songs, but hovered over the children when it came time for cake and ice cream. No sooner had they finished eating than he polished off the leftovers, including the balance of the birthday cake.

It wasn't long before the Arngrims, fellow Canadians, began including Bea, John Phillip Huck, and Lord Button in their activities. A show-business family, Norma and her husband, Thor, had worked in stage productions in Canada; on Broadway, Thor had appeared in *Luther*. Ten-year-old son, Stefan, was active in television.

Whenever their schedules allowed, Bea and her inseparable companion, Lord Button, would join the Arngrims at the Plush Pup, an open-air hot dog stand on Sunset, across from the Marmont. "They served only junk food," Norma remembered, "but Bea loved to eat there. She adored the atmosphere, it amused her." One day, while reminiscing, Bea made a swooping gesture with her hands and fell backward off her stool into the bushes. For a second, no one realized she had disappeared, then panic set in. "We looked at each other with blank faces," Norma said. "She was sitting there, then she wasn't—gone in a flash!" It didn't take long to find Bea. She was covered with leaves, having the time of her life. A grand joke, she called it.

As close as Beatrice Lillie was to her "very lordly" Lord Button, she could not be bothered taking him for walks. Instead, several times a day she would carry the little Pekingese to the front door in the lobby, set him down, and let him run out to the grassy garden, where he would relieve himself. After that, he would run back to her arms to be carried upstairs.

(An incident often blamed on Lady Peel actually happened to Trentje Bom. "Miss Bom Bom" had two enormous bassett hounds that, by all accounts, weighed at least sixty pounds each and resembled huge brown bolsters. One night, after checking into the Marmont for the first time, Trentje headed for the elevator, carting straw baskets, suitcases, and her two dogs. As she was waiting for the elevator doors to open, one of the hounds squatted at her feet, leaving a mound worthy of a dog its size. A former desk clerk, who witnessed the scene, recalled: "Miss Bom never blinked an eye. She simply took a scarf from her neck, scooped up the pile, put it in one of her bags, and nonchalantly entered the waiting elevator.")

While wandering around the Marmont, Beatrice Lillie also became friendly with several staff members, including switchboard operator Carmel Volti. One evening, Bea asked Carmel to join her and John Philip Huck for an evening of theater. Carmel eagerly accepted, even though she wasn't quite sure what was in store; Bea had only said, "How would you like to see The Wild Fuck?" It wasn't until the trio arrived at the theater that Carmel discovered she was to see *The Wild Duck*.

During the filming of *Thoroughly Modern Millie,* Bea was approached to appear on several TV variety shows originating from Hollywood. She refused. "Television," she said, "is just summer stock in an iron lung." One offer, however, fascinated her. John Phillip Huck wasn't as sold, but he was willing to hear more about it.

James Doolittle was producing a Cole Porter revue at Hollywood's Huntington Hartford Theater. Cast members Thor Arngrim and Ben Bagley had already been set, but he needed a headliner. Doolittle felt that Beatrice Lillie, with her unique talent, was the ideal choice. If arrangements could be worked out, she would be his star.

One Sunday afternoon, Thor and Norma Arngrim, Bea Lillie, and John Phillip Huck drove to Doolittle's house in Trousdale Estates, an exclusive residential community (the world's most expensive subdivision), located in the highlands above Beverly Hills. Bea sat silently as the car made its way through winding Trousdale streets, past the magnificent, modern mansions of gleaming white marble and glass. Many of the homes featured marble columns in bold contemporary designs, slabs rather than traditional cylinders. When Doolittle greeted his guests at the door, Bea's first words were, "What time's the funeral?" The meeting did not go well.

In her suite at the Marmont, Bea often amused herself at her easel. She turned to painting as a hobby, she said, during World War II, "to take my mind off things." Friends described her earthy style as "quite accomplished," but *unusual* may have been more fitting. Bea's technique varied from day to day. When she tired of using brushes, she would apply the paints with her fingers, the palms of her hands, even clenched fists. She admitted that she could work as well on all fours as she could standing up.

More than anything, however, Bea loved to ride in cars. Twice a week, at least, she would ask the Arngrims to take her for a drive. She knew exactly what she wanted to see and where she wanted to go: only the Hollywood Hills would do.

With Thor at the wheel, John Philip Huck pointing the way, and Lord Button wrapped in Bea's arms, they would drive up and down, back and forth, along twisting treacherous streets, some so narrow that only a single car could pass safely. "I was terrified," Thor remembered. "We had just come out from New York, and I had never driven in the hills before. It would have been frightening enough during the day, but we could only get away after work in the evenings."

Bea knew no fear. She sat regally in the back seat, chatting continuously while searching out homes and landmarks from her early days in Hollywood. She mentioned names from the past, dear friends Fanny Brice, and Gertrude Lawrence; how she missed them, she said. "No matter how long we had been separated over the years, we could always pick things up without skipping a beat."

Reviving memories may have been the real reason for the repeated rides. Prior to Bea's arrival at the Marmont, she had signed a contract to write her autobiography. She fought doing it, but she didn't want to return the advance, which she admitted was sizeable. Hell would freeze over, she said, before she would part with a cent.

Bea Lillie departed Chateau Marmont in early 1967, but she and John Philip Huck were back several years later, following the publication of her book. This time her arms were empty; Lord Button did not make the trip. "My precious little Oriental gentleman in gone," she said, with a faraway look in her eyes.

Bea no longer swept through the lobby or wandered the corridors in search of new friends. She refused to ride the elevator. There were no quips, no little songs. As Hermione Baddeley remembered: "Bea turned down all invitations to parties. She was rather content to stay put. But she was very kind to my dog."

Housekeeper Daisy Grossen and switchboard operator Carmel Volti at the front desk, late 1960s.

Two windows overlooking Marmont Lane, at the far end of the main-floor drawing room, were boarded up to keep out trespassers.

# Chapter 15

## The Natives Are Restless

## With A Cast Of Thousands

The glamor of old Hollywood and its fabled haunts, long the attraction of the Sunset Strip, was slowly fading. In its place came more colorful and contemporary attractions. Pandora's Box, a screaming coffee house, just a stone's throw from the Marmont, changed its exterior decor—from purple to orange to shocking green—with alarming regularity. Across the street sat the Plush Pup, hot-dog heaven, with its mouth-watering smoke signals. Down the way were the Strip Thrills boutique, Alfie's Sidewalk Cafe, the Brotherhood of the Source (a "microbiotic" cafe), Kelly's Kick (with its "Funk and Blues Cocktail Hour"), the Body Shop (the "sexiest garage in Hollywood"), and the Classic Cat, a most unusual watering hole that offered topless and *bottomless* divertissements.

By 1966, the Sunset Strip was no longer the playground of Hollywood's elite. It had become a mecca for the young, hip, and restless—and the scene of numerous demonstrations and riots protesting America's involvement in Vietnam.

The situation at the Marmont was equally unsettled. On Sunday, December 11, 1966, the *Los Angeles Times* carried the headline: CHATEAU MARMONT TO BE AUCTIONED. A short report followed. It read: "Chateau Marmont Hotel, a Sunset Strip landmark, is featured in the public auction of $4 million of income properties on Friday. The auction will be conducted at 1:30 by Milton J. Weshow Co. in the Garden West Room of the Statler Hilton in Los Angeles."

The auction went ahead on schedule, but the Marmont remained unsold and the property of Loughridge, Ltd. Bids had been tendered—low bids. Too low.

Throughout 1967, Loughridge continued to seek a buyer and, in late December, one was found: a group of Beverly Hills attorneys headed by Marvin Rowen, Paul Levinson, and Harold Klein. They called their new partnership Chateau Marmont, Ltd.

Several months prior to the sale to the attorneys, as the Vietnam war reached its height, a particularly large gathering of long-haired, bearded, and beaded young people began to form along the curve of Sunset Boulevard, just below the hotel. By early evening, the body count had swelled to thousands. They raised their voices, placards, and fists, as they overflowed the sidewalks onto the street, choking traffic. The darkening sky seemed to bring out their anger. Battalions of police arrived, armed with clubs and tear gas, to set up barricades—but not before a bus had been toppled. As if on cue, a film crew appeared to film the riotous action. The footage would be used the following year in an exploitation movie called *Wild in the Streets*.

There was concern that the unruly anti-war demonstrators might spread up the hill. Men from the Sheriff's department stood guard in the Marmont lobby and garage, just in case. All guests and visitors were screened before entering; anyone wanting to leave was urged to stay put. "It was like a war zone," Norma Arngrin recalled.

Few guests wanted to venture outside. They had only to take to the hotel's balconies and fire escapes for the best—and safest—view in town. And that they did. As the evening progressed, the terraces became crowded with fascinated onlookers, who turned the occasion into more of a celebration than one of impending disaster. They sipped wine, ate cheese and Triscuits, and traded banter befitting the moment. Overheard from one balcony to another: "The peasants are revolting."

"Let them eat cake!" came the reply.

On another terrace, a visitor from Canada, seemingly bored with the proceedings below, let her eyes wander the Marmont's exterior from floor to floor. Across the way she spotted a familiar face gazing intently at the frightening spectacle along the boulevard. "My God," she shrieked, "it's Myrna Loy!"

Riots, protests, and marches continued throughout the coming months, much to the dismay and inconvenience of the Marmont's guests. At night, Flower Children sneaked into the hotel through two lobby windows along

Marmont Lane, finding their way into the kitchen in search of food. Corinne Patten came upon two of them one morning; they were clutching slices of bread in their hands. "She gave them hell," said a staff member, "Then she ordered them out and threatened to call the police." When word of the incident reached Beatrice Lillie, she became upset. Earlier she had reportedly had words with John Philip Huck, who had told her, "Those hippies ought to be hosed off the street." "How dare you talk like that?" she snapped back, "They're human beings too!"

The two Marmont Lane windows were boarded up in an effort to keep the Flower Children out of the hotel. They got in anyway to beg for crumbs and write their messages of Peace and Love on the corridor walls. When one startled guest discovered a small group of them, serenely sitting on the stairs near the second-floor landing, she retreated to her room until they were removed.

Dennis Hopper, a loyal Marmont guest, was nearly refused admittance when a new employee on the front desk failed to recognize him. The young actor was thought to be a hippie because of his "scruffy" street-look appearance.

Robert DeNiro didn't get past the desk when he first came to the Marmont. He had asked to see the penthouse, but the night manager sent him on his way. "Do you know who that was?" another staff member asked, somewhat aghast. "A bum," the night manager replied. DeNiro received a call, and an apology, through his agent the next day. He didn't return to the Marmont immediately, but once he did, he became one of the hotel's confirmed regulars.

There were other prominent guests during these tumultuous times: mastre de ballet, Edward Villella; dancer-choreographer Peter Gennaro; Jordan and Sybil (the ex-Mrs. Burton) Christopher; artist Roy Licktenstein; top models Lauren Hutton, Cybill Shepard, Jaclyn Smith and *Get Smart's* Barbara Feldon; photographer Richard Avedon; Isabelle Collin-Dufresne (Andy Warhol star, Ultra Violet); George Plimpton; the Howard Koches; French director Jacques Demy; Carly Simon; Bill Cosby; actresses Tuesday Weld, Sharon Tate (and her director husband, Roman Polanski), Margot Kidder, Faye Dunaway; and actors Melvyn Douglas (with his wife, Helen Gahagan), Luther Adler, Arthur Hill, Hal Holbrook, Ken Howard, David Birney, and Woody Strode.

The Marmont registry also recorded its share of known activists and protestors: the Timothy Learys, Dick Gregory, Germaine Greer, Joan Baez, Judy Collins, Buffy Sainte-Marie, John and Yoko Lennon, (shortly after

"If it weren't for the baby, we would stay," Sharon Tate told a neighbor at the Marmont.

Tab Hunter and Tuesday Weld were among the young stars at the Marmont during the tumultuous 1960s.

the release of their *Two Virgins* album, with its controversial cover shot showing them in the buff), and Donald Sutherland. On the move again, Sutherland had departed Bungalow A to take up residence in the main building, with his future *Klute* co-star and old friend along the anti-war trail, "Hanoi-Jane" Fonda.

## The Housekeeper And Her Daughter

Daisy Grossen was the proud owner of what Corinne Patten described as "the Marmont's most intelligent cat." (Corinne liked to talk, but she did not toss labels around loosely.) Corinne came to that conclusion one day following a private performance in Daisy's room, where she discovered the cat, a female Siamese, curled on top of Daisy's television set. That was the animal's favorite place, Daisy explained, because when the TV was on, which it was constantly, the surface was warm, and the cat could listen to voices and music while Daisy was attending to her housekeeping duties. What really amazed Corinne was the cat's reaction to one particular program. "Whenever *Lassie* came on," Corinne explained, "the sound of purring filled the room. But if Lassie barked, the show was over. That smart little cat would look up, as if thinking 'Oh! Oh!', reach down with her paw and push the off button, then curl up again!"

Even if Daisy hadn't owned such a remarkable cat, she would have earned a spot in the hotel's annals. Daisy Grossen was not the typical housekeeper. When she started the job around 1962, she was well past seventy years old (some said eighty). She may have been "too old to be working, as Franchot Tone once commented to her face, but she had more than enough strength and stamina to compensate for her advanced age, whatever it was. Daisy was a mountain of a woman. For all of Joe Leigh's muscle, he wouldn't have lasted three rounds with her. Her parents, perhaps believing they had sired a delicate little flower, had judged wrong. They should have named her Samsonia.

Although Daisy made her home in 2E with her pet Siamese, she was rarely there. She spent most of her time in the linen room behind the front desk, a cozy cubbyhole where she planned her daily activities, read, relaxed, and mostly fortified herself. As a co-worker at the Marmont remembered: "Mrs. Grossen *always* seemed to be in the linen room—from early morning till late at night. Occasionally she would go to 2E, feed her cat, and grab a can of spaghetti or ravioli to bring downstairs. She would eat it cold, right out of the can, along with some root beer. She drank a lot of root beer. There was a machine around the corner from the linen room."

In between, Daisy would tend to business. She saved the heavy work for late at night, when she was less likely to be in the way. It was not unusual to find her lugging loads of dirty linen through the halls at 2:00 A.M. Guests could always hear her coming. She wore a huge bundle of keys strapped to her waist, which clanked with every step. In many ways, Daisy was like the Bea Lillie character, Mrs. Meers, in *Thoroughly Modern Millie*.

Having her "office" so close to the front desk made Daisy the logical candidate to fill in whenever anyone wanted to take a break from the desk or switchboard, especially during the evening, when a skeleton staff was on duty. Carmel Volti always hesitated asking Daisy to relieve her. "As late as the 1960s, Carmel says, "the Marmont still had an old-fashioned switchboard, with cords and plugs. The way Daisy pushed the plugs and pulled the cords, it's a wonder the old board survived. She was so strong she almost wrecked it whenever she answered a call."

Once in awhile, Daisy's daughter, Josephine, who lived in Los Angeles, would come to visit. (Another daughter lived in San Fransico.) Like her mother, Josephine was very tall. At close to six feet, in flats, she towered over most men. Josephine was also unmarried.

One day in April, 1968, a beefy ex-jock from Florida checked into the Marmont for a month's stay. He and Josephine were soon dating, though no one paid much attention. It wasn't until several years later that their relationship, even though brief, became the talk of the hotel. By then, Josephine's ex-beau had become one of the hottest actors in Hollywood. His name was Burt Reynolds.

# Mr. & Mrs. Polanski

On February 19, 1968, less than a month after their marriage in London, actress Sharon Tate and Polish screenwriter-director Roman Polanski checked into Chateau Marmont. They arrived carrying a fuzzy Yorkshire Terrier puppy, a gift from Sharon's parents. Roman had named it Dr. Saperstein, after the sinister character in his latest movie, the yet-to-be-released *Rosemary's Baby*.

On their brief return to Hollywood, the Polanskis had lived for a short time in a glitzy apartment-hotel on Sunset Boulevard, near the mid-point of the Strip. Sharon hadn't been happy there; she had yearned for a place with "more character." What she had had in mind, her husband soon found out, was the Marmont. She had discovered the hotel during her first days in Hollywood and claimed that it was "her favorite hangout."

"For Americans, to whom anything a few decades old seems romantic, it held a special appeal," Polanski remarked later. "Sharon loved its run-down appearance and old-world atmosphere, not to mention the crazy layout of its rooms. She felt at home among the actors, musicians, and writers that constituted its regular population. You could sense, simply by walking down its corridors, that the place had its quota of real-life dramas . . ."

The newlyweds took a fifth-floor suite, 5D. It had a wondrous view, spacious rooms, ample closet space, and a terrace, but, more than anything, Sharon was thrilled to have her own kitchenette. Polanski proudly admitted: "She's a born housewife."

From the day they moved in, Sharon prepared lavish communal breakfasts for her husband and two of his friends, Simon Hessera and Brian Morris, who appeared at the hotel early each morning, dressed casually in bathrobes. The men were appreciative of a hearty meal to start their days. Both were unemployed. Hessera had recently lost his job with a firm that made television commercials; Morris was a would-be entrepreneur, currently involved in trying to open a fashionable nightclub, Bumbles.

Another ritual that gave Sharon pleasure was cutting her husband's hair. It was a skill she had learned from her former lover, Beverly Hills hairstylist Jay Sebring.

One of Hermoine Baddeley's favorite friends and playmates at the Marmont, Peter Sellers, was a frequent guest of the Polanskis as well. In fact, it was through the Polanskis—Roman, in particular—that Sellers was introduced to Mia Farrow. A short passionate romance soon developed.

Mia Farrow had starred as the unsuspecting young wife in Polanski's *Rosemary's Baby* following the breakup of her marriage to Frank Sinatra. At twenty-three, Farrow was a delicate, fragile sort. She not only had the gentle look and manner of a Flower Child, but the philosophy as well. She became one in a big way, clinging to her new identity as if she had received word from Above. Actually, she did have a calling. No sooner did she complete her role in the Polanski picture than she was off to India for a month of transcendental meditation with her guru, Maharishi Mahesh Yogi. She returned, still a Flower Child, but steeped in the wonders of spiritual mysticism, which she shared with Sellers.

Mia Farrow and Peter Sellers never failed to attract attention, whenever they strolled through the Marmont lobby to visit the Polanskis. Dressed outlandishly in beads, chains, and wildly colorful psychedelic prints, they looked like misplaced East Indian potentates (or "rich hippies," as Corinne Patten put it). But it was Sharon Tate who received the enviable glances. With her sun-kissed beauty and dazzling, long-limbered figure, revealed to full effect in skintight miniskirts, she looked every bit the up-and-coming movie star that she was. She had appeared in four films, including the much ballyhooed *Valley of the Dolls*, and had recently signed as one of the leads in *The Wrecking Crew*, opposite Dean Martin, as the James Bondish Matt Helm.

In late spring 1968, the Polanskis departed the Marmont for the South of France, where they attended the Cannes Film Festival. They traveled on to London and Rome before checking back into their Marmont suite on June 2, just in time to read the laudatory opening reviews for *Rosemary's Baby*. If Polanski felt that the film's highly promising reception would result in lucrative new offers, he had to be disappointed. His studio, Paramount, was in turmoil, thanks to a trio of costly, star-studded box-office duds. Cutbacks, not new assignments, were the order of the season. Polanski was the first to admit that his wife's career appeared to be more promising than his own.

To keep busy, Roman began work on a new screenplay, and in early December, he flew to London to arrange overseas financing. He was barely back in Hollywood when Sharon announced that she was pregnant. "Roman appeared rather numbed by the news at first," a mutual friend recalls. "His reaction was probably surprise more than anything, because they hadn't planned on starting a family so soon. But Sharon was ecstatic, absolutely thrilled at the thought of becoming a mother. She had to tell everyone she knew at the hotel *immediately*, and that included almost everyone. Even at that early stage, she was reading books on childbirth and baby care. She even began shopping for a layette."

For nearly a year, Sharon and her husband had called Chateau Marmont "home." Now, as future parents, they talked of moving. Roman wanted larger living quarters, more space in which to raise their child. That wasn't Sharon's concern. One morning, she told Donald Spackman, her across-the-hall neighbor: "If it weren't for the baby, we would stay. But I want my little boy or girl to be born in a house, not in a hotel."

It was around the first of February when Sharon learned that her friends, young impresario Terry Melcher and Candice Bergen, were vacating the furnished country home they had been renting in the hills off Benedict Canyon. Sharon had been to the house on Cielo Drive, and had liked it.

She tracked down the owner. On February 12, 1969, Sharon and Roman leased the property.

As moving day approached, Sharon seemed to have mixed feelings about leaving the Marmont. It was difficult, she said, to tear herself away from the place where she and Roman had spent their honeymoon year. In the next breath, she spoke of the lovely new house and its flower-filled garden, and of the bright future that awaited them.

At the time, no one paid much attention to the activities in a house on Monteel Road, directly behind the Marmont, where members of two Terry Melcher-managed rock groups, the Nitty Gritty Dirt Band and the Peanut Butter Conspiracy, were living—or to the unkempt and untalented musician-songwriter named Charles Manson, who showed up on occasion, only to be turned away. Nor did anyone take much notice when two oddly dressed and curious young girls wandered into the Marmont one evening to gaze about. Former night auditor, John Howell, remembered: "They passed through the lobby, walked upstairs, came back down, and left. They didn't stay long, hardly more than a few minutes. It wasn't until later that we found out they were two of Manson's followers."

Several weeks after the Polanskis' departure from the Marmont, their dog, Dr. Saperstein, was struck by a car and killed. The hotel staff members were saddened by the news. Said Pam Hughes, who worked at the front desk during the Polanskis' stay: "Sharon adored that little dog, and we all felt so sorry for her. Little did we know what was to come."

Elsie Ferguson Pendleton (*left*), Billy Barnes, and Connie Nelson
help carry on the tradition at Meemi's Memorial Picnic, 1977.
(*Courtesy of Connie Nelson*)

View from the penthouse, late 1970s.

# PART V

# ABOVE THE SUNSET STRIP

There was little reason to celebrate as the Marmont began its fortieth year of operation in 1969. Sunset Boulevard, the once-grand entryway to the hotel, had fallen on hard times. The Strip had turned into hippie heaven, a gathering place for the anti-Establishment "Now" generation. Hundreds of long-haired hitchhikers, young and old, clustered on streetcorners in their tattered, funky clothes, awaiting rides to who knows where. Others camped out (even made love) on sidewalks next to boarded up store-fronts. Every block had an astonishing number of business closures. Store owners who struggled to remain open had to wonder why. (They were forever replacing expensive windows following destructive nightly melees). Only the rock clubs, record stores, and food joints seemed to be thriving.

Above the Sunset Strip, Chateau Marmont reflected the deterioration of the boulevard below. The hotel too had become a fading flower. Longtime staff members, recalling the elegance of the glory days, looked about forlornly. "So much neglect," Corinne Patten cried one day. "Things just *have* to improve."

Judging by the names on the guest list at the time, no one would ever suspect that the Marmont wasn't the epitome of Hollywood chic. Among the regulars were Maximillian Schell, Hermione Baddeley, the Joseph Cottons ( Patricia Medina), Tony Randall, Donald Sutherland, Mildred Natwick, Jo Van Fleet, and Lee Grant. Newcomers included Jon Voight, Louis Malle, Perry King, Bette Midler, Cicely Tyson, Francis Ford Coppola, Michael Cimino, and Stacy Keach.

During the tumultuous late Sixties and early Seventies, many screenwriters also arrived at the Marmont. They came to work in seclusion, often requesting a suite on the quiet back side of the hotel. William Goldman wrote *Butch Cassidy and the Sundance Kid* at the Marmont. Graham Ferguson penned *Downhill Racer.* Robert Stone adapted his novel, *Hall of Mirrors,* for Paul Newman's *W.U.S.A.* Leonard Gardner wrote *Fat City.*

Carole Eastman, known professionally as Adrien Joyce, struggled for years in her Marmont "hideaway" before hitting it big with her collaborative screenplay (with Bob Rafelson) for *Five Easy Pieces.* Eastman also introduced a number of her friends to the hotel: Jack Nicholson, Dominique Sanda, Jeanne Moreau.

There is no record of Brooke Hayward having stayed at the Marmont with her former husband, Dennis Hopper, during the Sixties, but she did check in on her own in 1976. She came to work on what would become her best-selling autobiography, *Haywire,* the story of growing up in a celebrated but ill-fated family. (Hayward's mother was actress Margaret

Sullavan; her father, the famous producer, Leland Hayward.)

Reliving her past took its toll on Hayward, as former desk clerk Inger Simonsen recalled. "Often she would come down into the lobby in the evenings, after having worked on her book most of the day. She was white-faced, drained looking, her eyes were red and swollen. There were times when she didn't answer her phone. Her friends became so concerned that they began stopping by to check up on her. Everyone worried about her."

John Crosby didn't arrive at the Marmont until later, "but I had heard of it for years as the trysting place for Bogart and Betty Bacall, and also as the haunt for Robert Benchley. Robert's son, Nat (author Nataniel Benchley) used to talk about it as a great hangout for all the more raffish Hollywood community, like his father and (screenwriter) Herman Mankiewicz." Crosby traveled to the Marmont from his home in Virginia to discuss writing the screenplay of his novel, *Party of the Year.* "I used to walk down the street to a delicatessen and buy salami sandwiches and milk to eat in my room, something you can't imagine doing in Beverly Hills."

Other authors who stayed at the Marmont during the Seventies included George Plimpton, Margaret Truman Daniel, John Kobal, Gore Vidal, S.J. Perelman, and Richard Schickel. For the majority of writers, Chateau Marmont was a quiet oasis in the midst of Hollywood madness. As Tom Shales noted in his *Washington Post* column, following a visit to the Marmont in 1979: "There is a tolerant decorum comparable to no other hotel . . . It's the Marmont that's home, and everything else that's away."

It's amazing that "a tolerant decorum" prevailed despite an ongoing abundance of children. At times, the Marmont seemed to be overrun with kids, just as once there had been indications of a pet explosion. "The concerns were needless," claimed one veteran Marmontphile. "Yes, there were children, but unless you actually saw them, you seldom knew they were around. For the most part, the youngsters were exceptionally well behaved. If they got into trouble, it was *quiet* trouble."

Lynn Redgrave's stay at the Marmont lasted so long that she enrolled her two children in the Gardner Street School. Desk clerk Inger Simonsen's son, Oliver, also attended school there. As Simonsen remembered: "Miss Redgrave's little boy was in Oliver's class, and her nanny would often pick up Oliver when she collected the Redgrave children. Oliver stayed with them many times until I finished work for the day. Most of the guests were marvelous. One time, on Christmas Eve, Maximillian Schell offered to pick up Oliver for me, then let him stay in his suite till I got off work. Another time, Donald Sutherland and a friend wound up playing hide-and-seek with Oliver all over the lobby.

"Then there was Richard Gere, an extremely likeable guy with a great sense of humor. He was so kind to Oliver. He would spend time with him and even take him out for treats."

T.C. Jones loved children, too. He and his wife, Connie, had only a pet poodle to call their own, but T.C. was seldom without the companionship of youngsters. They may not have called him "Daddy," but "Uncle T.C." suited him just fine.

One summer day, in 1968, T.C. offered to take the children of his Marmont friends to Griffith Park, where they could play on the swings, dangle their feet in a trickling stream, and lie in the shade under lush, flowering branches of jacaranda, crepe myrtle, and California pepper. Trees were especially important to T.C. Coming from New York City, he hadn't seen many as a child.

The outing soon developed into more than just a day in the park. A picnic was organized, and several grown-ups were asked to tag along. Pianist Calvin Jackson, who was appearing down the street from the Marmont at Villa Frascati, joined in with his daughters. So did Jackson's wife, Joyce, and Connie Nelson with her two children. And Meemi Ferguson, never one to miss a get-together, also *had* to join the group at Griffith Park.

T.C. didn't know what he was starting. "The kids had such a great time— everyone did—that it became a yearly tradition," says Connie Nelson. "But not without help from Meemi. She was really the one who kept it going."

Over the next few years, the little group began to expand. Billy Barnes showed up, along with friends Ken Barry, Jackie Joseph, Joanne Worley, Earl Holiman, Tom Hatten, Bob Mackie, Bob Rogers, and Ray Aghayan. There were others as well. Some even brought their children. (The toddlers were already beginning to take a back seat in the proceedings.)

The guests were each expected to bring their own dinner and drinks, but Meemi, who was nearing eighty, insisted on providing much of the food. "She was the world's worst cook," her granddaughter admits, "but she had her table of six boys, and she wanted to feed them. One year, she prepared a 'hot' rice and tuna casserole and forgot to turn on the oven. It was a mess, really awful, but no one complained. They were all good sports."

Meemi was still living in her modest accommodations at the Marmont when T.C. Jones first led his troops into Griffith Park that bright summer day. By 1973, however, she had moved into a small apartment a few blocks from the hotel, just south of Sunset. "I should never have made the change," she admitted at the time, "but I'm here now, and I'll have to make the best of it. What else can I do?" A short while later, as she was walking home from the bank, she was approached by two men. They robbed and beat her; she received a strong blow to the head. Meemi didn't make it through the summer.

The picnic was very nearly canceled that year, but the regulars decided to carry on in Meemi's memory. Now, as they have every year since 1973, Meemi's friends—as well as scores more who never knew the former Marmont manager—gather on the second Monday in August to celebrate Meemi's Annual Memorial Picnic. "Last year, we had nearly 150 people," Connie Nelson reported. "Most are working in shows, that's why Monday—usually a dark night—is best. Friends bring friends. It keeps mushrooming."

The invitations still designate "in the swing area" of Griffith Park. "Grandmother loved it there," said Connie, "and it's her night. We think it's a super way to remember somebody."

The news of Meemi's death had stunned everyone at the Marmont. Fortunately, for Corinne Patten, an event taking place at the hotel helped soften her grief. "A star is born today . . . *me!*" she jotted in her journal. "A new movie, *Blume in Love,* is being shot here, and I'm going to make an appearance. George Segal and dear Shelley Winters will be in it with me."

Carmel Volti hadn't been asked to appear in the film, but she did not feel slighted. During her long association with the Marmont, she claimed to have "seen and heard just about everything"—including a prediction from the housekeeper that she would one day leave the hotel "in the twinkling of an eye." Ridiculous, Carmel thought at the time. But in 1973, following a senseless to-do with Corinne, the housekeeper's words came true.

"It happened on a Sunday," Carmel reflected. "Corinne came up to me, wanting to discuss religion, and I not only didn't have the time, but I wasn't interested. Besides, we weren't supposed to talk about such things on duty. When I reminded her that the management wouldn't approve, she said, 'That's too bad about them' and really started in. I wouldn't have minded her tirades once in a while, but I had heard them for ages. That woman could make stone cry when she got on her soapbox.

"There I was on the switchboard, trapped behind the front desk, and she was prattling on and on. Instead of doing the sensible thing—contacting the manager—I acted on impulse. I buzzed the relief operator, told him I wouldn't be in anymore, and cleared my drawer. It was just as the housekeeper had predicted. After forty-three years, I was gone 'in the twinkling of an eye.'"

Following Carmel's departure, producer James Hill commented: "Carmel knew everything that was going on. She was like a housemother. She worried about you. I'm sure she knew more about me than I did."

Said Walter Matthau: "The strongest impression in my memory [of the Marmont] is the gentility, decency, intelligence, and friendliness of Carmel Volti. I used to call her 'Carmen,' and there wasn't a more comforting voice and manner to be heard anywhere."

With the Marmont ladies now reduced to one, Corinne Patten did her best to carry on and spread a little joy. That wasn't always easy, but she had some help from incoming merrymakers.

Flip Wilson, who rarely made a move about the hotel without his big, burly bodyguard, lived for a time in the penthouse. Bill Cosby occupied one of the bungalows, as did (later) David Letterman. In fact, it was in a Marmont bungalow that the show bearing Letterman's name was born.

Two *Laugh-In* loonies signed the guest registry: Alan Sues, who had appeared onstage in *Tea and Sympathy* with Tony Perkins ("I'd heard so much about the place I had to check it out") and Judy "Sock it to me" Carne. From the *Steve Allen Show* came Don Knotts and Tom Poston.

Producer Loren Michaels started coming to Chateau Marmont in 1972, three years before the premiere of *Saturday Night Live*. "I was doing various TV shows," he remembered, "writing, then producing. I lived all around in the hotel, moving from room to room, depending on the show I was doing. If I had the money, I moved to a larger suite. It not, I took a smaller one." Between shows, Michaels subsisted on white toast and canned orange juice. His future may have seemed uncertain at times (he kept his place in New York, just in case), but he remained at the Marmont. "I felt very safe there," he said. "The hotel had seen better days, but it still had a dignity and warmth." By 1975, based on the work he had done to date, including several shows with Lily Tomlin, Michaels was asked by NBC to produce their new late-night offering out of New York, *Saturday Night Live*.

It was through Loren Michaels that SNL's resident cast of characters was introduced to the Marmont. Gilda Radner arrived first, followed by Chevy Chase and Dan Aykroyd, Jane Curtin and John Belushi. "Chevy had lived in Los Angeles," Michaels recalled. "He would come back to visit his girlfriend, as well as for the Emmys and other awards shows. We all made the trip from time to time." Chase continued to visit the Marmont even after he left the show in 1976.

So did John Belushi.

The cast of *Saturday Night Live,* and other funsters who roamed the Marmont—Andy Kaufman, Dudley Moore, Dick Gregory, and the Monty Python gang—provided a refreshing contrast to the grim sights on the teeming boulevard below. Yet like the neighboring roadway, the hotel had seen better days. Life at the Marmont, high above the Sunset Strip, may not have been as elegant as in its golden years, but it still had an appeal, one that was uniquely its own.

Corinne's Corner. (*Photo by David Strick*)

Small garden bugalows on adjoining property.

# Chapter 16

## Echoes From The Hills

### A New Beginning

Throughout the early Seventies, the Marmont continued its steady decline. The hotel's magnificent antique furniture, brought in by Albert E. Smith, was gone. The glorious murals, adorning the high main-floor ceilings, had faded to a colorless blur. The priceless Persian rug lay in shreds (thanks to a drunken Mario Lanza who had trampled it with his cleated golf shoes). The impressive wrought-iron decorative lamps, flanking the Gothic archway at the hotel's entrance, had "disappeared mysteriously."

The lack of quality furniture had been a problem for years. Carmel Volti remembered: "People would come in off the street at night in their stocking feet and steal things—antiques, pictures off the walls, whatever they could get their hands on. It was easy because there were so few people on staff. By the time the steel gate was put up at the entrance, it was too late."

Outsiders weren't the only thieves. A former manager had held a garage sale, which seemed a good excuse for moving out precious objects. Most of the good pieces, however, such as the remaining antiques, were moved all the way to his home. A guest who came to know the man well recalls: "He invited me to see his house one day, and when I walked through the front door, I couldn't believe my eyes. I thought I was back at the Marmont."

The shortage of furniture had always been a problem at the Marmont. Meemi Ferguson, in her day, was often forced to take on decorating chores out of desperation. Said Donald Spackman, "Meemi would borrow furniture from one suite and put it in another, trying to make do with what was available. A really important guest would get the 'fix up treatment.' But she could only do so much."

That held for the rest of the staff as well. Cut to bare bones during the Brethauer-Popper period, it had never been augmented, resulting in don't-hold-your-breath service. Laundry, once sent out, was being hauled to a local laundromat. Telephone service was almost non-existent. As author Thomas DeLong recalled: "One of the biggest drawbacks at the Marmont was the lack of direct phone dialing. All outside calls had to go through a single operator at the switchboard, which was a museum piece. Getting the operator took forever. It was agony." Maximillian Schell always kept a novel handy when he used the phone in his suite. He admits, "I never made a call without a book to read."

Inger Simonsen wasn't yet working at the Marmont when she came to visit a friend in 1969. She hasn't forgotten her first impression. "The place was like something out of an old film," she said. "Spooky describes it best. Coming into the dark cool lobby from the dazzling California sunshine outside, the atmosphere was one of past glory and quiet gloom. I can't remember who was at the desk, but I do remember passing old Mrs. Grossen jangling her big bundle of keys." After being hired, she came to know the hotel better: "It was eccentric to the extreme. Only four of us worked the front desk over a twenty-four-hour period, and we had no lunch break. Many of the guests felt so sorry for us. I remember the family of Graham Nash [of Crosby Stills Nash & Young] bringing me afternoon tea and biscuits, so I would have something to eat."

"The hotel was a joke in those days," said former desk clerk Pam Hughes. "If you needed anything, you had to track down poor old Daisy Grossen. If you needed *anything,* even toilet paper in the middle of the night, you had to wake up Daisy. She was the only one with keys to everything. That's the way she wanted it. One guy was put in a room without sheets. Nobody could find Daisy, and the houseboys couldn't speak English."

Few guests complained about the hotel's deteriorating conditions. Perhaps they didn't want to burden the already overworked staff; more likely they figured it would be easier, and far faster, to take matters into their own hands. Jo Van Fleet "borrowed" a throw rug to cover a gaping hole in her carpet. The Carl Esmonds rearranged the furniture in their suite to conceal worn spots. Andy Warhol star Ultra Violet draped sheets over her stained and frayed sofa and chairs. Glynis Johns prevailed upon Donald Spackman to drive her to The Akron, a discount emporium, so she could "purchase little touches to freshen her tired decor."

An advertising executive from New York cleaned up the mess when a large chunk of plaster fell from the ceiling in his suite during the night. Myrna Loy and Gram Parsons carried on as though nothing had happened, after lobby chairs collapsed under them.

With the Marmont's lost elegance, it is surprising there weren't more defections. Actually, only one of the hotel's most distinguished longtime guests departed for cleaner pastures: Sam Weisbord, president of the William Morris Agency. "We felt very sad when Mr. Weisbord moved out," Mrs. Volti reflected. "He had lived at the Marmont for years. He was so much a part of the hotel."

No sooner did Mr. Weisborg depart than his suite was occupied by a new arrival. Management had no problem whatsoever with vacancies; the hotel was continually booked from top to bottom. Business on the Strip may have hit the skids, but Chateau Marmont was riding high.

It is easy to understand why the owners were hesitant to spruce up the place. Why bother when no one complained? With so much plastic and glitz along the Strip, they had every right to believe that part of the Marmont's attraction was its slightly tarnished splendor. An incoming New Yorker compared the Marmont to a theatrical backdrop. "It's the stars who are supposed to glitter," she said, "not the sets."

The prevailing conditions made Chateau Marmont target for every possible sleazy rumor, however. When Bea Lillie heard that the hotel might be torn down, she didn't bat an eye. She simply shrugged and said, "Why not!"

No one knew what to believe when the Los Angeles papers announced in March, 1975, that the Marmont had been purchased by two Southern California builders and developers, Raymond Sarlot and Karl Kantarjian. "Some of us were scared," a staff member admitted. "We didn't know how much longer we would be working or what would happen to the hotel, especially with *builders* and *developers* taking over. We had visions that it really might be leveled and replaced by a shopping center or condominium—even a savings and loan. Look what happened to the Garden of Allah."

No such fate awaited Chateau Marmont. Follow-up articles told of the new owners' ambitious plans for grand-scale restoration, "in a manner that will preserve the atmosphere that has led numerous Hollywood personalities to make the hotel their home."

Something *had* to be done. As one columnist pointed out: "Chateau Marmont could do with a facelift. The good basic bone structure is there—handsome arches, vaulted and painted like European cathedrals, high, beamed ceilings, and a profusion of private balconies. All that is needed are a few tucks, a good firming up, a paint job, and some minor refurbishing."

Minor?

"When we bought the Marmont," Sarlot said, "the bank was ready to foreclose. Bills hadn't been paid in months, and the building was in total disrepair. The corridors were lined with red and black carpeting—only the black was shiny patches covering the holes. It was even worse by the elevators, shreaded and threadbare. The walls had peeling wallpaper with criss-crossed Scotch tape. Plastic Hawaiian light fixtures hung from the ceilings. Karl and I would walk up and down the smoke-filled halls and shake our heads. You could cut the smell of marijuana with a knife. People were wandering in and out of open doors. The place looked like a dungeon. Or worse. It was so bad I wouldn't have stayed free for a one-nighter."

In April, one month after the hotel changed hands, Sarlot moved into a suite on the fifth-floor. From there, he and his partner began their campaign to bring the Marmont "back to Normandy."

Up came the patched and shredded carpeting. Down came the peeling wallpaper. Out went the plastic lampshades and dilapidated furnishings. Wainscoting was installed in the corridors to enhance the period look. A sprinkler system was added for fire safety. Artisans were brought in to restore the once-magnificent murals in the lobby and drawing room. The swimming pool, long neglected, was rebuilt. A new, modern switchboard replaced the museum piece, and a sophisticated security system was installed. The exterior of the building was sandblasted and repainted, the grounds relandscaped and freshly planted. An unused anteroom off the lobby was turned into a breakfast room. In 1978, it was named Corinne's Corner.

Although Corinne Patten had officially retired the previous year, she had remained at the hotel, living in 1F, a bright, unfurnished single only steps from the lobby, and supervising the breakfast nook. From her favorite table in the cozy plant-filled room, she could easily "keep her eyes on things," especially the comings and goings through the front door across the way. "I was so thrilled when the coffee shop was named after me," Corinne noted in her journal. "This is where I meet and gab with guests from all over the world—some coming back to the Marmont for many years. I love this place!"

There were other additions. A wine cellar was built and stocked with the finest California and French wines. ("We happen to be two crazies who love good wines," the partners confessed. "It's not the biggest cellar or the smallest, but it's very decent.") Adjoining property to the east was acquired, containing small garden bungalows, increasing the accommodations from forty-eight to sixty-two. The inadequate, overworked staff was augmented.

"There was so much to do, so many decisions to make," Sarlot commented. "Karl and I were rarely out of each other's sight. We became like Mutt and Jeff. Inseparable. We had to be to get things done."

Getting things done didn't necessarily mean quickly; the project would stretch on for years, primarily because the Marmont remained open—and generally full—during restoration. Had the hotel shut down, workmen could have moved about at will. As it was, they had to wait until guests vacated to get into the individual suites and rooms, cottages, and bungalows.

Sarlot wasn't complaining, not about the occupancy rate, at least. "Occupancy had never been a problem," he said, "but when we bought the hotel, it was losing some $2,000 a month. Rates were as low as $12 for a single room and $26 for a two-bedroom suite. Those were the *publicized* rates. From there, deals were made."

Many of the restoration's artistic concepts were created and supervised by Regina Sarlot Bernstein, internationally known Palm Springs-based interior designer. "Regina's knowledge of European art and design was instrumental in helping to reestablish the hotel's original appeal," said Kantarjian. "She brought in antiques—authentic period pieces—luxurious imported fabrics and, rich color harmonies. It was her intention, as well as Ray's and mine, to return the Marmont to its previous splendor, without sacrificing comfort. Our aim was to create an extension of 'home.' We wanted our guests to feel they were *coming home*—not to a hotel room."

With all the turmoil, that wasn't always easy. But there were visible signs of progress, and unexpected boosts. "Neil Simon became our patron saint," admitted Sarlot. "He had written a story called *Gable Slept Here,* about a New York actor who comes to Hollywood and puts up at the Marmont in a room that, he discovers, Gable once used. The hotel's phone number was even used in the script for authenticity. Robert DeNiro and Marsha Mason were to star. Mike Nichols was to direct. A big, big movie. The title was later changed to *Bogart Slept Here,* then the project died. But the early publicity was tremendous. There were billboards in London, full-page color ads in the trades, articles from coast to coast—all featuring an illustration of the hotel."

Another boost came when the Los Angeles Cultural Heritage Board classified the Marmont as a Historic-Cultural Monument. In the Board's proclamation, the hotel was cited as "one of the few remaining landmarks to remind us of the glitter of Hollywood's past."

In 1979, Chateau Marmont, entered its fiftieth year. The glitter of old Hollywood was missing, but the hotel had regained much of its original grandeur. There was still work to be done before the restoration would be complete. Few guests, however, could deny that the Marmont had turned the corner in its return to Normandy.

# Mr. Polanski

In April of 1977, Roman Polanski returned to Chateau Marmont for the first time in over eight years after he and his young wife, Sharon Tate, departed the hotel in February, 1969. They had lived only briefly in their new home when Sharon was offered a co-starring role with Vittorio Gassman, Orson Welles, Terry-Thomas, and Lionel Jeffries in the feature, *Twelve Plus One* (also released as *13 Chairs*), to be filmed outside Florence, in London, and in Paris. She accepted, despite her pregnancy, and left almost immediately for Europe. She was accompanied as far as London by Roman. According to director Nicolas Gessner: "Sharon hadn't told anyone [connected with the film] about her condition. Not me, not the producer [Claude Giroux], no one. But after a time, she began to show, and we had to find devices to conceal her changing figure. We shot many scenes in close-up, put her behind furniture, and had other actors cross in front of her.

"By the last few days of shooting in late July, we all felt attached to the baby. She was in her eighth month, and it was due in only weeks. I wanted her to stay in Europe to have it. 'Go to one of those film star clinics like Sophia Loren,' I told her, 'then come back for the rough cuts. She wouldn't hear of that. 'No, no, no,' she said emphatically, 'I've got to have my baby at home!' By that time, no airline would take her, so Roman arranged for her passage on the *Queen Elizabeth II*.

"After the tragedy, we had to make many changes in the movie before it could be released. It was hard to edit, as there were problems at every turn. Scenes with partial nudity had to be deleted. There was a scene where Sharon takes a knife and slashes the tires on her car; we didn't know whether to leave that in or not. And in the final scene, one of the players had long, wild hair. We knew we couldn't use that. He looked too much like Charles Manson."

Since Roman's last visit to the Marmont, his life had been a series of incredible highs and devastating lows, an emotional rollercoaster. Certainly, nothing could erase memories of the gruesome multiple murders of Sharon and her friends at the hands of the Manson "family" members, although there were some bright moments, particularly the stunning commercial and critical success of his stylish movie melodrama, *Chinatown*. Following the bloodbath at the Polanski home on Cielo Drive, Roman had abandoned Hollywood for Europe. He had returned to the West Coast for occasional work and to visit friends but never to Chateau Marmont. The memories had been too painful.

Had the circumstances been any different that spring day in 1977, it is doubtful Roman Polanski would have checked into the Marmont. His arrival was far from joyous.

He had come to Hollywood some weeks earlier to start production on a new film for Columbia, *The First Deadly Sin*. Arrangements had also been made for him to photograph a layout for the French edition of *Vogue* Magazine while in town. It was following that photo session, held at Jack Nicholson's secluded hillside home, that the nightmare began. The next evening, as Polanski was readying for a theater date, he was arrested on drug and rape charges. His accuser was the thirteen-year-old girl who had been his model on the *Vogue* assignment.

Within days, a grand jury had indicted Polanski on six counts, ranging from furnishing a controlled substance to a minor to having unlawful sexual intercourse. He suddenly found his world crumbling once again, much as it had that black August day when he had learned of the Manson murders. This time, however, public sentiment ran against him. He became the butt of Hollywood jokes ("Heard the title of Polanski's next picture? *Close Encounters with the Third Grade*"), his agent abandoned him, and his Columbia film project was scuttled.

Since his arrest and release on bail, Polanski had taken refuge in the Coldwater Canyon home of an associate. But he found he could not stay in hiding, so he turned to Chateau Marmont where, he reasoned, he would be among friends while retaining his privacy.

Corinne Patten remembered that Polanski was "somewhat hesitant to leave his suite at first," but as media attention began to subside, he became less inhibited. Still, he guarded his actions like a hare pursued by hounds. An advocate of exercise, he remarked that he no longer felt safe jogging on public streets "for fear of being recognized and accosted." A ballet studio on Melrose Avenue, run by an old friend from Poland, became a frequent hideaway. There, in the quiet of evening, after the students had departed for the day, he would go through the paces of his workout ritual.

There were times too when Polanski would venture down to the Marmont garage to chat with Noelly or whoever was on duty. Often he carted snacks with him for the staff to enjoy during their visits. As one employee recalls: "With all his troubles, and you could tell he was hurting inside, Mr. Polanski was always going out of his way to be nice to people."

In mid-April, Roman Polanski was formally charged on all six counts of the indictment; he pleaded not guilty. Immediately upon renewal of his bail, he requested, and received, permission to travel to his home in London. He was back at the Marmont within days, and on April 19, he was joined by his former lover, seventeen-year-old Nastassja Kinski. Although Polanski and Kinski were no longer romantically involved, a strong bond still existed between them. The earlier relationship, and Kinski's tender age, prompted Polanski's counsel to caution his client never to be seen alone in the young German actress' company—and never to be caught entering or leaving one another's suites. The admonition really wasn't necessary. Polanski acted as though he had known for some time that he was under surveillance, if not by the law then certainly by the press. He regarded strangers with suspicion. He avoided the Marmont lobby and sidestepped unfamiliar faces, as he made his way along the corridors. He moved quickly in and out of the hotel, wary of anyone who loitered by the entrances.

The weeks dragged on, as Polanski awaited his next court appearance; the delay did little for his morale. His legal fees were escalating rapidly, and, with the controversy continuing to rage about him, he began to believe that he was no longer bankable and, worse, "a complete Hollywood outcast." It came as a surprise, then, when producer Dino DeLaurentiis sought his services to direct a remake of the 1937 hit, *The Hurricane*. The assignment, with its million-dollar contract and built-in lead for Nastassja Kinski (if she could master the English language in time), helped ease Polanski's mind. Still, he had the jitters. More than anything, he confided to friends at the Marmont, he wanted to be able to remain in the United States to live and work. Fear of deportation haunted him.

On August 8, the eighth anniversary of Sharon's death, Polanski roared into the Marmont garage and, in uncustomary fashion, stalked off for the elevator, without even a nod to his pals in the parking area. Later, it came out that he had been to Holy Cross Cemetery. While placing flowers on Sharon's grave, a photographer, who had been lurking in the shrubbery, began recording the touching scene on film. Roman had been lost in the moment and hadn't seen the man, but he did hear the familiar sound of a clicking shutter. Infuriated by the invasion of his privacy, he turned on the photographer, yanked away his camera, and exposed its contents.

Six days prior to Christmas, Polanski was sentenced to ninety days in the prison facility at Chino, north of Los Angeles, for the drug and sex charges. By the end of January, after serving less than half his sentence, he was released on probation and was back at the Marmont. If Roman was thrilled by his freedom, he didn' t show it. There was talk that the judge was "getting too much criticism" over Polanski's premature release and talk that he might have to return to Chino to serve "an indeterminate sentence" or, at least, complete the original ninety-day term in full. The judge would yield to public pressure, Polanski felt certain. He regarded him as hostile. After all, hadn't the judge referred to him as *"a sick dwarf?"*

In his suite at Chateau Marmont, Roman Polanski was kept apprised by his counsel of the judge's latest plans. The reports often varied from day to day; usually they were at odds with statements released to the press. One constant soon began to emerge, however: Polanski would be allowed to go free after serving his full ninety days at Chino, *if* he agreed to voluntary deportation.

Polanski had heard enough. On the day he was scheduled to report to Santa Monica courthouse for sentencing, he hurriedly packed his belongings and drove instead to Los Angeles International Airport. There he boarded the first available flight to London.

Later he confessed: "I simply knew I would rather do anything than go on living the way I had in the past year. I had endured disgrace and press harassment, lost two director's jobs, and done time in prison. What had I to gain by staying?"

## March 5, 1982

"I was swimming in the pool with British actress Jacqueline Pearce, remembered Alex Gildzen, "when a policeman came down the steps from the upper bungalows toward the pool area. Jacqueline asked him if anything was the matter. He said not to worry, but that someone had died. Not much later, I was off to Schwab's for a paper, when I noticed a television news van pulling up Marmont Lane. I didn't connect it with the report of the death. By the time I had returned from Schwab's, however, the Marmont was surrounded. An officer stopped me at the front door. It was the first time in all the years I've stayed there that I had to show my room key

John Belushi.

Publicity-shy Robert DeNiro kept his
doors closed to outsiders.

New owners Raymond Sarlot (*left*)
and Karl Kantarjian announced plans
for grand-scale restoration. (*Photo by
David Strick*)

to get back into the hotel. Inside, I asked a young woman at the desk what was wrong. She said only that there had been a slight disturbance. The Marmont is famous for observing the privacy of its guests, but I found her remark a bit much, since the local stations were broadcasting live. I went immediately to my room, turned on the tube, and learned that John Belushi had died. Then I went out to the tower that overlooks the bungalows, where I would often go alone at night to observe the Hollywood lights, and watched the circus that was beginning."

Raymond Sarlot and Karl Kantarjian were having lunch at the Friar's Club in Beverly Hills when the news broke. They rushed back to the hotel to find the surrounding streets clogged with cars and curiosity seekers and the Marmont overrun with radio and TV film crews, reporters, and police. "It was bedlam," said Sarlot. "The place was swarming with outsiders, the switchboard was lit up, and our manager (Suzanne Jierjian) was in panic." Jierjian, too, had been away from the hotel when the story broke; she had had a doctor's appointment that morning. It wasn't until she had returned that she learned of Belushi's death. Assistant manager Tom Rafter told her of the grim happening and tried to fill in the details. At that point, however, little was known. The only sure thing was that Belushi was dead. His nude body had been found in his bungalow bedroom.

"John was a super nice person," Sarlot commented, "and we were all stunned by the tragedy. But we had to think about our other guests as well, and how to protect them from the blitz of news people. The continuing privacy of the hotel's guests became a major concern."

To that end, Sarlot virtually locked up the hotel. Except for the garage, where guards were on round-the-clock duty, all entrances to the building were closed. Additional security was brought in. A barricade, manned by police, was set up at the foot of Marmont Lane. Only hotel guests and residents of the area were allowed through. Reporters were barred.

"Through all the turmoil," Sarlot said later, "the names of our other guests were never known. Tony Randall was living next door to Belushi, in the adjoining bungalow, and no one ever found out. We certainly didn't want to have Tony disturbed or hassled, and he wasn't. No one was."

There was one notable exception.

Less than twelve hours before Belushi's body was discovered, the comedian and two of his pals, Robert DeNiro and Robin Williams, were spotted stage-side at the Roxy, a popular Sunset Strip nightspot. A television newsman, having learned of Belushi's final public appearance, apparently decided that DeNiro would make a fascinating exclusive interview.

Somehow he and a camera crew made it past the guards to the upper floors of the Marmont, where they positioned themselves before the entry to DeNiro's suite. With lights glaring, hand-held camera rolling, and a live microphone at the ready, the reporter set the scene for his television audience, then rapped loudly on DeNiro's door and called out the actor's name.

For the reticent, publicity-shy DeNiro, the moment must have been horrendous. Not only was the reporter announcing to the world that he lived at the Marmont, but his gleaming suite number was clearly within camera range.

DeNiro's door remained shut. Seconds passed, but the reporter would not be discouraged. If anything, he became more determined to rouse a response. His raps grew increasingly forceful, and his voice stronger. Vamping for time, he recapped the tragic happening a half dozen different ways.

His patience finally paid off. "Go away," a voice from within hollered. *"Go away!"*

As the red light on the camera flashed off, the reporter was heard to say: "I guess he doesn't have any comments."

Outside, reporters and a camera crew cornered one of the Marmont's gardeners; he and Belushi's trainer had discovered the body. At the time, no one else was in the two-bedroom bungalow. Earlier, around 8:00 A.M. a young woman, later identified as Cathy Smith, had called room service to order breakfast. By the time the two men had entered the premises, she was gone.

"There were no signs of foul play," the gardener told the reporters, speaking with expertise. "Mr. Belushi was lying in bed with his clothes neatly folded and put away, as though he had gone to bed for the night. The man was overweight. It looked like he had a heart attack."

"The gardener suddenly became the authority on Belushi's death," Sarlot commented later, still shaking his head. "He had the whole country believing John had died from a heart attack. Everyone was after him for interviews."

Actually, the gardener's testimony seemed logical. As Sarlot remembered: "When Cathy Smith left the bungalow that morning, she totally cleared the pullman and dresser top. No drugs or paraphernalia were found anywhere." Still, Sarlot wasn't particularly pleased that the gardener had taken it upon himself to play doctor. He dubbed him "Doctor of Gardens" and banished him from the scene. The gardener was reassigned to Sarlot's valley home for a week to pull weeds.

The heart-attack story held up throughout the afternoon, as no one could offer a better explanation for the cause of death. The police would only state that "nothing out of the ordinary" had been found in Belushi's bungalow. "New York went crazy," Sarlot recalled. "John's friends there knew it had to be drugs." Indeed, the incoming calls from the comedian's friends and personal manager in the east were non-stop; they all wanted to know *exactly* what had happened. There were desperate outgoing calls as well, in an attempt to reach Belushi's widow, Judy.

The first indication that things were not as they appeared came about an hour after the coroner and his staff departed. Cathy Smith returned to the hotel in Belushi's rented Mercedes, to hand over to the police assorted drug paraphrenalia. She admitted that they had been used the night before, and that she had taken them with her when she had left the bungalow earlier in the day. She was led away in handcuffs.

The first people to occupy Belushi's bungalow after it had been reopened for occupancy were a reporter and photographer from one of the tabloids. They had been rushed to Hollywood from the east coast to record "the actual scene where John Belushi lived and died." Photo after photo was taken, details were observed and noted; nothing escaped their attention. What they didn't know was that the bungalow had undergone a transformation. "By the time the tabloid people arrived, it was no longer the same unit," Sarlot confessed. "The decor, everything, had been changed. We didn't want the place to become a cult symbol."

The security guards hired by the hotel remained on the job for a full month. While they kept out the curious, they also served as a reminder of that dreadful day when, for the first time, the Marmont was suddenly thrust into the national spotlight. "It was just so sad," manager Jierjian later told a television interviewer. "It was an unfortunate incident, but one that could have happened anywhere."

Many stars took to the Marmont's staircase to slip quietly in and out of the hotel. (*Photo by David Strick*)

The Bay City Rollers introduced Rollermania to the Marmont.

# Chapter 17

## Those Glorious Memories & Traditions

### Star Struck

Corinne Patten made no secret of the Marmont's privacy. It was a point she often stressed to celebrity newcomers. "At the Marmont," she would say, "you can keep your anonymity. We're more like a private club."

The stars who came to Chateau Marmont preferred keeping a low profile. Being paged in hotel lobbies and around pools was not their style. Once they checked in at the front desk, there was no need for anyone to see them again.

Most of the guests appreciated that. Myrna Loy once pointed out: "In our profession, actors are all comrades. If there's anything we need, it's privacy. At Chateau Marmont, everyone religiously respects the privacy of every other guest."

"To show *exactly* how private the hotel is," said Lisa Eichhorn, "I was there for several weeks before I found out that John Heard [her co-star] was staying there too. We finally ran into each other at the front desk, while picking up messages."

Some celebrities went to extremes to protect their privacy. Howard Hughes, Fanny Brice, and Greta Garbo often took to sneaking downstairs and exiting through back doors. Stars like Faye Dunaway laid out "hush money" on arrival to make sure her calls were thoroughly screened. Another generous tip was forthcoming upon her departure.

There were times, however, when nothing worked.

Bud Cort became a death cult hero, thanks to his role as the suicide-obsessed youth in *Harold and Maud*. For months following the picture's release, he would find small, hand-carved tombstones at his door, left by spooked fans who would sneak into the hotel at night. Others would wait in hearses outside to catch a glimpse of him.

When former desk clerk Inger Simonsen returned to the Marmont for a visit, after moving back to her native Norway, she found a group of young girls camped out on the front lawn. "It was the only time I ever saw autograph hounds at the hotel," she says. "They were all waiting for Joe Cocker."

Cocker's coterie of patient fans paled beside the hotel's lone invasion of groupies. They swarmed into the lobby one day in 1976—scores of seemingly desperate teenage and prepubescent girls—in search of five lads from Scotland known as The Bay City Rollers. The hottest group to come from overseas since the Beatles, the Rollers had created a phenomenon known as Rollermania, and their young fans had it good. There was no stopping them or calming them down. They screamed, they cried, they clutched at the air (and everything else their idols might have breathed upon), they looked ready to faint.

Even the sight of another music superstar, Art Garfunkel—of Simon and Garfunkel fame—failed to faze them. As one eyewitness recalls: "Garfunkel appeared in the lobby with some chick, right at the peak of the madness. The groupies completely ignored him, as if they didn't know or care who he was. That didn't made Garfunkel happy *at all*! In fact, he really got ticked off. Maybe he wanted some attention to impress his lady, but he didn't get any. He just stood there with his mouth hanging open— and this guy's usually a fast talker. So what does he do? He starts carrying on so the kids would notice him. He actually made a scene!"

Several years later, Duran Duran's fans made it into the hotel too, but in smaller numbers. Still, they left their mark by carving their initials into the walls of a brand new elevator. Mirrored strips had to be installed to cover the damage.

For days, a determined young man with "a heavy Brooklyn accent" stood in the street beneath Robert DeNiro's window hollering, "Hey, Bobby . . ., *Bobby* . . ., Hey, *Bobbeeeee*!" If he had thoughts of eliciting a response from the reclusive DeNiro, he had to have been disappointed. It's not certain which gave out first, his stamina or his voice.

Debra Winger also had an interest in DeNiro. When she first came to the Marmont for her role in the 1980 film, *Urban Cowboy*, she lived in "the tiniest room in the hotel," one that not only flanked DeNiro's suite but shared a common foyer. Winger has admitted to having cracked her door at frequent intervals, hoping to catch a glimpse of the ladies in DeNiro's life.

Tim Curry, star of the outrageously kinky *The Rocky Horror Picture Show,* received many late-night phone calls at the Marmont after he registered in 1978, but few ever got past the switchboard. The only words his fans heard were: "Tim Curry *who?*"

Handsome Maximillian Schell was hounded for months by a woman from New York. "She followed him across the country," John Howell remembered. "At first, he was nice to her, because she was a fan, but she became a real problem. She charged things to his accounts. She trailed him everywhere, and called constantly. She tried everything to have an affair with him. She even left notes that would say things like, 'I want to have your child.' One time, she came by in a cab to see him, and she didn't have the fare. I don't know how Mr. Schell put up with her as long as he did, but when she really started going overboard, he got rid of her. I should say he had the staff get rid of her. She didn't discourage easily, but then, she didn't like being treated rudely either."

Maximillian Schell had another admirer at the Marmont—Marlene Dietrich. She visited him in the late summer of 1960, during the production of *Judgement at Nuremberg.*

"The first time I saw Miss Dietrich come in," noted Carmel Volti, "she was wearing beautiful, grey slacks. She looked wonderful, and I was hoping we would have a chance to talk. But she never stopped at the desk, not even to ask the way to Mr. Schell's suite. She already knew. It seems she was always carrying something when she came to visit." (That "something," Max Schell later admitted was hot soup.) The warm friendship that developed between the two stars at the Marmont was a lasting one and ultimately resulted in Schell's 1984 Oscar-nominated documentary, *Marlene.*

At the Marmont, the guests themselves were frequently the biggest fans of stars. Tab Hunter, the movies' Golden Boy of the 1950s, often sat stargazing for hours in the lobby. Roddy McDowell roamed about with his camera. Richard Chamberlain liked staying at the Marmont "because I once ran into Lauren Hutton in the elevator."

"You never knew *who* you might run into at the Marmont," said Mrs. Volti. She certainly wasn't expecting to find one of her favorite movie stars wandering on the seventh floor. "I was delivering a manuscript—slipping it under someone's door—when I looked up, and there was Cary Grant. I was thrilled, but I think he was a little embarrassed. He acted like he wished I hadn't seen him, a little naughty, almost as if I had caught him with his hand in the cookie jar. I don't know who he was going to visit, and I'm sure that's the way he wanted it. Neither one of us said a word."

The first time Jack Benny walked into the Marmont to visit his producer-director, Ralph Levy, Carmel Volti was standing at the front desk. Without thinking, she blurted out his name. "It just came out—*Jack Benny*—as loud as could be," admitted Carmel. "He smiled and went on upstairs. As soon as he was gone, the night maid, Margaret, walked over to me. She happened to be in the lobby, so she had heard my outburst, and she couldn't stop laughing. 'You should have seen your face,' she giggled. I told her I couldn't help myself. I adored that man!"

Meemi Ferguson's grandson, Lee was secretly—and *madly*, according to his sister, Connie—in love with "the complete animal," Anna Magnani. He constantly prowled the hotel for a glimpse of her and spotting her, he would hover in the background, careful not to be seen. One day, Lee found Magnani in the lobby. He quickly took cover in the phone booth, then stood staring at the earthy Italian star through a small glass panel in the door. Magnani could not help but notice "the suspicous looking character" casting glances, but she didn't let on. Nor did she let her explosive temperament get the best of her. She simply walked calmly to the front desk and, in a low voice, asked the clerk to call the police. Lee was still eyeballing his great love when an officer arrived. No charges were filed, but Lee's snooping days were over. As for Magnani, she seemed pleased to discover that the culprit was a smitten young man.

Of all the techniques to discourage star-gazing, the most direct came from Esther, one of the maids, who found herself the target of an overly inquisitive guest. After weeks of being badgered with "Tell me, *tell me*. You must know *everything* that goes on around here!" Esther replied, as tactfully as possible, "If I knew everything, I'd have seen you coming—and I'd have been long gone!"

# Oscar Nights

Every year, months before the Academy Awards presentation, the Marmont is booked solid for Hollywood's big event. For some stars, it has become tradition to stay at the hotel during Oscar week. For others, a touch of superstition might be the lure. "I'm hoping this place brings me luck," Margaret Wycherly confided to Ann Little, prior to the 1941 awards. It didn't for Miss Wycherly, but it just might have for some of the others who followed.

For fifty-plus years, the Marmont has played host to scores of Academy Award winners, nominees, and presenters. Among the earliest guests touched by Oscar were Ronald Colman, Billy Wilder, James Hilton, Helen Hayes and Charles MacArthur, Lillian Hellman, Martha Scott, Humphrey Bogart, Conrad Nagel, Dorothy Parker, Orson Welles, and John Van Druten. Others soon followed.

Oscar nights—and days—at Chateau Marmont begin with excited phone calls from well-wishers and telegrams of congratulations, sent in advance "just in case." Then come the visitors, everyone from delivery boys bearing champagne and floral bouquets to family members and friends, many coming from long distances to offer moral support to their celebrity loved ones. In between, there are smiling hairdressers and make-up artists, personal secretaries, publicists, and agents. No one arrives empty-handed or without words of encouragement. As the day progresses, the chatter becomes increasingly less meaningful; laughter dissolves into nervous giggles. By late afternoon, Marmont Lane is lined with long, black limousines. It is not unusual to find the procession of sleek, chauffeured vehicles stretching all the way down to Sunset Boulevard.

In early 1956, Maurice Chevalier returned to the Marmont, after an absence of twenty years, to entertain at the Academy Awards. It was his first invitation to appear on the program. The jaunty boulevardier, whose French accent and jutting lower lip set feminine hearts aflutter, had left Hollywood in a huff in the mid-1930s, when Irving Thalberg insisted he take second billing to co-star Grace Moore in his next film. He doubted that he would ever come back, especially to make movies. He returned in 1948 with his one-man show, but that was only briefly, and he stayed with the Charles Boyer in their Beverly Hills home. He was heading back to Hollywood with another show in 1951 when he was refused entry into the United States for having signed the "Stockholm Appeal," a Communist-inspired document that proposed the banning of nuclear weapons.

"It's been many years since I've stood here," he told a friend from his terrace at the Marmont. "When I left as a film star, Hollywood was a small town with fields that reached to the studios. Today there are houses and shops and buildings, and people rushing, rushing, rushing." Chevalier, who was accustomed to an unchanging Paris, was not particularly pleased with the view that greeted him. Nor was he pleased with an incident that happened following the Academy Awards ceremony in 1956. At the post-

Awards party, he had been seated next to the evening's star attraction, Grace Kelly. Three months earlier, Kelly had announced her engagement to Prince Rainier of Monaco and her retirement from films. She was scheduled to depart Hollywood the following day for New York, then on to Monaco for her wedding. "Grace Kelly was a Dresden doll," Chevalier commented later, "with a kind of platinum beneath the delicate porcelain, a beautiful girl who I feel was always in control of her world. When I asked her to dance, she replied with a quiet dignity that she had decided to dance with no one until she danced again with Rainier in faraway Monte Carlo." Chevalier told the future princess that her decision was admirable. Relating the story back at the Marmont, however, he spoke as if he had been snubbed.

Maurice Chevalier's Hollywood film career had been in limbo for two decades. That was to change during his 1956 visit. While at the Marmont, he received a phone call from director Billy Wilder with an offer to appear opposite Gary Cooper and Audrey Hepburn in his production, *Love in the Afternoon*. Other films quickly followed: *Gigi, Can-can, Fanny,* and more. Chevalier returned to the hotel many times over the next few years, not only for picture assignments but to appear at the 1958 awards ceremony (held in 1959), where he received an honorary statuette "for his contribution to the world of entertainment for more than half a century."

Burl Ives, one of America's top balladeers, had been living at Chateau Marmont for several years, off and on, when he won an Oscar as best supporting actor for his performance in *The Big Country* (1959). Finding his way back to the hotel from the Pantages Theater in Hollywood, where the ceremony was held, wasn't difficult. It was later that problems developed, when he headed for "home."

With Ives' Academy Award came increasing offers for him to appear in films as a dramatic actor. He and his family moved into the Marmont, and there they remained for the next nine years. Returning to the hotel each night from the studio became so routine that when he bought a house, he found himself "in trouble." As Ives confessed, "I had lived at the Marmont so long that I automatically pointed the car for the hotel, not my *new* home. That happened time after time. It was almost impossible for me to break the habit."

Diahann Carroll did not accompany Sidney Pointer to the Academy Awards in 1964. But she was waiting for him at the Marmont when he returned, clutching his golden statuette, after being named Best Actor for *Lilies of the Field*. "My going alone," he commented later, "was a decision mutually arrived at, out of consideration for our delicate situation."

The night Maximillian Schell was named Best Actor for *Judgement at Nuremberg*, he returned to the hotel with his Oscar and quietly adjourned to the main-floor drawing room, where he serenaded himself at the piano.

Peter O'Toole has been nominated for Best Actor seven times to date and has never won. But he showed good sportsmanship following one Award's ceremony, when he entertained friends by tap-dancing on a table top in the lobby.

Margaret Herrick never won an Oscar either, but she reportedly named it her first day on the job at the Academy of Motion Picture Arts and Sciences, when she saw the statuette and quipped, "Why, it looks like my Uncle Oscar!" Herrick, who founded the Academy's world-famous research library (later named after her), and subsequently became a powerful Academy figure, checked into Chateau Marmont on August 22, 1951, to wage a scorching alimony battle against her husband of five years, baby-food executive Philip A. Herrick. At the time, she vowed that she would never return to their once-happy Hollywood home—and she never did.

Poet Alex Gildzen attended the Academy Awards during a visit to the Chateau in 1981, the year Robert DeNiro won Best Actor for *Raging Bull*. The day following the ceremony, Gildzen found himself unexpectedly standing face to face with the big winner. "I was in the elevator at the Marmont when Robert DeNiro got on. I don't make a habit of speaking to people I don't know, but the hotel elevators are so small, and I had been to the Oscars the night before—and we were sort of neighbors. So I looked over at him and said congratulations. He smiled and thanked me. He even looked back when he got out, smiled again and waved."

The most publicized Oscar night at the Marmont never took place. According to published reports: "Patricia Neal, Melvyn Douglas, Martin Balsam, and Sidney Poitier were all holed up at the Chateau Marmont one year [some accounts have them checking in simultaneously], departed for the Santa Monica Civic Auditorium, and returned carrying an Oscar apiece." All four stars were frequent guests at the Marmont, but on that night in question—April 13, 1964—only Sidney Poitier returned to the hotel a winner. Melvyn Douglas was working in Spain (Brandon de Wilde, who *was* at the hotel, accepted the award for Douglas). Patricia Neal was in England. And Martin Balsam wasn't even a nominee. He won his Oscar two years later.

That's Hollywood!

## Holidays & Other Celebrations

During the late autumn of 1984, ninety-one-year-old Ann Little reminisced at her Park LaBrea apartment in Los Angeles. Her face brightened at the mention of holiday celebrations at Chateau Marmont. More than four decades had passed since she had resigned her position as manager to become a Christian Science practitioner (her *third* switch in careers, she liked to remind visitors, following her highly successful start on the silent screen), but memories of those happiest of times still flooded her thoughts. "They were such festive occasions," she smiled, "especially for the children."

She talked of Easter egg hunts on the front lawn, of Fourth of July displays, and lavish Christmas fetes hosted by the Albert Smiths. "At Christmas, the lobby was decorated with garlands and wreaths, and a huge, twinkling tree stood at one end of the drawing room. Each year, the kitchen was busy for days, preparing delicious holiday treats for the big celebration. Everyone was invited—staff members, their families, and our wonderful hotel guests. We served a special dinner, then passed out presents, which delighted the little ones to no end. Many guestss arrived with gifts for their favorite employees. They were quite generous."

With the arrival of Drs. Brethauer and Popper, the "frivolous holiday spending," as they called it, came to an abrupt halt. Traditional Christmas dinners were no longer held, Easter egg rolls were stricken from the spring schedule, anyone interested in pyrotechnic displays had to travel elsewhere to see them. The only show of spirit during the tenure of the highly conservative Germans, and for years afterward, was a minature Christmas tree positioned in the lobby. Fresh and green to start, it was replaced in time by one of plastic.

Over a period of some thirty years, guests and employees alike had to generate their own holiday excitement. Some of the most memorable times were usually unplanned.

Halloween at the Marmont found the youngsters parading in costume. "I was dressed as the devil, and my brother, Stefan, was the hunchback of Notre Dame," recalled Alison Arngrim, "We would ride the elevator and roam the halls, scaring people. Then we would knock on all the doors. Trick-or-treating was great. We collected lots of loot."

Little Channing Lowe was introduced to trick-or-treating at the Marmont. Unfortunately it was not a positive experience for the young son of Carol Channing and Charles Lowe. As a family friend remembered:

"Channing was making the rounds, accompanied by the Lowes' housekeeper, when they came to Estelle Winwood's suite. He knocked, held out his little hand and waited. When the door opened, Estelle and Judith Anderson were standing there. Channing took one look at Winwood's bulging eyes and started screaming. He thought she was a witch!"

Myra Robinson worked for a time as manager. She was an odd choice because she had an intense dislike for show people (their open displays of affection made her cringe), but Dr. Brethauer and Dr. Popper were very fond of her. One day shortly after Thanksgiving, Mrs. Robinson entered the lobby to find Walter Matthau leaning over the desk, kissing Carmel Volti; a friendly peck on the cheek, nothing more. She gasped at the sight but said nothing, not to Matthau, anyway. She waited until he departed for the elevator, then turned on Volti. "Christmas is coming," she said frostily, "why don't you stand at the front door and kiss *all* the guests as they come in?" Volti forced a little smile. "Maybe they would like it," she replied, "but I wouldn't"

Debra Paget's mother, Mrs. Griffen, was noted for her magnificent holiday displays and generous gift-giving. The Christmas trees in her luxurious second-floor suite (decorated Harlow-style in white and gold) were the talk of the Marmont. Each year they appeared to be larger and more splendid than ever. How she continually outdid herself, no one knew.

Beatrice Lillie and Hermione Baddeley were noted for their trees too, mainly because they left them up most of the year, no matter how limp and barren they became. "One of Bea's trees was the most amazing little thing," Norma Arngrim recalled, "full of ornaments, but no needles. Bea thought it was so beautiful. She kept it on a table near her easel. She even started to do a painting of it."

Some guests liked to have wreaths on their doors over the Christmas holidays. Not Bea Lillie. Whenever she spotted one as she walked down the halls, she would crack, "Who died?"

One Christmas afternoon, composer Fritz Loewe wandered into the lobby, in search of a friendly face. He found the place even quieter than usual. The only voices to be heard came from behind the desk, where Meemi Ferguson and Carmel Volti were on duty. As Mrs. Volti remembered, "He joined in our conversation, then confessed, 'I am the loneliest man in the world. I have no relatives, no one. He seemed so sad. And he writes such beautiful music."

The Marmont ladies—Carmel, Meemi, and Corinne—often worked holidays before joining their families. One Christmas, however, Meemi

Larry Bordeaux, James Haake ("Gypsy"), and Hermoine Baddeley were among the many guests at the Marmont's anniversary gala.

Staff members and their families gather for gift-giving and buffet at annual Christmas celebration.

was missing. "We were frantic," said her granddaughter, Connie. "No one had seen her all day, and when she didn't show up for Christmas dinner, we really began to panic. Meemi *never* missed Christmas dinner." It turned out that Meemi, an avid bridge player, was lost in cards with some of her cronies. Small wonder that the time and importance of the day had completely escaped her. Rarely, if ever, has a more unusual foursome been known to gather around a card table. From the Marmont, along with Meemi Ferguson, came the ever-intriguing Christine Jorgenson. From the Crescendo, a swinging Sunset Strip nightspot, came the bombastic (and bawdy) Frances Faye. And from the Metropolitan Opera, came the celebrated coloratura, Lily Pons.

Christmas wouldn't have been Christmas without a visit from Louella Parsons' driver. He arrived on schedule each year to gather gifts from the stars for the famed and powerful gossip columnist. For the most part, the offerings were unsolicited. They were *expected,* however, from performers eager to remain in Louella's good graces—and from those seeking a mention in her well-read column. The haul was at times so bountiful that a single pick-up could not accommodate all the packages.

In December, 1981, Lisa Eichhorn and her husband, make-up artist Ben Nye, Jr., turned their sixth-floor suite into a wonderland for their baby daughter's first Christmas. They bought a huge tree, boxes of ornaments, strings of lights, and pots of bright, blooming poinsettias. Stockings were hung in the living room; candy canes and other seasonal goodies, made by Lisa in her kitchen, were scattered about, along with mounds of ribboned boxes. The baby may not have been as impressed with the festive decorations as the dozens of grown-ups who attended the Nyes' New Year's Eve celebration that year. They reportedly stayed through the night, dancing and partying.

From 1943 to 1974, the Marmont lobby had the sparkle and warmth of a ten-watt bulb over the holidays. With the arrival of new owners Sarlot and Kantarjian, however, the room brightened considerably. Not only did they purge the hotel of its vinyl lampshades and furnishings, they got rid of the lifeless "forevergreen" artificial tree. As they are quick to admit, "We put an end to the reign of plastic garbage."

"We started out by having one of the staff order our trees," said Ray Sarlot, "but they weren't what Karl and I had in mind, so we would send them back. Now we have a new ritual. On the first of December, early in the morning, Karl and I get in our little truck, and down the road we go. We bring back the best tree we can find." The tree is always enormous, reaching to the high ceiling, while spreading across the floor.

With the rebirth of holiday spirit in 1975 came a revival of the annual Marmont Christmas party for employees, their families, and friends. Each year, one-hundred or so guests gather around the tree for a candlelit buffet dinner and caroling. Huge wicker gift baskets filled with turkeys, hams, cheeses, wines, and fruit await everyone.

The main-floor drawing room has also been the site of other gala happenings. During his three years at the Marmont, Loren Michaels celebrated his thirtieth birthday with one of the liveliest bashes ever held on the lobby level. "It took place just before I started work on *Saturday Night Live*," Michaels said, "so none of the cast members was there." Even without them the place was overflowing with guests, mainly friends from the hotel, who whooped it up till four in the morning.

Billy Barnes' spectacular opening-night parties at the Marmont attracted not only "the Barnes people" (his multi-talented repertoire company), but much of movieland's hip "in" crowd.

But the party to end all took place in late 1977 to honor the upcoming fiftieth anniversary of Chateau Marmont's groundbreaking. As Corinne Patten, last of the Marmont ladies to depart the hotel, noted in her journal:

"Our $10,000 gala had all the glamor of a Hollywood premiere. So many famous faces, guests at one time or another, turned out to enjoy cocktails and hor d'oeuvres on the penthouse roof garden, while an orchestra played romantic songs throughout dinner in the downstairs drawing room. In the Jean Harlow suite, a guitarist strummed softly, while Larry Bordeaux's father, a very noted astrologer, held readings. Reporters, many from overseas, were everywhere asking questions and taking pictures. It was so wonderful seeing our friends again, and remembering those who couldn't be with us."

The guests included veteran actors, young rock stars, writers, artists, and a few executives from other hotels. Carol Lynley returned to the Marmont for the festivities, and happily confessed that she had "lived in just about every room in the hotel."

Actor Henry Wilcoxon could not recall when he had last set foot inside the Marmont, only that he was with screenwriter-producer Sydney Box at the time. "I had brought Sydney here from England to write a version of *On My Honor* for DeMille," he said wistfully. "I was to be his co-producer on that film."

Also present were the Arngrim family (Alison, Stefan, Norma, and Thor), Jill Jackson, Hermione Baddeley, James Haake ("Gypsy"), Richard

B. Schell, and the Marmont's charter guest, Nellita Choate Thomsen.

Nellita nearly stole the show. In her mid-eighties, looking fit and trim in a print silk dress and flaming bouffant wig, she seemed forever lost in mobs of friends and strangers, many a quarter of her age, who had sought her out, hoping to hear about the early days at the Marmont and the celebrated visitors she had known. Nellita didn't disappoint them. Her stories of Jean Harlow, Mary Astor, Stan Laurel, and Raquel Torres prompted one young reporter to inquire if she had ever been a part of the movie industry herself. "Oh, heavens, no," she replied with a titter. "The only acting I did was with the Nine O'Clock Players of the Assistance League. We would rent theaters and think we were real artists. We lived in a world of our own."

Nellita never once hinted about her *other* world. Decades had passed, but she still found it impossible to talk about her glory days as a reporter for the Hearst papers, or to at last reveal the true identity of her alter ego, Pauline Payne.

## The Front Desk

Scarcely a corner of Chateau Marmont was ignored during the hotel's much needed restoration. About the only thing left untouched was the ornamental wood facing of the Gothic-inspired front desk. (Even a bullet hole from a thwarted robbery attempt, some thirty-odd years ago, remains unfilled and intact.) It is still, as one European visitor remarked recently, "like the quaint little counter in a village corner shop."

No village corner shop, however, has been frequented by such a steady stream of celebrities over the years. To paraphase Earl Carroll's famous legend: "At this counter have stood—or leaned—the most famous people in the world." Even MGM's heyday roster pales by comparison. And MGM, as Louis B. Mayer wanted moviegoers to believe, had "more stars than there are in the heavens."

Here are a few memorable happenings that have taken place at and around the Marmont's venerable symbol of times past and one of the few remaining links to legendary Hollywood, the front desk:

German director Oskar Karl Weiss was standing at the desk one day when young Joanne Woodward, dressed comfortably in culottes, strolled through the lobby. She had only recently made her screen debut and wasn't yet well known. "Who was *that*?" Weiss asked Carmel Volti. "Joanne Woodward,"

Volti replied."She's going to be a big star some day." Weiss shook his head. "I'd never let her on *my* stage," he said. "She's not glamorous at all!"

Around the Marmont, few stars were.

Shirley Booth often picked up her mail with her hair in curlers. Maria Schneider, Marlon Brando's lovely co-star in *Last Tango in Paris,* thought nothing of stopping at the desk with a green face mask smeared over her countenance. Peter O'Toole was rarely seen in anything except a velour jogging suit. Tony Perkins got in the habit of stopping at the desk, removing his shoes, then adjourning to the telephone booth, where he would sit on the floor in his socks. Like Garbo, actress-model Lauren Hutton's favorite "at home" look is shorts and no make-up. Richard Gere opts for jeans and a tee-shirt.

When Buddy Hackett first came to the Marmont, he lived not far from the front desk in 1F. Every morning, he would come out in his yellow terry cloth bathrobe, step to the lobby water cooler, and get a drink. Then he would wander by the desk, crack a few jokes, and disappear. "He hadn't done much of anything yet in Hollywood," Volti remembered. "He was just a goodnatured, roly-poly guy, who always kept us laughing."

Betty Buckley had starred on Broadway in the hit musicals *1776* and *Pippin,* in the London company of *Promises, Promises,* and in the films, *Hair* and *Carrie,* when she began a four-year stay at the Marmont, while appearing in the long-running television series, *Eight is Enough.* In many ways, Buckley was like the Abby Bradford stepmother character she played—strong-willed, dedicated, and appealing. Then, again, she was her own unique character. A student of the Jain Eastern philosophy and a vegetarian, she was constantly dieting. To find her strolling through the lobby in sweatshirt and slacks, sipping a concoction of maple syrup and lemon juice, wasn't unusual.

Nor was it unusual to find celebrated guests in the lobby at odd hours. One evening, well past midnight, Myrna Loy caught John Howell with his head in his arms, asleep at the front desk. She said nothing to him at the time; she saved her reminders, and playful razzing, for future visits.

Former football star Lance Rentzel wasn't quite as controlled. He and a friend were taking some luggage to their car, late one night, when Howell waylayed them. "They hadn't stopped at the desk to pay their bill, and I thought they were skipping out," Howell remembered. "I didn't want to accuse them of that so I asked if I could be of help. I guess they knew what I was thinking, because Mr. Rentzel turned and really let me have it. I thought he was going to take my head off."

Howell thought he had learned his lesson earlier. Shortly after he had been hired, he was asked to show George Segal one of the suites. As Howell recalled: "We were going from room to room, and it seemed a little stuffy, so I decided to open a window. That was my mistake. I pulled and struggled but the window wouldn't open. It was stuck. In disgust, I mumbled, 'Shit!' After that, Mr. Segal lost interest. When we got back to the desk, he excused himself by saying he had been offended by my foul language." Some years later, Segal returned to the Marmont for the filming of *Blume in Love,* and, according to Howell, more than a few choice words were overheard while observing the actor at work.

Gloria Vanderbilt stopped at the Marmont for years, as did her aunt, Lady Thelma Furness. Despite Gloria's many marriages, her sign-in signature never varied; it was always *Miss Gloria Vanderbilt.* Soon after her marriage to Wyatt Cooper, a former acquaintance of Cooper's at the hotel commented: "And to think it wasn't that long ago that he was living in Carleton Carpenter's garage. Wyatt's a great guy, but you just don't go from living in a room the size of a table to marrying Gloria Vanderbilt."

Teenagers Susan Strasberg and Steffi Sidney always "checked out the celebrities" when they signed in. "The hotel kept a list of names by the switchboard," Sidney remembered, "and it was fascinating to catch a peek at who was staying there. Susie and I always made a game out of it."

John Belushi did the same thing, hoping to spot the names of friends. If he didn't find any, he would leave to check out another hotel's register.

Kevin McCarthy often stopped at the front desk to quote Shakespeare "and other things." According to one of the former clerks, "He was always very entertaining." (McCarthy's young friend at the Marmont, Stefan Arngrim, remembered the actor as being "extremely supportive. He knew what was going on with everybody, and he took a real interest in their careers. He struck me as a man who dearly loved his profession.")

Quentin Crisp had never been to the Marmont prior to his 1981 cross country tour to promote his book, *Doing It with Style.* The dapper dilettante, who arrived wearing bluish-gray eye shadow to match his hair, was introduced to the hotel by his co-author and associate, Donald Carroll. ("I had told Quentin: 'When we get to Los Angeles we must stay at the Marmont. It's not a fishbowl—and it doesn't have Lysoled tapes over the toilets.' ") Crisp's visit appeared to get off to a good start. Awaiting him in his fourth-floor suite was a basket of fruit and a bottle of wine (Joseph Phelps Cabernet Sauvignon) from the Marmont wine cellar. Crisp, though not a wine expert, was most appreciative; Carroll, a definite connoisseur, was highly impressed. ("He believes in wines the way other people believe in salvation," noted Crisp.)

The introductory glow quickly faded, however, when an interviewer failed to show on schedule. Crisp's crowded itinerary left little room for error. There were reporters to see, appearances on talk shows, bookstore signings, and a large reception for friends. But Crisp remained calm; he had been through "the wars" before. Not Carroll. After a suitable period of waiting, he called the front desk to discover that the interviewer had indeed made an appearance, only to have been turned away.

It seemed another Mr. Carroll had recently checked out, resulting in some confusion. "He wanted to see *me . . . us!*" Crisp's frenzied friend shouted into the phone. "We' re here! *We're here!*" For good measure, Carroll added, "Stop doing this!" then banged down the receiver.

A minute later, the phone rang in Crisp's suite. It was the desk calling back to apologize. The desk clerk wanted to talk with Carroll, but Crisp had answered. "Oh, take no notice of my associate," he said serenely. "He didn't mean anything." The caller knew better; in the background, she could hear Carroll ranting, 'I *did* mean it. I *did!*" She all but insisted on speaking with Carroll, when Crisp interrupted to say, in his understated British way: "I don't think that's too wise at the moment. Possibly under calmer circumstances."

As it turned out, things didn't calm down much, but they did run more smoothly. Crisp even found a few moments to relax. One day, while in the lobby awaiting his chauffeur, he fell asleep on a sofa in the drawing room. Guests wandered in and out oblivious to the impeccably dressed little man—in suit, ascot, and eyeshadow—sprawled out like a baby. The next day, Crisp and Carroll checked out.

Later, the Marmont began receiving a flurry of phone calls from New York. "We couldn't understand why we were getting so many inquiries," said Ray Sarlot. "Then we found out about the article in *The New York Times.*" By-lined by Quentin Crisp, it was a lengthy remembrance of his all-too-brief visit to Chateau Marmont. "I could gladly have lived there for the rest of my life," Crisp wrote, "but on a promotion tour, there are no forevers, except forever moving on . . . "

Few quests maintained their composure as well as Quentin Crisp. Carol Channing came to the desk in a dither one day; she had lost a contact lens. Bette Midler became completely unglued when she thought she had lost her address book. "Miss Midler didn't know what to do," one of the clerks reported with amusement. "She was running around in circles like a chicken with a hot foot."

It's impossible not to know when dynamic Margot Kidder checks in at the Marmont. Word is she arrives "like gangbusters," anxious to know if her favorite suite is ready.

Bianca "ex-Jagger" (as Louis Malle affectionately called her following her divorce from rock rage, Mick Jagger) was at the Marmont in October, 1978, "putting my affairs in order" before seriously launching a film career. One night, she appeared at the front desk, looking stunning, dressed for an evening's festivities. All she needed to complete "the look" were her jewels, which she kept locked in the lobby safe. Unfortunately, the clerk on duty didn't know the combination. Other staff members were quickly called in to try their luck, but without success. As the minutes passed, and Jagger grew more desperate, Ray Sarlot and Karl Kantarjian walked in—to the rescue! They had been down the street having a drink and were in such a happy state that the magic numbers to the lock suddenly and completely eluded them. "Don't worry about it," Sarlot said, brimming with confidence, "we'll get it open." Jagger seemed reassured. With Sarlot's background in construction, there was really no need to panic. He disappeared briefly, before returning with chisels, wrenches, a crowbar, and drill. He hammered, he pried, he dug, he twisted. Nothing happened. He pulled, he yanked. The safe remained sealed tight. Jagger looked at Sarlot, then slipped into the night. She still looked gorgeous, even without her jewels.

For a time, Debra Winger had trouble getting enough warm water to fill her bathtub. When the pipes wouldn't deliver all she needed, she tried closing the bathroom door and turning up the radiator full blast. That helped, but she had to plan ahead, *way* ahead (about three hours for each soaking). Eventually, she discovered a faster way. She had only to call downstairs to the front desk, and order tea—with pots and pots, and *more* pots, of hot water.

Walter Matthau stopped at the front desk one evening, just as a wire was coming in on the teletype. It happened to be for him—brief and to the point— from his wife, Carol. It read: "What are you doing and who are you with?" Carol, It seemed, liked to keep tabs on her Walter.

Elaine May and her daughter, Jeannie Berlin, were at the desk talking with Carmel Volti, when a slight young man passed by. Carmel commented how much he looked like Berlin's friend, Bud Cort. "Everyone looks like Bud Cort," May hissed.

Other guests had special comments too. Burl Ives frequently visited

Carmel Volti when she was alone at the desk in the evening. He made a habit of saying, "Well, if we don't have any troubles, we'll find some."

Mildred Natwick could not leave the hotel at night without advising the desk clerk, in rather dramatic fashion: "I'm goin' *gout!*"

Mort Sahl rattled Carmel almost as much as her comic idol, Jack Benny. "He walked in one night, and I flipped," she remembered. "I didn't blurt out his name, because seeing him made me speechless, but once I caught my breath I had to tell him about my son. 'My friends call him the poor man's Mort Sahl,' I noted with motherly pride. Mr. Sahl didn't crack a smile. He just said, 'I'm still poor.' "

One evening, a persistent intruder kept wandering by the front desk while Inger Simonsen was on duty. "It was one of those nights when everything was happening at once," she reported. "To top it off, a dog kept roaming in and out of the front door, which had me running outside with it, hoping it would go back to wherever it belonged. I was about at my wits end when Kate Jackson and her boyfriend, Edward Albert, walked in to pick up their messages—followed by the dog!" According to Simonsen, Jackson took an immediate liking to the animal. "It was her birthday, and she said she had wished for a dog. It appeared that her wish had come true." Jackson and Albert took their newfound friend upstairs, promising that they would try and find its rightful owner. A few nights later, Simonsen received a call from a man wanting to know the whereabouts of his dog. She took his name and number, and passed them along to Jackson. The next day, the grateful owner came in to claim his dog. "Not much later Kate Jackson and Edward Albert were gone too," Simonsen said. "But I seem to recall someone telling me that she got herself a puppy."

There were other celebrated twosomes who passed the front desk. Former California Governor Jerry Brown and Linda Rondstadt frequently rendezvoused at the Marmont. (Brown had a home in the hills above the hotel, and Rondstadt drove in from Malibu). Louis Malle and Susan Sarandan were often seen in each other's company, as were Jessica Lange and Sam Shepard, and Marianna Hill and David Groh.

One night, a guest called the front desk for a taxi. Mrs. Volti was on duty, doubling at the desk and switchboard. Ten minutes later, she heard "a terrible honking in the street." She left her position and went out to the curb to tell the driver that the noise wasn't at all necessary; *she* would announce his arrival. In the middle of her reprimand, the honker stepped from the car. It was Frank Sinatra. "I was mortified," she recalled. "He had come to pick up a lady friend, I believe, and I greeted him with a tongue-lashing! 'Oh, I'm so sorry, Mr. Sinatra,' I apologized. He glared at me and stormed into the hotel for the elevator. Later that night, one of our guests, a very prominent actor, dropped by the desk, and I told him about my horrible blunder. He just shrugged and said, 'Don't be silly. He looks like a cab driver, doesn't he?' "

Then there was the time two gentlemen from New York stopped at the front desk to check out. One of them had a bottle of whiskey in his hand; the other carried a small envelope. They were gifts for Mrs. Volti, tokens of appreciation for her kindness during their stay, they said. After they had gone, as she recalled: "I opened the envelope and out rolled two marijuana cigarettes. Corinne (Patten) looked at me as if I were a criminal. Well, I knew she drank, so I gave her the bottle, which kept her quiet. Then I took the cigarettes home and put them in a stew. My husband couldn't tell the difference!"

Hermione Gingold seldom lost her sense of humor, even after an exhausting day at the studio. She would all but drag herself across the lobby, throw her arms on the desk, and sigh, "Oh, let's end it all!"

Everyone thought hotel guest, Mr. Holiner, had "a macabre sense of humor." A strange little man, he would purposely come to the desk each afternoon to tell Corinne Patten, "I'm going to kill myself." Corinne eventually became so tired of listening to Holiner that one day she waved him off by saying, "Well, just don't mess up your room." Holiner nodded and went upstairs. Several hours later, he was found dead in his bathtub. "The poor man did exactly as he was told," another staff member recalled. "Corinne was beside herself for months."

Fortunately for Corinne, she had "her stars" to help ease her guilt. Few things in life pleased her more than chatting with celebrities, and to have her picture taken with them was, in her own words, like "presents under the tree." Not long after the Holiner incident, Joanne Woodward and Paul Newman were at the front desk when a camera-carrying guest requested a shot. Corinne remembered: "Paul obliged by jumping on top of the desk, and, as the shutter clicked, he reached over my head to get the mail out of his box. Now *that* was one for the fan magazines!"

Fred Horowitz at the front desk during 1986 reception.

Courtyard view of Chateau Amboise, showing L-shaped structure.

# Epilogue

## Return To Normandy

Toward the end of 1985, a location manager from Warner Bros. arrived at Chateau Marmont to arrange for rooms to be used during the shooting of a feature film at the hotel. He was met by the Marmont's manager, Suzanne Jierjian. "I'm Doug Horowitz," he said, introducing himself.

Suzanne welcomed him, then started for her office. She had taken only a few steps when she stopped. "By any chance, are you related to Fred Horowitz, the man who built the Marmont?" she asked.

Doug smiled. "He is my great uncle."

"*Is* your great uncle?" she repeated, almost in disbelief. "We had no idea . . ., after all these years."

"It has been a long time," Doug acknowledged.

"Mr. Sarlot would love to talk to him. Could he possibly attend a small get-together we're having at the hotel in a few weeks?"

"I think that can be arranged," Doug replied.

On the night of January 22, 1986, ninety-one-year-old Fred Horowitz returned to Chateau Marmont as guest of honor at a dinner reception. It was his first visit to the hotel since 1931.

After an absence of fifty-five years, most of which had been devoted to his highly successful law practice (at one time, he had worked as a prosecutor for the Attorney General of the United States), Fred Horowitz saw little that appeared truly familiar to him during a brief tour. The sight of the shield on the exterior tower wall, containing a large baroque letter "H," brought a genuine flash of recognition; it still impressed him. Most of all, however, he enjoyed meeting new friends and posing for pictures at the front desk in the lobby.

Having the opportunity to meet Fred Horowitz enabled Raymond Sarlot and Karl Kantarjian to ask him a question that had gone unanswered since they purchased the hotel. They knew that the Marmont had been patterned after a chateau in France, yet they were unable to discover its name and precise location. Unfortunately, Fred Horowitz could not tell them. The secret of the hotel's inspiration had faded from memory.

Two months later, Sarlot and his wife, Sally, were vacationing in France, traveling through the Loire Valley. At the edge of a forest, rising from the crescent of a promontory, a castle with massive towers and intricate sculpted decorations caught their attention. Soon they were standing in the courtyard of Chateau Amboise.

Built on the site of a former Roman camp, Chateau Amboise had originated as a feudal fortress, dating back to the Eleventh Century. In time, it became not only the first leisure residence of the kings of France, but the home of Leonardo da Vinci.

While Chateau Marmont was not an exact duplicate of Chateau Amboise, Sarlot discovered undeniable similarities. The L-shape of the two buildings; high windows opening onto balconies (on the Amboise's front side); colonnaded entryways flanked by Gothic arches (also on the Amboise's front side); and rugged stone lacework. Arnold A. Weitzman, architect for the Marmont, had liberally borrowed the Amboise's most distinctive features and incorporated them into his design.

"I can't express the deep feeling I had as I stood before Chateau Amboise," Sarlot said. "It was as if I had come home. I had found what Fred Horowitz had found. Now I can't help but believe that the genius of Leonardo da Vinci lives on, six thousand miles away, through the talented entertainers and creators who come to Chateau Marmont.

Since that long ago day when Fred Horowitz stood on a barren hillside overlooking Los Angeles, surveying the land with a photograph of his beloved faraway chateau in hand, Hollywood has seen many changes.

The great stars have come and gone, replaced by newer names and faces. Many of the giant studios, once the dream factories of the world have dwindled or disappeared. The great movie moguls—Mayer, Cohn, Zanuck, Warner, and others—no longer rule. The Garden of Allah, the glittering nightclubs, the fabled Brown Derby, and Schwab's are but a memory. Few landmarks remain.

Chateau Marmont, like Hollywood, has somehow survived. The years

Vaulted ceiling in the state room at Chateau Amboise (*above*);
entryway at Chateau Marmont (*below*).

have been crowded with glamorous highs and despairing lows, storybook romances, fast times and wild parties, overnight successes and failures, even tragedies. Through them all, however, the Marmont has remained Hollywood's authentic Grand Hotel—and one of its best kept secrets, much to the joy of its celebrated clientele.

Not too many years ago a *Newsday* journalist cornered Jill Clayburgh sipping coffee in Corinne's Corner. Following the usual career questions, she was asked to comment about her stay at the Marmont. "Oh, don't mention the hotel," she said, crinkling her face. "Then all the tourists will come." A moment later, Clayburgh was on her way, but not before leaving the journalist with a final thought. "If you must say something about this place," she said, "say it's terrible. *Please* say it's terrible."

The hills surrounding Chateau Marmont are no longer desolate and uninhabited. The panoramic view from its terraces has become, if anything, even more spectacular. A reflection, perhaps, of a new spirit in the land of make-believe. Ciro's may be gone, but it has been replaced by the Comedy Store; Preston Sturges' The Players has become Imperial Gardens; Sunset Tower, abandoned for more than a decade, has been transformed into St. James' Club; and The Whiskey rocks again.

Today, Chateau Marmont stands imperiously above the resurging Sunset Strip, a proud legacy of times past. The memories of Garbo, Gable, Harlow, Monroe, and so many others, are linked irrevocably with the lives of everyone who has had—or will have—the pleasure of residing, if only for a night, at the historic and very magical Marmont.

# Index

# INDEX

# INDEX

# INDEX

Hill, George Roy 25, 97, 172,
Hill, James 209-11, 260,
Hill, Marianna 294,
Hiller, Wendy 231,
Hilton, Conrad 6,
Hilton, James 29, 281,
Hines, Cortland S. 63,
Hirschfeld, Al 77,
Historic-Cultural
    Monument 267,
Hitler, Adolf 48, 56, 76,
    86,
Hock, John Phillip 223,
Hoffman, Dustin 177,
Holbrook, Hal 247,
Holden, William 65, 68,
    70-1, 113,
Holiman, Earl 258,
Holiner, Mr. 295,
Holloway, Stanley 231,
Hollywood 8, 19, 31,
    63-4, 76, 115, 120, 129,
    143, 245, 281,
Hollywood *Citizen News*
    74,
Hollywood and Vine 19,
Hollywood Athletic Club
    44,
Hollywood Boulevard 217,
*Hollywood Wives* 205,
Hollywood's Walk of
    Fame 167,
Holman, Libby 93-4, 96,
    162-3,
Holmes, Ralph, 94-5
Holy Cross Cemetery 270,
*Hook, Line and Sinker*
    180,
Hope, Bob 215-16,
Hopkins, Miriam 98, 121,
Hopnon, Lena 29,
Hopper, Dennis 125, 139,
    141-2, 147, 247, 256,
Hopper, Hedda 143,
Horn Avenue 69,
Horn, Paul 223,
Horowitz, Doug 297,
Horowitz, Fred 1-3, 5-7,
    20-21, 297-8,
Horowitz, Jay 5,

*Horse Feathers* 97,
House Un-American
    Activities Committee
    133,
Houseman, John 76, 138,
    144,
Hover, Herman 78,
Howard, Ken 247,
Howard, Trevor 231,
Howard, William R. III
    215,
Howell, John 199, 219,
    227, 253, 279, 290-1,
Huck, John Philip 239,
    240-3, 247,
Hudson, Rock 120,
Hughes, Howard 103-8,
    147, 277,
Hughes, Pam 253, 264,
Humane Society 151,
*Humoresque* 132,
Hunnicutt, Gayle 232,
Hunt, Martita 231,
Hunter, Tab 279,
Huntington Hartford
    Theatre 242,
Hutton, Lauren 247, 279,
    290,
Hutton, Robert 89,
Huxley, Aldous 97, 155,
Hyde-White, Wilfred 231,
Hyland, Diana 225,
*I Am A Camera* 97,
*I Can Get It For You
    Wholesale* 212-14,
*I Love Lucy* 91,
"I'm Glad I'm Not Young
    Anymore" 222,
*Illegal* 139,
Imperial Gardens 300,
*In a Lonely Place* 138,
industry strikes 120,
Inge, William 158, 177,
*Inside Daisy Clover* 143,
Ireland, John 144,
Irens, Priscella 87,
Iribe, Judith 52-3,
*Irma La Douce* 214,
Isherwood, Christopher
    97, 236,

*It's A Mad Mad Mad Mad
    World* 211,
Iturbi, Jose 76, 219,
Ives, Alexander 150,
Ives, Burl 129, 150, 213,
    222, 238, 282, 293,
J. Geils Band 226,
Jackson, Anne 131,
Jackson, Calvin 258,
Jackson, Jill 122-3, 148,
    201-2, 206-7, 211-12,
    234, 288,
Jackson, Joyce 258,
Jackson, Kate 294,
Jackson, Sam 180,
Jacobi, Lou 169,
Jaffe, Henry 213,
Jagger, Bianca 293,
Jagger, Mick 226, 293,
James, Rick 226,
Jameson, Joyce 217-18,
*Jane Eyre* 199,
Janis, Conrad 116,
Jay Ward Productions 166,
Jean Harlow suite 288,
Jeans, Isobel 232,
Jefferson Airplane 226,
Jeffries, Lionel 231, 268,
Jenkins, Allen 61,
Jennings, Mrs. Talbot 78,
Jierjian, Suzanne 273, 275,
    297,
*Johnny Guitar* 138, 144,
Johns, Glynis 192, 231,
    236, 264,
Johnson, Rita 77,
Jolson, Al 60,
Jones, Christopher 137,
Jones, Quincy 222,
Jones, Ricki Lee 219, 226,
Jones, Shirley 147, 222,
Jones, T.C. 148, 234, 258,
Joplin, Janis 227,
Jorgensen, Christine
    148-9, 287,
Joseph, Jackie 258,
*Journey for Margaret* 83,
Joyce, Adrien 256,
*Judgement at Nuremberg*
    279, 283,

—*306*—

# INDEX

# INDEX

# INDEX